Seventy
Years
of
BBC Sport

Seventy
Years
of
BBC Sport

ANDRE
DEUTSCH

Damon and Graham Hill race to the bookshop to purchase *70 Years of BBC Sport*

Edited by
BRIAN GEARING AND PHIL MCNEILL

Designed by
ROBERT KELLAND AND ADRIAN WADDINGTON

With thanks to
Dave Crowe, Louise Dixon, Tim Forrester, Peter Baxter, Audrey Adams, Lynda Raymond, Rob Harborne, Wallace Grevatt,
Ken Vaughan, Alistair Tait, Eve Cossins, Joe Crowe, Catherine McNeill, Mark Peacock, Paul Sudbury, Audrey Todd and Godfrey Warde

First published in Great Britain in 1999 by André Deutsch Ltd
76 Dean Street, London W1V 5HA
www.vci.co.uk

Printed and bound in Great Britain
by Jarrold Book Printing, Thetford

Contents

The BBC justly looks back with pride, but now...
The challenge lies ahead
JOHN INVERDALE PREPARES TO COME OUT FIGHTING

Italia 90. The World Cup. A junior reporter dispatched across the maelstrom of the International Broadcast Centre in Rome to interview a renowned manic commentator from Radio Caracol of Colombia.

The red carpet had never been unfurled so quickly. I was from the BBC, the "King of Broadcasting Organisations" as they put it. My every wish was their command. I left, interviews in hand, and unsteady on my feet after several drinks of whatever they give royalty in Bogota.

But after 70 years, the House of Reith, perhaps like the House of Windsor, has reached a crossroads in its life. A time to reassert its position of pre-eminence in the marketplace, but also to realign itself more with the public mood. And while anniversaries offer a chance to look back with pride and fondness, as the Millennium beckons, this is also a golden opportunity to plan for the future.

Seventy years of coverage, 50 years of *Sports Report* on the radio, 40 years of *Grandstand* on the television – programmes indelibly imprinted in the national psyche, as

the Beeb has established a worldwide reputation for integrity, honesty, fair-mindedness and excellence.

Captain H.B.T. Wakelam can't have imagined, as he became the first play-by-play commentator on England against Wales at Twickenham in January 1927, that he was establishing a dynasty that through domestic television and radio, plus the incomparable World Service, would be renowned from Alaska to Adelaide. John Snagge, Freddie

Grisewood, Harold Abrahams, Peter Dimmock, Sir Peter O'Sullevan, Bill McLaren, Harry Carpenter, David Coleman, Des Lynam, all of us have a BBC voice and face that shaped the way we felt and feel about sport as a whole.

Dimmock, together with Paul (now Sir Paul) Fox, was behind the immensely influential programme *Sportsview* that formed public perception of sport from its inception in 1954. For 50 years, fans have left football grounds around the country to race for a radio in time to hear the words "Five o'clock and time for *Sports Report*". Those at home have watched expectantly as the teleprinter has chattered out the results on *Grandstand* since it was launched in October 1958.

Sales of television sets soared during England's victorious World Cup campaign in 1966, when *Grandstand* broke the mould of sports coverage, and actually used action replays for the first time.

As the BBC's coverage has developed and grown, so have we grown with it. But the world moves on, and as the 21st Century waves us in, what price honesty, integrity and an unrivalled reputation in Bogota? The BBC's

Left: Welsh miners
in Tonypandy listen
to the radio commentary
as their former workmate
Tommy Farr challenges
Joe Louis for the world
heavyweight title in 1937.
Below left: John Snagge
became famous for his
commentaries on
rowing events

status as a sports broadcaster has been undermined in recent years, even if in reality the quantity and quality of the output remains at the top of the Premiership. In purely football terms, most people get their weekly injection of action through *Match of the Day* – still the jewel in the BBC crown.

Of course, there is more than ever on television and radio these days and, in the digital age, who knows how coverage will diversify and how long it will take before everything from show jumping to synchronised swimming is on pay-per-view. That in many ways is why the challenges that lie ahead are the greatest ever faced by those charged with upholding the ethos of Public Service Broadcasting. But the House of Windsor appreciated the need to adapt and adjust as the hyper-ravenous vultures gathered overhead. And so must the House of Reith.

In the world of sport, it's time for the BBC to come out of its corner fighting and reclaim its title.

Cynics will say that this collection is more an obituary than a celebration, a lament for a lost empire. Nothing of the sort. It's an acknowledgement that society as a whole, and sport in particular, would have been infinitely poorer over the past 70 years without the men and women who set the standards for others to follow.

An old bird remembers...

The birth of sport broadcasting

BY ONE OF THE BBC'S FIRST COMMENTATORS

It is a pleasure to contribute to Seventy Years of BBC Sport seeing that, at 91, I suppose I might be the last survivor of the early days of sports broadcasting. I began in the autumn of 1934 by contributing weekly talks on Saturday evenings to what was then called the BBC Empire Service, giving a résumé of what had happened in British sport over the preceding week to far-flung parts of the Commonwealth and Empire.

I made my first cricket running commentary of a county match at The Oval between Surrey and Lancashire on 31 August 1938. This came about because I was determined to see Test matches in South Africa in 1938/9, and to broadcast them home. "Lobby", the head of outside broadcasts – otherwise known as S.J. de Lotbinière, the great pioneer of the developing art of talking sport over the air – was trying me out.

As it happened, my half-hour (no scorer, of course) included 10 minutes between innings faced by an empty field. I talked through that period and Lobby was quite congratulatory afterwards.

Thus I became the first person to go abroad on a cricket assignment for the BBC. On my return I covered the three Tests of 1939 against the West Indies alongside Howard Marshall and Michael Standing. We gave most of the game to home listeners and ball-by-ball all day back to the West Indies.

I was lucky to work with these two. Marshall, who had only been allowed to progress from eye-witness to running commentary in the summer of 1938, had the voice, the pace and the knowledge of the game to set a high standard. Both he and Standing became famous names in other fields, including coronations and the D-day Landings in Howard's case, and lively outside broadcasts by Michael such as *Standing on the Corner*!

The contrasting personalities of broadcasters were, I think, evident enough, though we all implicitly followed certain inviolable rules.

> •The opening of the broadcast football season will mean thrilling Saturday afternoons for sports enthusiasts.•
>
> RADIO TIMES
> 9 SEPTEMBER 1927

'Lobby' – a real pioneer in the art of talking sport over the air

That was certainly true of those with whom I shared commentaries and summaries after the war, notably John Arlott and Rex Alston. Those rules included never being late on the delivery of the ball, and always giving the score and scorer when a run was scored.

> 'The story of Aintree and Putney, of the Grand National Steeplechase and the University Boat Race, will be heard by listeners all over the country on Friday and Saturday of this week. In 1927 these two broadcasts were among the most successful and popular of the year. This week's Radio Times deals specially with the two races, each a classic in its own category. You will find plans of the courses on page 593, and on the previous page articles by Geoffrey Gilbey and G.O. Nickalls, this year's commentators.'

RADIO TIMES, 23 MARCH 1928

When televised cricket started in 1950, I alternated 50-50 between the two media, at first on television with Brian Johnston and Peter West, and later, as soon as they retired, with Denis Compton and Richie Benaud, who is happily still performing. I broadcast every home Test, and many from Australia, South Africa and the West Indies up to my retirement from *The Daily Telegraph* in 1975.

It was hard work combining the writing and the talking but I loved the game and I loved communicating my picture of it to all

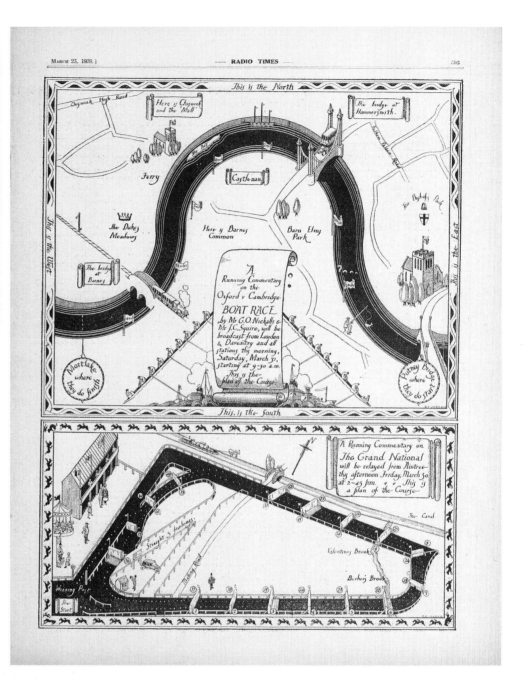

Radio Times went graphic with two illustrations depicting major sporting events in 1928. The top illustration showed the route along the Thames for the Boat Race between Oxford and Cambridge Universities, while the bottom drawing gave readers an unusual look at what horses and riders experience in the Grand National at Aintree. Note the borders on the two drawings – waves surround the top picture while horses border the bottom illustration who would read and listen. I don't think one can do the job justice unless one does have, despite all the troubles that spring up, a deep affection for the game.

Lobby, although he was an administrator and not a performer, was such an expert on the techniques of every sort of outside broadcast that he gave what was rated a notably successful teach-in to us all at Broadcasting House in November 1951.

Here is the full cast of those attending, some of whom are still well-remembered nearly half a century on: Harold Abrahams, Rex Alston, Eamonn Andrews, W. Barrington Dalby, Michael Barsley, Patrick Burns, Jack Crump, Richard Dimbleby, Peter Dimmock, Charles Gardner, Arthur Gilligan,

Howard Marshall (left) and Raymond Glendenning set high standards

Raymond Glendenning, Billy Griffith, Michael Henderson, Robert Hudson, C. A. Kershaw, John Lane, David Lloyd James,

Howard Marshall, Richard North, Daphne Padel, C. Parker, Robin Richards, Max Robertson, Audrey Russell, Berkeley Smith, John Snagge, David Southwood, E. W. Swanton, Wynford Vaughan Thomas, Graham Walker and Peter West.

A final thought, if I may: when Teddy (H.B.T.) Wakelam was about to make the first broadcast at Twickenham on January 25, 1927, his producer, one Lance Sieveking, introduced to him a blind man from St Dunstan's and said: "Don't worry about your audience, just tell our friend here what's happening." It was a stroke of genius, for the prime truth of all broadcasting is that you are talking not to the wide world but to one person at a time.

1927 • THE ARRIVAL OF THE RUNNING COMMENTARY

'Back to square one...'

It's a phrase heard all over the world, but very few people are aware that its origins are part of the birth of BBC Radio sport broadcasting in Britain. In January 1927, with the arrival of 'running commentaries' on sporting events, BBC Radio sought ways of making the accounts easy to follow. For football and rugby, *Radio Times* printed a chart showing the pitch divided up into eight numbered squares. The commentator was then able to refer to the chart as he described the action – "Play is now in square five", for example. And when the ball was passed to the goalkeeper, it was "Back to square one."

In the 1920s, *Radio Times* created charts with eight numbered squares to help listeners follow the action

The artist may have drawn on his imagination for some of the details of this picture, but this is the actual Derby course, so use this drawing when you listen to the Derby broadcast.

An early illustration in *Radio Times* imaginatively depicts the course for The Derby

The Twenties

HELEN WILLS-MOODY

WALTER HAMMOND

THE 1920S WERE AN AGE OF SPORTING HEROES.
BOBBY JONES, HELEN WILLS MOODY, JACK DEMPSEY,
JOE DAVIS, GORDON RICHARDS, BABE RUTH, DIXIE DEAN,
WALLY HAMMOND, TAZIO NUVOLARI, JACK HOBBS
AND EVEN A DOG CALLED MICK THE MILLER...
MANY OF THE CHARACTERS WERE LARGER THAN LIFE,
AND THEIR FEATS BEYOND BELIEF

Main photo: Bobby Jones thrills the gallery at St Andrews in 1927,
where he won the Open Championship for the second year in a row.
Above: Helen Wills Moody and Wally Hammond dominated their
respective sports of tennis and cricket during the late 1920s

Above: Finland's Ville Ritola
won two Gold medals at
the 1924 Olympics.
Right: Jack Dempsey and
Gene Tunney in their
famous 1927 title fight,
when Tunney was saved
by 'the long count'.
Main photo: Ted Ray's
Great Britain & Ireland team
set sail for the United States
to contest the inaugural
Ryder Cup in 1927,
which the US won 9½ - 2½

Twenties Diary

BEGINNING WITH A FAMILIAR SCORELINE FROM HIGHBURY...

1927

Broadcasting history is made on 22 January 1927 when BBC Radio features Arsenal v Sheffield Wednesday live from Highbury. The game ended in a 1-1 draw.

The FA Cup Final is also broadcast live on BBC Radio. A crowd of 91,206 see the Cup leave England for the first and only time when Cardiff City beat Arsenal 1-0.

Boxing's infamous long count: Gene Tunney retains the World Heavyweight Championship when the referee delays starting the count after Jack Dempsey floors the champion. Tunney gets $1 million for the fight.

The year of BBC sporting firsts continues with live radio commentary from Wimbledon, where Helen Wills Moody wins the first of her eight titles.

A British team captained by Ted Ray lose golf's first official Ryder Cup to Walter Hagen's America in Worcester, Massachusetts. The great Bobby Jones wins The Open Championship with a record-breaking total of 285, a year after winning both the British and US Opens.

Babe Ruth breaks his own record by hitting 60 home runs – a record that will stand until Roger Maris's 61 in '61.

1928

Dixie Dean wins Everton the League title with a record 60 goals, overtaking the 59 scored the year before by George Camsell for Second Division Middlesbrough. But even Dean can't match the 66 scored by Jimmy Smith for Ayr United – a Scottish record that may never be broken.

Scotland humiliate England at Wembley, thrashing them 5-1, but Wales win the Home Championship for the third time in the decade (while Scotland won it seven times).

Women compete in the Olympics for the first time at the Amsterdam Games. Germany's Lisa Rodke wins the 800 metres – an event scrapped after several women finished in pain. She thus held the title until 1960.

Wally Hammond takes an unprecedented 78 catches in the season, including 10 in a match for Gloucestershire against Surrey. Both records still stand today.

Don Bradman (below) makes his Test debut against England at Brisbane. After scores of 18 and one he is dropped for the only time in his career. Hammond scores 905 Test runs in the series as England retain the Ashes 4-1.

PLAYER'S CIGARETTES

D. G. BRADMAN (N. S. WALES)

1929

Fred Perry becomes the first Briton to win the table tennis World Championship, breaking the domination of Hungary, who won it for nine out of 10 years from its inauguration in 1926. Perry later became the last British man to win Wimbledon, taking it three times in a row (1934-36).

Legends of the Golden Age
THE TWENTIETH CENTURY STARTS HERE...

GIANTS OF THE '20s

Sport in the 1920s was so colourful, it demanded to be heard on the air. Here are a few of the heroes whose deeds inspired the early broadcasters

By Peter Matthews

Batting master

JACK HOBBS, known to all simply as 'The Master', was the supreme batsman of his era. Although he was later surpassed in Test match run-scoring by Don Bradman, Hobbs amassed 61,237 runs in first-class cricket – a record that will surely never be matched. His career lasted 30 years from his belated debut aged 22, but five of those were lost to the Great War.

Of his record 197 centuries, 98 came after the age of 40. Our picture shows him in 1926, the year after he passed W. G. Grace's 126 centuries. It was in 1926 that his partnership with Yorkshireman Herbert Sutcliffe reached its high point, helping England regain the Ashes lost before the War.

His classical style delighted all who watched Hobbs play for England and Surrey. He was also a superb cover fielder and, in 1953, became the first professional cricketer to be knighted.

Left: Jack Hobbs was the greatest run-scorer in cricket's history.
Right: Hobbs in 1926. His style was founded on a perfectly correct stance, and he retained an unerring eye for line and length until he retired at the age of 51

Snooker's Mr Cool

JOE DAVIS was the personification of snooker for some 30 years, popularising the game as it emerged from the shadow of billiards – a sport at which he was a four-time World Champion.

Davis initiated and won the first World Snooker title in 1926 and remained unbeaten (apart from handicap matches) until 1955. Indeed, such was his superiority, he retired from World Championship play after winning the title for the 15th time in 1946. If this was to allow his younger brother Fred to succeed him, it did not work, as Fred was beaten by Walter Donaldson in the 1947 final, before taking the title for the first time a year later.

Joe continued to win other major tournaments and, in 1955, became the first man to make a maximum break of 147 under championship conditions.

Spurred to victory

GORDON RICHARDS rode a record 4,870 winners in Britain between 1921 and 1954. This amazing figure was 2,000 more than the previous record; he was also Champion Jockey a record 26 times from 1925 to 1953. He only lost that title in 1926, to Tommy Weston, in 1930 when Freddie Fox beat him by one, and in 1941, when he broke a leg.

He surpassed Fred Archer's season's record with 259 winners in 1933 and improved that record to 269 in 1947, with 12 years at 200 or more. His domination is shown by the fact that the runner-up in 1933 was Bill Nevett on 72!

Yet there was no Epsom Derby winner for Richards in his younger days. Then, in the autumn of his career, he had a hugely popular win on Pinza in 1953, just a few days after it was announced that he was to be knighted for his services to the sport.

HELEN WILLS MOODY

Helen Wills Moody won Wimbledon eight times, and so dominated the game that she was unbeaten at the world's top tennis championship from 1926 to 1933. In fact, she did not lose a set in singles play for six years.

She won 31 major titles, including 19 at singles. But she was not a crowd-pleaser, because her relentless run of successes came with no visible display of emotion.

Also a fine artist and illustrator, Helen Wills Moody died at the grand old age of 92 at the beginning of 1998.

of the Twenties

MICK THE MILLER

The king of greyhounds, Mick the Miller was so famous that on his death in 1939, his body was embalmed and sent for display to the Natural History Museum in London. He had come a long way. Bred by a parish priest in Ireland, he won 15 of 20 races there before going to England in 1929, where he promptly became the first dog to win the Greyhound Derby twice, in 1929 and 1930. Two days after his second triumph he won the Cesarewitch.

He won 46 of his 61 races in Britain, including 19 in a row in 1929-30. In his last race, at Wembley in October 1931, he won the St Leger over 700 yards, the longest distance he ever raced. He set numerous national and world records and was at his best at distances from 525 to 700 yards. He starred in the film of his life, *Wild Boy*, in 1935.

A perfect gent

WALLY HAMMOND's glorious cover drive thrilled cricket lovers and was cited by coaches of young cricketers as perfection.

A rather stern figure, Walter Hammond was a good all-rounder. As a batsman he was exceeded as a run-scorer from the 1920s to the 1940s only by Don Bradman. He was also a brilliant slip fielder who took a season's record 78 catches in 1928 for Gloucestershire and England, and a fine medium-fast bowler who took 732 first-class wickets, including 83 in Tests. He scored 50,551 runs in all, and his average in 85 Tests from 1927-47 was a superb 58.45 for a then record total of 7,249 runs.

With 336 not out in 318 minutes against New Zealand in 1933, he set the then highest Test score, and having scored 227 in the first of the two Tests, his 563.00 is the highest ever average for a Test series. He changed status from professional to amateur and became England's captain in 1938.

Jack the lad

JACK DEMPSEY won the World Heavyweight Boxing Championship in 1919 by savagely defeating fellow American Jess Willard – who was four stones heavier. Dempsey's manager, Tex Rickard, made the flashy Manassa Mauler one of the best-known heavyweights ever. He defended his title six times in seven years before massive crowds, but was badly out of shape when he lost the title to former light heavyweight champion Gene Tunney in 1926.

The rematch was a year later. Dempsey floored Tunney in the seventh round, but took several seconds to realise he had to go to a neutral corner before the referee could start the count. Tunney remained on his knees for 15 seconds, but got to his feet on a count of nine and went on to win on points. The fight became known as 'The Long Count'.

Tunney retired undefeated. Both men prospered in business, living into their 80s.

Above: Jack Dempsey (right) fights Tom Gibbons

Baseball's all-American hero

BABE RUTH was to baseball what Don Bradman was to cricket, although he had a very different personality. A larger than life character in every way, he was a hero to millions of Americans, who mourned when he died from throat cancer in 1948, three weeks after the premiere of the movie *The Babe Ruth Story*. Ruth began his career as a pitcher with the Boston Red Sox, but in 1920 he was traded to the New York Yankees, where he shifted to playing right field.

Already known as a good batter, his abilities blossomed and he became the game's greatest power hitter. He was widely considered to have 'saved' baseball, regenerating interest after the betting scandal of 1919.

He hit 60 home runs in 1927 and 714 career home runs. He is still the all-time leader on slugging average.

Millions of Americans mourned when Babe Ruth died of throat cancer in 1948

'The University Boat Race is one hundred years old today. What is the secret of it? One would love to know. Perhaps it is just that this is such a decent piece of sport. It represents so great, but yet so unindividual a physical effort. There is no prize in it save honour. No man in it rows for himself, but for his crew and his University. Of necessity, being British, the spirit of the thing appeals to us.'

RADIO TIMES, MARCH 15 1929

Bobby dazzler

BOBBY JONES was the first man to do the golf Grand Slam – except it was then called the Impregnable Quadrilateral, and consisted of the British and American Open and Amateur Championships. After that stunning coup in 1930, Jones retired at the age of 28, although in later years he would play each year in the great tournament he founded – The Masters at Augusta in his home state of Georgia.

A supreme stylist, he finished eighth in the US Open when only 18. In his last nine US Opens he was first four times and second four times; he also won the US Amateur five times. He won three of the four British Opens he contested, with a qualifying round of 66 at Sunningdale in 1926 – an unheard-of feat at the time.

A popular and erudite man with degrees in literature and law, he later suffered from a spinal cord disease which kept him wheel-chair-bound for a decade to his death in 1971.

Above: Tazio Nuvolari driving an Auto Union – a team he joined in the latter part of his career. He won his first motor racing Grand Prix in 1927 and his last, at the age of 54, in 1946

DIXIE DEAN

Ferrari's favourite

TAZIO NUVOLARI was the man that Enzo Ferrari described as the greatest driver of all – yet he actually started out by racing motorbikes from 1923 to 1929. Small and wiry, he was known as Il Campionissimo, 'The Great Champion', and his feats made him a big hero in his native Italy.

By 1930 Nuvolari had made the jump to motor racing, which was a very different sport from the high-tech procession of the 1990s. There was much more scope for the skill and panache of the drivers to be recognised, and Tazio was the greatest star of that era.

Just as he had become a living legend on motor cycles, he did the same on four wheels, with a large number of major wins up to his last race in 1950. In the 1930s he won most of the major Grand Prix races, usually driving Alfa-Romeos. His win at Nurburgring in 1935, driving an Alfa designed by Ferrari against superior German cars, was rated one of the greatest ever.

William Ralph Dean, nicknamed 'Dixie' because of his swarthy complexion, scored 60 goals in 39 League matches for Everton in the 1927/28 season to set a record which still stands today. Bill Dean's total that season in all competitions was 82.

The previous season he uniquely scored at least twice in each of his first five internationals (12 goals in all). Amazingly, this feat came just months after a motorbike accident in which he broke his skull.

With the advent of stopper centre-halves, the goals came more slowly, and in all he scored 18 times in 16 internationals for England. A robust centre-forward, he was renowned for the power and direction of his heading, and scored 473 goals in 502 first-class matches. While he was with Everton, they won the Football League in 1928 and 1932, and the FA Cup in 1933. Sadly, his right leg was amputated in 1976 and he died at Goodison Park after an Everton v Liverpool match in 1980.

Flying Finns

and Chariots of Fire

The Paris Olympic Games of 1924 were dominated by the 'Flying Finns', led by the legendary Paavo Nurmi. He won a record five Gold medals, including a unique double of the 1500 and 5,000 metres which he ran within 100 minutes on the same afternoon. He also won the 10,000m cross country race on a day when the temperature rose to over 40 degrees Centigrade and more than half the 38 starters in the field failed to finish. And if he had not been excluded from the 10,000m track race, which

Right: Ville Ritola leads fellow Finn Paavo Nurmi.
Below: Britain's Eric Liddell set a new world record in the 400m relay.

JEUX OLYMPIQUES DE 1924
ARRIVÉE DU 100m FINALE GAGNÉE PAR ABRAHAMS

386

A.N PARIS

**Above: Britain's Harold Abrahams wins the 100 metres.
Right: Paavo Nurmi after winning the 10,000 metres cross country in 40-degree heat.
Far right: The Prince of Wales congratulates a robed Harold Abrahams after the first round heat for the 200 metres**

was won by his countryman Ville Ritola, he probably would have taken that too.

An unusual situation occurred in the long jump, when the world record was beaten in the pentathlon by Robert LeGendre (USA), who had not made his team for the individual long jump itself.

But in British hearts this Games has been immortalised by the Oscar-winning film *Chariots of Fire*. Harold Abrahams and Eric Liddell were unexpected victors in the 100 metres and 400 metres, with 100m specialist Liddell setting a new 400m world record. Abrahams later became a distinguished commentator for BBC Radio.

Left: The flags are raised on the 1928 Olympic Games in Amsterdam. Below: Olympic Games founder Baron de Coubertin was against women participating in the games

Women liberated
A 16-year-old steals the show

the founder of the modern Olympic Games, Baron de Coubertin, was against the participation of women in the Games, and was supported by many governing bodies. Nevertheless, there were half a dozen female competitors in tennis at Paris in 1900, and swimmers were allowed in 1912.

Women athletes had to wait until 1928 for their turn, after de Coubertin had resigned from the Presidency of the IOC

due to ill health. At Amsterdam there were only five women's events, and Great Britain boycotted them as a protest against the limited number. World records were broken in all five disciplines – 100 metres, 800 metres, sprint relay, high jump and discus – but there were such distressing scenes at the end of the longer race that the 800 metres was banned from the Olympics for the next 36 years.

A 16-year-old American student, Betty

Robinson, won the 100 metres to become the first female Olympic athletics champion, and remains the youngest winner of that event.

Scotland's sweetest success
England 1 Scotland 5

England against Scotland was the big match throughout the inter-war period, and Scotland came out much the better, with 11 wins to six for England and three draws.

The high spot for Scotland came on 31 March 1928, when a Scots team later termed the 'Wembley Wizards' destroyed England 5-1. Making better use of a wet pitch, the visitors thrashed the bigger Englishmen with a display of skilful possession football.

From the right wing the brilliant Alec Jackson scored three goals. He was one of a legendary forward line of Jackson, Dunn, Gallacher, James and Morton, none of whom was over 5 feet 7 inches in height.

Alex James and James Gibson were the other scorers for Scotland, and Robert Kelly scored England's goal from a last-minute free kick. The one worrying point for Scottish football was that eight of this team were 'Anglos', playing their football with English clubs.

The Scots take Wembley in 1928. The English goal was bombarded as Scotland cruised to a 5-1 win. This photo shows centre-forward Hughie Gallacher (on the ground) narrowly missing the English net

The Thirties

It may have been the age of the Great Depression, but the 1930s were also a decade of great sport. Jesse Owens upstaged Hitler at the 1936 Olympics. Fred Perry won Wimbledon, Stanley Matthews made his debut, and Bobby Jones did golf's Grand Slam. Cricket was ruled by Bradman; and divided by Bodyline. And the BBC began to cover sport on television...

Main photo: Fred Perry in action during Wimbledon.
Above top: Italy celebrate winning the 1934 World Cup Final.
Above left: Don Bradman set many cricket records in the 30s.
Above right: Jesse Owens shone in the 1936 Berlin Olympics

1930

New Zealand's cricketers play their first Test match, losing to a second-string England touring party. The main England XI, with Bill Voce, Les Ames and Patsy Hendren, are held to a 1-1 series draw in the West Indies, whose backbone is George Headley (703 runs in four matches).

Bobby Jones does the golf Grand Slam.

The first ever Commonwealth Games are held in Hamilton, Canada. Then known as the British Empire Games, the event involved 11 countries. Women competed at swimming only, and the star of the show was English hurdler Lord Burghley, who won three Gold medals to add to the 400 metres hurdles Gold he had won at the 1928 Olympics.

Bill Tilden wins his third Wimbledon singles title, 10 years after the first. He had also won the US Championship seven times in the Twenties.

Uruguay win the first World Cup Final.

Sir Henry Segrave dies after breaking the world water speed record when his boat crashes on Lake Windermere. Segrave, who in the Twenties had been a successful motor racing driver (and the first to wear a helmet), had clocked up a speed of 98.76 mph.

In a sign of things to come, Don Bradman reaps revenge for his first Test disappointment by scoring 974 runs in his first series in England at an average of 139. The Don scores an unbelievable 300 in one day at Headingley, en route to a Test record of 334.

1932

Wales win the first four-nation 'Five Nations' after France are barred from rugby union's International Championship for breaching amateur rules. They returned in 1947.

Australia's slow left-armer Bert Ironmonger takes 11 wickets for 24 runs on a 'wet sticky' at Melbourne as South Africa total 81 in two innings – the lowest ever. Bradman averages 200 as Australia win the series 5-0.

Above: Ted Drake goes for a run at Highbury shortly after scoring seven goals for Arsenal in a 7-1 rout of Aston Villa in 1935. Right: Bill Tilden in action at Wimbledon

J. B. HOBBS (SURREY)

D.G.BRADMAN
NEW SOUTH WALES.

Stanley Matthews makes his debut for Second Division Stoke City in a glamorous fixture against Bury.

Controversy hits cricket as England attempt to win the Ashes using the 'leg theory'. Questions are asked in the Parliaments of both countries, as the England quicks, Larwood and Voce, pepper the Australian batsmen with the kind of hostile bowling never seen before. England win despite The Don battling to average 56.57 in the series.

1933

Wally Hammond averages a record 563 on a tour of New Zealand. His final innings of 336 not out – the fastest 300 ever – was the hightest Test score at the time.

Gordon Richards rides an incredible 246 winners in his best ever season, in his eighth year as Champion Jockey.

Fred Perry captains England to Davis Cup victory.

Boxing fans are shocked when Jack Sharkey is beaten by unfancied Primo Carnera – the first (and last) Italian World Heavyweight Champion.

1934

Jack Hobbs scores his last first class 100, his 197th, at the age of 51.

Italy become the first European side to win the World Cup when they beat Czechoslovakia 2-1 in Rome. Defending champions Uruguay choose not to attend.

A unique double: Golden Miller wins both the Grand National and the Cheltenham Gold Cup.

1935

Arsenal win their third League title in a row, a year after the death of inspirational manager Herbert Chapman. Ted Drake hits seven goals for Arsenal v Aston Villa, equalling the First Division record set in 1888 by James Ross of Preston North End. The record still stands.

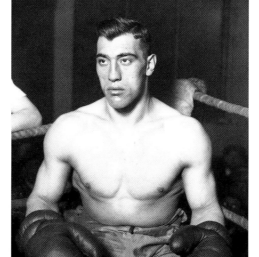

1936

Arsenal do a unique double. Having hosted the first ever radio sport broadcast in 1927, they are now the home team for the first televised football game. The visitors are Everton.

Hitler's plans for a stage-managed German Olympics triumph are upset when black American Jesse Owens storms to four Golds.

Great Britain stage an upset by winning the Olympic ice hockey for the only time.

1937

The Brown Bomber, Joe Louis, begins his reign as World Heavyweight Champion by beating James J. Braddock.

A British record crowd of 149,547 people cram into Hampden Park to watch Scotland beat England 3-1 – but the home championship goes to Wales for the last time.

Welshman Tommy Farr's heroic attempt to take Joe Louis' title ends in disappointment when he loses on points.

1938

Jimmy McGrory retires after scoring a record 550 goals for Celtic, Clydebank and Scotland. His 50 for Celtic in 1935-36 remains that team's highest tally ever.

A year of TV firsts: BBC screens its first coverage of rugby (England v Scotland for the Calcutta Cup), cricket (the Second Ashes Test at Lord's, a draw in which Hammond scored 240) and swimming (the European Championships from the Empire Pool, Wembley).

1939

The first TV golf: BBC screens action from a 72-hole match from Coombe Hill, Surrey, between young South African Bobby Locke and 1938 Open champion Reg Whitcombe.

Time is called on the last 'Timeless Test'. After 10 days, MCC are 42 runs short of victory against South Africa in Durban when rain stops play. They pack up and go home.

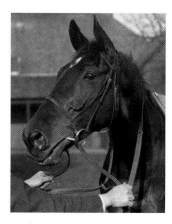

Above: Stanley Matthews as a teenager for Stoke City in 1933.
Top: Golden Miller was the world's greatest steeplechaser.
Above left: Italy's Primo Carnera was world heavyweight boxing champion from 1933-34

Cricket's most bitter controversy
The battle of Bodyline
AUSTRALIA v ENGLAND 1932: WHEN THE GAME TURNED NASTY

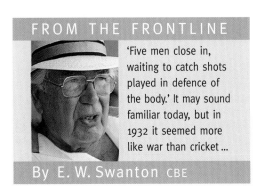

'Five men close in, waiting to catch shots played in defence of the body.' It may sound familiar today, but in 1932 it seemed more like war than cricket ...

By E. W. Swanton CBE

The word 'Bodyline' was probably coined by an Australian journalist covering the 1932-33 Test series between Australia and England. It is thought to have come from telegraphese, a form of shorthand, to describe the fast bowling tactics used by the England bowlers on the orders of captain Douglas Jardine (pictured right).

Though the word was resented by many, it presented a fair picture of the tactics which caused the biggest upset in the game's history. Bodyline consisted of fast bowling pitched short on the line of the batsman's body and rising to the ribs, chest or shoulders, sometimes head high. There were five men, even six on occasion, fielding in a crescent at close range around the bat, waiting to take catches from strokes played in defence of the body.

The affair climaxed in the third Test at Adelaide, where crowd reaction was so fierce that mounted police were on hand in case spectators invaded the field. Their presence was justified following casualties, one involving national hero Don Bradman.

The tactics, as used by Harold Larwood, the fastest bowler of the day, and his fast left-arm county partner Bill Voce, were considered before the MCC team left England. Those who discussed the matter included Jardine, Notts captain A. W. Carr, and P.G.H. Fender, former captain of Surrey. It was under Carr's encouragement that Larwood and Voce had bowled at times in an intimidating way – a tactic much resented by other counties – though not to an "umbrella" field.

The object now was to reduce the effectiveness of Bradman, who as a young man of 21 had broken all records on Australia's 1930 tour of England. In his last Test innings at The Oval, after rain had made the pitch spiteful, Bradman was deemed to have been uncomfortable with the short, fast ball, even though he had scored 232, to add to his scores earlier in the series of 131, 254 and 334. Hence the experiment.

Bodyline succeeded to the extent that the victim's average fell from 139 in England to a human 56. It also allowed England to recover the Ashes by a margin of 4-1. But the cost in terms of relationships between not only the

PLAYER'S CIGARETTES

D. R. JARDINE (SURREY)

players, but the Australian and English publics was immense. At the height of the Adelaide Test, the Australian Board of Control sent the first of many cables to and from the MCC. The first outlined their concerns:

"Bodyline bowling has assumed such proportions as to menace the best interests of the game, making protection of the body by the batsmen the main consideration.

"This is causing intensely bitter feeling between the players as well as injury. In our opinion it is unsportsmanlike. Unless stopped at once it is likely to upset the friendly relation existing between Australia and England."

The MCC's first response deplored the cable with its allegation of bad sportsmanship, and said they "would consent but with great reluctance" if the board considered cancellation of the tour desirable. In a third cable the ABC retracted the word unsportsmanlike.

Between 18 January and 14 December 1933, 13 cables passed, the later ones concerning whether Australia would send a team to England in 1934, and if so with what guarantees. They did come, the tour taking place in a tense atmosphere which did not approach normality until G. O. Allen took

Bodyline in action – Australian batsman Bill Woodfull ducks a ball by Harold Larwood during the 1933 Test match in Brisbane. Note the legside 'umbrella' field

the next MCC side to Australia in 1936/7.

What fueled the controversy was, apart from press reports, the primitive communications of 60-odd years ago. The MCC remained almost completely in the dark about Bodyline until the England team returned home from a tour of New Zealand in May. By this time J. H. Thomas, Secretary of State for the Dominions, had begun talks on the matter

with Sir Alexander Hore-Ruthven (later Lord Gowrie), Governor of South Australia. On his return to Australia, Sir Alexander played a pacifying role with Jimmy Thomas and the MCC manager Plum Warner. The latter hated Bodyline, but didn't have the strength of character to influence Jardine.

People at home followed the issue through Jack Hobbs, Warwick Armstrong and Bruce

Harris, all writing for London evening papers, and Gilbert Mant of the Reuter/PA agencies.

Hobbs, the greatest name in English cricket, was still on the Surrey staff and Jardine was his captain. The team were his friends. How could he, with his background, make criticisms which would have been promptly wired back and headlined in the Australian press? He wrote factual reports,

Champion
of the Thirties

FRED PERRY

The most stylish man in Thirties sport first achieved fame when he won the World Table Tennis Championship. When he switched his attention to the outdoor game, Fred Perry did not do things by halves. He travelled to the United States to compete in the 1933 US Open – and defeated Wimbledon champion Jack Crawford in five sets, becoming the first Briton to win America's national championship since 1903.

The win set Perry on the road to stardom. He went on to win Wimbledon a year later, defeating Crawford again, to become the first British winner for 25 years.

Perry won again in 1935 and 1936, making him the first man to win three successive titles – a record that stood until Bjorn Borg reigned over Wimbledon in the Seventies.

though when he returned home he condemned Bodyline in *The Star*.

Armstrong's reports were critical but he had not endeared himself as Australia's captain in England in 1921, and was seen as a hostile witness. Mant was an Australian and agencies were by custom non-controversial.

There was Harris of *The Evening Standard*, a respected sports reporter who knew nothing of cricket. He aimed naturally to keep close to the captains and Jardine was shrewd enough to use him as a mouthpiece. Harris accordingly took a pro-Bodyline stance, later writing a book called *Jardine Justified*, with a foreword by Jardine! Harris wrote what English people wanted to hear: The Aussies were squealers and our boys were the objects of hostile colonials who couldn't take a beating.

When the true nature of Bodyline sank in, the MCC were obliged to make illegal what was defined as 'Direct Attack'. On this basis

agreement was reached for the 1934 tour of England to go forward. The MCC agreed to issue the invitation by only eight votes to five.

In the 1934 edition of Wisden, editor Sydney Southerton deplored the tactic "because it makes cricket a battle instead of a game" and wrote a thorough appraisal of 'The Bowling Controversy'. He ended with this clear and succinct epitaph:

"For myself, I hope that we shall never see fast leg-theory bowling as used during the last tour in Australia exploited in this country. I think that (1) it is definitely dangerous; (2) it creates ill-feeling between the rival teams; (3) it invites reprisals; (4) it has a bad influence on our great game of cricket; (5) it eliminated practically all the best strokes in batting."

There was no broadcast coverage of Bodyline. What if Test Match Special had been on, let alone exposure on TV? It would have made riveting watching, that's for sure.

English captain Douglas Jardine (centre) leads his side out to face Australia in the controversial 1932-33 series

Golden Miller's golden year
The only horse ever to win the National and the Gold Cup

In the 1930s Golden Miller brought National Hunt racing to a new peak of popularity. He first achieved fame in winning the 1934 Grand National. Ridden by Gerry Wilson, this great horse set a race record time of nine minutes 20.4 seconds despite carrying a top weight of 12 stone 2 lb. The victory completed a unique double, for the previous month he had taken the third of his record five straight wins in the Cheltenham Gold Cup, with four different jockeys.

Bred in Ireland, Golden Miller was trained by Basil Briscoe between 1930-35 and then by Owen Anthony. After two wins as a three-year-old, he was bought by the Honourable Dorothy Paget in 1931. While he lost his jockey, Ted Leader, in his first National (1933), Golden Miller never fell and won 29 of his 55 races between 1930-39.

A statue of him was unveiled at Cheltenham in 1989.

Right: Golden Miller in action at Aintree en route to winning the 1934 Grand National.
Above right: Gerry Wilson rides Golden Miller to the winner's circle after winning at Aintree

Uruguay set the ball rolling

Home advantage plays a big part in the first two World Cup finals

Above: Winners Uruguay. Right: French soccer boss Jules Rimet (left) with the Jules Rimet Trophy, or World Cup

england, Scotland, Wales and Ireland did not contest the first World Cup; indeed only four European teams undertook the long boat journey to Uruguay in 1930. All were soundly beaten by South American teams. Although Yugoslavia made the semi-finals, they were thrashed 6-1 by Uruguay. The host nation went on to beat Argentina 4-2 in the final in Montevideo.

Uruguay did not defend their title in 1934. Again the host nation, this time Italy, emerged victorious. The Italians defeated Czecho-

Right: Uruguayan players celebrate winning the 1930 World Cup.
Left: A massive crowd watched their 4-2 win over Argentina in Montevideo

slovakia 2-1 in the final. The British teams were not members of FIFA during the 1930s, and did not take part during that decade. However, England won all home matches against foreign opposition in that era, including the infamous 'Battle of Highbury' against world champions Italy in November 1934.

It was Italy's first international after their World Cup win. In a brutal match, Italy were reduced to 10 men when Luisito Monti suffered a broken toe after five minutes. England captain Eddie Hapgood, one of seven Arsenal men in the England team, had his nose broken on his home ground. England led 3-0 at half-time but Italy came back well with two goals from Giuseppe Meazza.

Above: Italian manager Vittorio Pozzo is carried from the field after Italy's 1934 World Cup win.
Right: Action around the Italian goalmouth during the infamous 'Battle of Highbury'

2.35 THE FOOTBALL ASSOCIATION CUP FINAL
ARSENAL v NEWCASTLE UNITED
  COMMUNITY SINGING
  Conducted by T. P. Ratcliffe. Accompanied by the Band of H. M. Welsh Guards, under the direction of Captain Andrew Harris. By kind permission of Colonel R. E. K. Leatham, D.S.O. Under the auspices of the Daily Express.
  A RUNNING COMMENTARY on the Match by GEORGE F. ALLISON (By courtesy of the Football Association). Relayed from THE EMPIRE STADIUM, WEMBLEY
  (IMPORTANT NOTICE – No unauthorised outside use may be made of a broadcast programme. In particular the copyright of all broadcast commentaries, and of all news supplied by the News Agencies, is strictly reserved. These broadcasts are for the private use of owners of receiving sets only and may not be communicated to the public by loud-speaker, lantern slide, printed slip or other device.)

RADIO TIMES, 15 APRIL 1932

The First Rugby International of the Season
Wales versus England: Broadcast from Cardiff Arms Park on Saturday, January 15

'A No.1 commentator such as Captain H. B. T. Wakelam is an unfailing source of wonderment to Rugby football crowds, and they take delight in crowding around him to see and hear him at work and, if possible, to secure his autograph. In Cardiff, however, the box is perched on the roof of the grand stand, over the halfway line and quite near the field of play. The only means of access is by a ladder from the grand stand. This ladder is taken away when play begins and the box is cut off from the world except by telephone.'

RADIO TIMES, 7 JANUARY 1938

W. H. WESTON

W. WOOLLER

1937 • BOXING

Farr fights Louis

The Welsh miner crossed the Atlantic to take America's 'Brown Bomber' the distance

August 31, 1937 and in the early hours the family and workmates of Tommy Farr gather together to crowd round their radios in the mining town of Tonypandy. Across the airwaves comes the BBC Radio commentary from New York's Madison Square Garden, where the Welsh miner is challenging American Joe Louis for the World Heavyweight Championship.

It was the Brown Bomber's first defence of the title he won two months earlier when he defeated James J. Braddock with an eighth-round knockout. The live commentary described how Farr boxed brilliantly to contain the champion's superior punching power. In a thrilling encounter, Farr took Louis the distance before losing on points.

Louis went on to 25 successful defences of his title, which he held until 1949, but the brave Briton had almost caused him to fall at the first hurdle.

Above: Tommy Farr's family gather by the radio in 1937 to listen to BBC commentary of his title fight

The Helen and Don show

Her eighth Wimbledon title, his first Grand Slam

W. T. TILDEN

the difficulties of travelling to Australia, France, Britain and the United States made it very hard for a player to achieve the Grand Slam prior to the days of air travel, but the tall, powerful American Don Budge finally achieved the feat in 1938. He won the French and Australian titles, became a triple Wimbledon champion for the third successive year, taking the singles without losing a set, and took all three titles at the US Open at Forest Hills.

He turned professional in 1938 and two years later was rated by Bill Tilden as "the greatest tennis player of all time".

In 1938 Helen Wills Moody won her eighth Wimbledon singles championship, 11 years after her first. In doing so she showed the same confidence and determination that had made her the dominant player between 1929 and 1935.

Wills Moody had a tough match against Germany's Hilde Sperling in the semi-final, whom she beat 12-10, 6-4, before easily defeating Helen Jacobs 6-4, 6-0 to secure a record eighth title.

Left: Don Budge became the first player to win the tennis Grand Slam when he achieved the feat in 1938. Bill Tilden (above) called Budge "the greatest tennis player of all time".

Far left: In the same year, 1938, Helen Wills Moody captured her eighth Wimbledon singles title

ALL ABOUT THE TEST FROM TRENT BRIDGE
'*Nottingham, where the first Test Match is being played. Howard Marshall will give eye-witness accounts of the progress of the game today and tomorrow at the lunch and tea intervals and at the close of play. Tomorrow is the last day of the match.*'

RADIO TIMES, 8 JUNE 1934

Owens four, Hitler nil
The Führer showed his disgust by stalking out

The 1936 Berlin Olympic Games had one main aim for the host nation: to glorify the Nazi regime of Adolf Hitler. But the dictator's dream of Aryan supremacy did not come true; Jesse Owens, a modest, 22-year-old black athlete from Ohio University, saw to that by winning four Gold medals.

He destroyed two world-class fields to win the 100 metres and 200 metres, he won the long jump, and led the United States to victory in world record time in the 400 metres relay.

Hitler's propaganda minister, Josef Goebbels, labelled Owens and the other American negroes "black mercenaries". After Owens' triumph in the 200 metres final the crowd rose to salute the world's greatest athlete. A fuming Hitler showed his disgust by stalking out of the stadium.

Above: The American Olympics team in Berlin for the 1936 Olympic Games. Owens is third from the right. Right: Owens on his way to four Gold medals

BABE ZAHARIAS

Mildred 'Babe' Zaharias is best remembered as a golfer – but she began her sporting career in athletics, as Mildred Didrikson. The Babe took three medals in the 1932 Olympics in Los Angeles. Good going considering she was only allowed to enter three events, much to her annoyance.

A typist from Texas, the 18-year-old won Gold medals in the 80 metres hurdles, where she set a world record, and the javelin. She also won Silver in the high jump.

After the Olympics, Mildred turned her attention to golf, becoming one of the game's greatest players under her married name of Zaharias. She won the US Open three times, her 1954 victory coming less than a year after an operation for cancer. Not content with that, Zaharias also played baseball and basketball professionally.

The Forties

PLAYER'S CIGARETTES

W. J. EDRICH

PLAYER'S CIGARETTES

D. C. S. COMPTON

It may have been the decade of the Second World War, but sportsmen and women excelled in the 1940s nevertheless, bringing colour to a drab world. Sir Stanley Matthews lit up the football field, Compton and Edrich brought glamour to cricket, Fanny Blankers-Koen stole the show at the 1948 London Olympics, Joe Louis ruled the ring – and Gussie Moran caused apoplexy at Wimbledon

Main photo: Fanny Blankers-Koen (near lane) wins the Gold medal in the 80 metres hurdles.
Above: Bill Edrich (left) and Denis Compton were the undisputed stars of English cricket

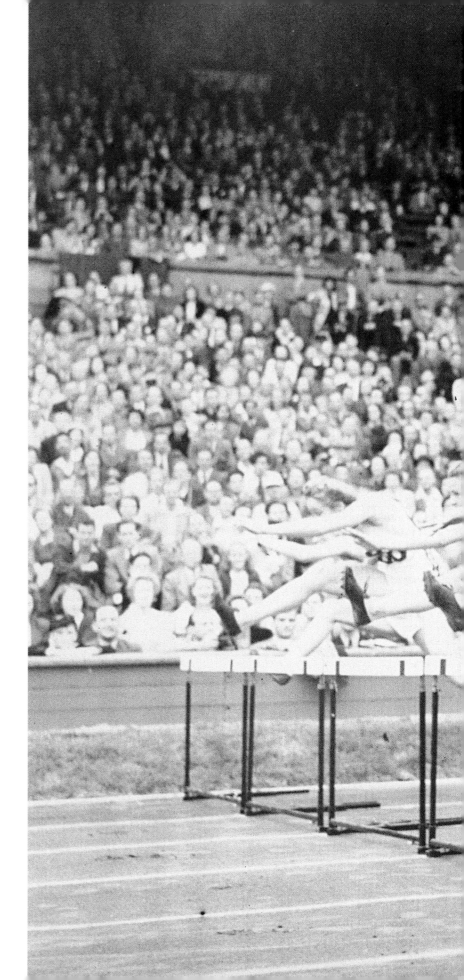

Forties Diary

1945

Former Manchester City player Matt Busby becomes the new manager of Manchester United. United had not won a major trophy since the First World War. Within three years they would win the FA Cup, and they then went on to win the League three times in the Fifties.

Australian rugby league legend Brian Bevan debuts for Warrington, beginning a career which brings him 740 tries.

1946

Tragedy strikes Bolton's Burnden Park when 33 are crushed to death during an FA Cup tie with Stoke City.

A gallant Freddie Mills loses out to American Gus Lesnevich in a battle for the vacant light heavyweight boxing title. The British fighter was knocked down eight times during 10 rounds of ferocious punching. Mills, who took Lesnevich's title two years later, was found dead from mysterious gunshot wounds in 1965.

1947

Double figures for England as they thrash Portugal 10-0, with Stan Mortensen and Tommy Lawton helping themselves to four goals each.

A landmark summer for the original 'Brylcreem Boy', Denis Compton, who scores 3,816 runs including 18 centuries. Compton's average was 94 from 753 runs against South Africa, which comprised six 100s.

The Brooklyn Dodgers initiate the long process of creating racial equality in American sport by signing the first black player, Jackie Robinson, to a Major League baseball team. The Dodgers swiftly follow with another bright young prospect, catcher Roy Campanella.

1948

Dutch golden girl Fanny Blankers-Koen stars in the London Olympics with four Gold medals.

Matt Busby's young team bring Manchester United the FA Cup for the first time since 1909, coming from behind twice to beat Blackpool 4-2.

The BBC carries the first television coverage of rugby league – the Cup Final between Bradford Northern and Wigan, from Wembley.

Don Bradman plays his last Test. After an emotional walk to the crease, the great man is bowled second ball and finishes with an unparalleled first-class average of 99.94.

1949

Juan Fangio makes his debut in European motor racing, notching up six victories.

Brian Close becomes England's youngest Test cricketer.

The great Joe Louis retires undefeated after successfully defending his crown 25 times.

England, on tour in South Africa, win two of the closest Test matches in history. The First Test is won by a leg bye off the last ball. In the Third Test, Dudley Nourse sets a target of 172 runs in 95 minutes and England lose seven wickets before getting there with one minute to spare.

Above: Don Bradman retired from Test cricket in 1948.
Picture postcard: An early baseball card depicts Jackie Robinson, the first black man to play professional baseball.
Right: Joe Louis, the Brown Bomber, trains for his 1947 fight against Jersey Joe Walcott.
Far right: Freddie Mills won the Light Heavyweight Boxing Championship from Gus Lesnevich in 1948, despite being badly beaten by Lesnevich two years earlier

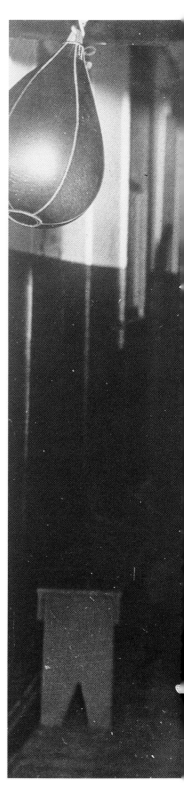

Denis Compton and Bill Edrich

The Middlesex Twins

BUCCANEERING DEEDS MADE THEM THE BEST-LOVED PARTNERSHIP IN CRICKET

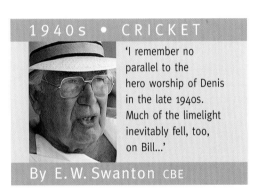

*	Matches	Innings	Not Out	Runs	Highest	Average	100s
COMPTON	515	839	88	38,942	300	51.85	123
EDRICH	571	964	92	36,965	267*	42.39	86

Cricket is rich in partnerships which have become household names, especially opening batsmen and bowlers: Hobbs and Sutcliffe, Lindwall and Miller, Woodfull and Ponsford, Trueman and Statham. Only the loftiest pinnacles carry a solitary figure: Bradman, Sobers, W.G. Grace.

In this illustrious company, Denis Charles Scott Compton CBE and William John Edrich DFC hold their high place – some might say a unique place – in the game's history.

They came together in 1937 and parted company – so far as Middlesex were concerned – at the end of the 1957 summer. Of course, war, arriving just when both were reaching their peak, took away six years, and Denis's knee troubles knocked many months off his. Nevertheless, what they achieved was still prodigious: 38,942 runs for Compton, 36,965 for Edrich, very many of them scored with the other man watching from 22 yards away.

In Tests there was a greater disparity. Denis played 78 Tests, scored 5,807 runs, and averaged 50, with 17 100s; Bill's figures were 39 matches, 2,440 runs, average 40, eight hundreds.

Each was at times more than useful as a bowler, though expensive overall. Denis (slow left-arm) had 622 wickets at 32 runs each, Bill (fast-medium right) 479 wickets at 33 apiece.

Both were highly popular, extrovert, sociable to a degree, enjoying cricket and life in equal measure. R.C. Robertson-Glasgow in the 1948 Wisden, hot upon their annus mirabilis, summed them up in a characteristically pithy phrase or two:

"Compton has genius, and, if he knows it, he doesn't care. Edrich has talent; or, more truly, he started with a number of talents and has increased them into riches."

Cricket gained much from the BBC coverage of the game on radio as soon as play resumed in 1946. Needless to say, the Middlesex Twins were constantly on air, ideal subjects for the commentator. In 1953 two events contributed greatly to the growing popularity of television: the Coronation and the Test series against Australia. The latter showed Denis and Bill

Compton has genius, and, if he knows it, he doesn't care. Edrich has talent; or, more truly, he started with a number of talents and has increased them into riches.

scoring the winning runs when England won back The Ashes at The Oval.

Denis was born at Hendon in north London, son of a cricketer father. It did not take him long to discover that the No.13 bus from his home would deposit him at Lord's Cricket Ground. In a schoolboys' match at the age of 14, he made 100 there under the eye of Plum (later Sir Pelham) Warner. Thereafter all was plain sailing. The MCC and Middlesex coaches found him marvellously endowed by nature, as indeed did their football counterparts at Arsenal.

When Norfolk-born Bill qualified by residence in 1937, Middlesex found themselves wonderfully blessed with ready-made substitutes for the famous partnership of J.W. Hearne and Pat Hendren. Which was the better? For a while opinion was divided, but not surely after Denis, having made 100 in the First Test against the 1938 Australians on a blameless pitch at Trent Bridge, saved England from highly probable defeat at Lord's with an innings of 76 not out on a pitch made truly spiteful by rain and sun. When that innings was recalled to him later in life, Denis always used to say it was his best. The coolest of 20-year-olds dealt as deftly with the lift and spin of O'Reilly as with the speed and fire of McCormick.

Denis became a Company Sergeant-Major and PT instructor in a gunner regiment in the war. Bill had a more glamorous role piloting daylight raids over Germany, and as a Squadron-Leader winning the DFC.

I remember no parallel to the hero-worship of Denis in the late '40s. Everyone wanted to forget the war, and the crowds were greater then ever before or since. The gates were closed for county matches everywhere. Denis was the man every mother wanted her son to be

Bill Edrich (far left) and Denis Compton were the ideal partnership, Edrich's courage matching Compton's flair

– good-looking, full of charm, enjoying every moment on the cricket and football field. Much of the limelight inevitably fell, too, on Bill.

Their most memorable year was, of course, 1947, that hot, dry summer wherein runs flowed from both bats with a profusion unparalleled. First Denis broke Tom Hayward's record 1906 aggregate of 3,518, then Bill followed. Denis's final tally, obviously unbeatable with modern fixture-patterns, was 3,816 with a record 18 100s and an average of 80. Edrich made 3,539. Seven times that summer they had partnerships of more than 200, headed by 370 in the Second Test against South Africa at Lord's. Poor South Africa were the chief sufferers. Denis's 753 is the most ever made by an Englishman in a Test series in England.

Compton's last innings in 1947 – 246 for Middlesex, the champions, against the Rest of England – carried a warning of trouble in store. He batted with his left knee strapped. It gave out the first signs of the wear and tear which pained and restricted him ever thereafter. But he still played 14 games for Arsenal that winter as they won the League Championship.

In cricket, several great innings lay ahead in the next 10 years culminating in 1957, his last season and Bill's last but one.

I should mention one attribute in which Bill had it over Denis: the art of captaincy. Denis was too disorganised to be a leader. But Bill was an admirable captain of Middlesex and later, with zest undiminished, of Norfolk until he was 55.

Neither lived to ripe longevity. Bill Edrich died at home following a fall, aged 70. Denis Compton struggled vainly against ill-health, dying on St George's Day, 1997, a month from his 78th birthday. Like his old friend Brian Johnston, he was honoured with a Thanksgiving Service in Westminster Abbey, and in both cases the church was filled to overflowing.

For one last time the gates had to be closed.

Fanny: The greatest of all?

The brilliant Dutch star lit up the post-war world

Fanny Blankers-Koen (far right) takes the Gold medal in the 1948 Olympic 100 metres final

The first Olympics since the Second World War were also the first main event to be broadcast live by the fledgling BBC Television service. They were hailed as a huge success, despite the strictures imposed by post-war austerity on Britain, the host nation.

Francina Blankers-Koen, a 30-year-old Dutch housewife and mother-of-two, arrived in London as world record holder in the high jump and long jump, but competed in neither. Instead she won four track events: 100 metres, 200 metres, 80 metres hurdles and the 4 x 100 metres relay.

Fanny's performances made her the most successful female athlete of all time. By the time she retired in 1955 she had set world records in *nine* different events. Naturally, she was the personality of the 1948 Games.

But Czechoslovakia's Emil Zatopek also provided a memorable contribution. He won the 10,000 metres by almost a full lap – then was just beaten to the Gold medal in the 5,000 metres after dramatically making up a deficit of 40 metres in the final lap in a despairing attempt to catch Gaston Reiff of Belgium.

'Six thousand picked athletes representing sixty-one nations have come to London from all over the world to compete in the great Olympiad which His Majesty the King will declare open at Wembley on Thursday. After the nine o'clock news on Wednesday the Prime Minister will broadcast a message of welcome. Listeners will then hear a description by Wynford Vaughan Thomas of the scene at Dover earlier in the evening as the Mayor receives the Olympic Flame from a naval runner and the Vice-Lieutenant of Kent despatches it on the last stage of its journey to London.

The Home Service broadcast of the Opening Ceremony on Thursday will last for one-and-a-half hours. Wynford Vaughan Thomas will describe the scenes for listeners in Great Britain and overseas. It is expected that 80,000 people will watch the athletes parade and see the lighting of the Torch; but many more will view the scene by television.

The broadcasting and televising of the London Olympiad will be the biggest operation of its kind that the BBC has ever undertaken.'

RADIO TIMES, 23 JULY 1948

Above: Fred Perry had turned professional before the war, but he remained a star in the 1940s.
Below: Brian Close became England's youngest Test cricketer when he made his debut against New Zealand in 1949 aged 18 years and 149 days. He scored a duck and took one wicket – and was dropped

Left: Emil Zatopek leads from the front in the 5,000 metres, a race he narrowly lost.
Far left: Zatopek had more success in the 10,000 metres, where he won Gold by almost a full lap. But an even greater triumph awaited him four years later...

Right: Jersey Joe Walcott tries to block a big punch from champion Joe Louis in their 1948 World Heavyweight fight at New York's Yankee Stadium.
Louis knocked Walcott out in the 11th round to retain his title.
Louis retired undefeated a year later after successfully defending his title 25 times.
The hard-hitting 'Brown Bomber' had been champion for 12 years – the longest reign of any Heavyweight Champion

STANLEY MATTHEWS

When the Footballer of the Year award was inaugurated in 1948, it was natural that the first award would go to Stanley Matthews. The 'Wizard of Dribble' made a habit of collecting 'firsts': he was also the first European Footballer of the Year (1956), the first footballer to receive the CBE (1957), and the first to be knighted (1965).

An immensely exciting and skilful right-winger whose command of the ball left opposing full-backs bemused, Matthews began playing for Stoke City at just 17. He moved to Blackpool in 1947 and a year later led them to the FA Cup Final. Although they lost 4-2 to Manchester United, Matthews was voted Footballer of the Year for his inspirational leadership.

Matthews played for England 54 times between the ages of 19 and 41, and did not retire until after his 50th birthday.

Henry the third
Cotton makes his mark

The weather looks bleak, but it was glory all the way for 41-year-old Henry Cotton at Muirfield in 1948 as he won his third Open Golf Championship. His second round of 66 took him well clear of the field, and his 72-hole total of 284 gave him a five-stroke advantage over Fred Daly. He had won in 1934, the first British win for 11 years, and again in 1937.

Cotton started playing in an era when professionals were kept firmly in their place by golf club members, but his achievements and demeanour did much to raise the status of the professional prior to the huge increase in enthusiasm for the game that came with the days of Arnold Palmer in the 1960s.

With Walter Hagen and Bobby Locke, he was one of the first three professionals to be accorded honorary membership of the Royal & Ancient Golf Club of St Andrews.

Right: Henry Cotton on his way to winning the 1948 Open at Muirfield, 14 years after he first won the trophy

T. H. COTTON

Portugal's rosy for Mortensen

25 MAY 1947 — Portugal 0, England 10. What an international debut it was for Stan Mortensen, the day before his 26th birthday as, playing at inside-right, he scored four goals. So too did centre-forward Tommy Lawton.

Mortensen had two more hat-tricks and a total of 23 goals in his 25 internationals for England between 1947-53. He also became England's first goal-scorer in the World Cup, against Chile in 1950. He initially signed for Blackpool in 1937 and played for them until 1955. He also scored a hat-trick in the 1953 FA Cup Final (the first ever in a Wembley final), the 4-3 win over Bolton Wanderers, a game remembered for the genius of Stanley Matthews.

Bradman bows out

Just four runs would have given him an average of 100...

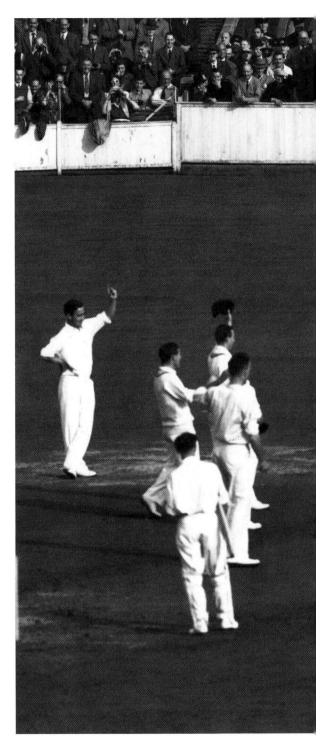

A famous scalp for Somerset's giantkillers

Yeovil's win over Sunderland in 1949 remains the greatest upset in FA Cup history. The Somerset club had reached the third round three times in the 1930s, but Liverpool had beaten them 6-2 in their only game against First Division opposition.

The 1948-9 run began with 4-0 victories over non-League Romford and Weymouth, then Second Division Bury were beaten 3-1. Thus it was that 15,000 packed Yeovil's ground, The Huish, to see mighty Sunderland play on its infamous sloping pitch.

The Southern Leaguers led after a goal from player-manager Alec Stock, only for Sunderland to equalise to make it 1-1 at full-time. Even England star Len Shackleton, the 'clown prince of football', could not score. Indeed his trickery was punished in extra time when his attempted overhead kick from halfway was pounced on by Eric Bryant, who scored Yeovil's decisive goal.

Anticlimax came in the fifth round, when Yeovil were trounced 8-0 by Cup-holders Manchester United.

england's captain Norman Yardley led his team in giving three cheers to Don Bradman on his arrival for his final Test innings at The Oval on 14 August 1948.

Were there tears in his eyes? Who knows, but he was bowled by leg-spinner Eric Hollies for a duck on only the second ball.

Just four runs would have given him a Test career total of 7,000 and an average of exactly 100. Nevertheless, his Test average of 99.94 and first-class average of 95.14 far surpass that of any other player in the history of cricket.

In 1948 his team, one of the greatest ever, swept England aside, winning four Tests by huge margins and drawing the other. In fact, in Bradman's final match, England collapsed 52 all out to the fast bowling of Ray Lindwall.

Don Bradman (far right) is cheered by the England side during the 1948 Test at The Oval

GUSSIE MORAN

There was a near riot at Wimbledon when American 'Gorgeous Gussie' Moran showed up for the 1949 tournament sporting a new item of fashion. The item in question was a pair of lace-trimmed panties which poked from beneath her white skirt. Needless to say, the All-England Club were not happy at the mob scene caused by press photographers vying to get a snap of Miss Moran's underwear.

Wimbledon had seen many changes in women's attire, starting in 1905 with May Sutton's knee-length skirt, and moving on to Suzanne Lenglen's bare arms and Helen Jacob's shorts – but Moran's panties caused a sensation. It will come as no surprise to hear that they were designed by Teddy Tinling, who went on to become the master of Wimbledon women's wear.

The Fifties

With the Coronation of Elizabeth II, sport caught the mood of the nation and celebrated with joyful successes. A Briton ran the four-minute mile, Stanley Matthews received an FA Cup winner's medal, and Lester Piggott rode his first Derby winner. But a snowy night in Munich left a gulf that not even sport could heal

Main photo: Rocky Marciano hammers Roland La Starza
in a 1953 title fight in New York.
Above top: The two Stans – Matthews and Mortensen.
Above left: Jim Peters' 1954 marathon collapse in Vancouver.
Above right: Lester Piggott made horse racing headlines

Fifties Diary

Above: Indian spin bowler Sonny Ramadhin was the undoing of England sides in the 1950s.
Right top: Australia's Peter Thomson dominated The Open, winning the title four times in the Fifties (and five times in all).
Right middle: Gordon Richards won The Derby in 1953, on his 28th attempt.
Right bottom: Manchester United and England star Duncan Edwards' career was cut short by the Munich disaster

1950

In one of the greatest upsets in World Cup history, little-regarded USA beat a star-studded England side 1-0 in Brazil. With Matthews sidelined, it's red faces all round for Mortensen, Ramsey, Wright and Finney.

The beginning of a golden era for Welsh rugby, as they win the Grand Slam and go on to win five more championship titles over the next seven seasons.

The first snooker on BBC TV: Walter Donaldson v Joe Davis from Leicester Square Hall.

Continuing a disappointing season of English sports, solid batting by Worrell, Weekes and Walcott, and bowling by the young spinners Ramadhin and Valentine, give the West Indies their first series win over England.

The first fully representative British Lions team tour the Antipodes, losing in New Zealand and winning in Australia.

1951

Oxford University suffer the embarrassment of sinking in the Boat Race.

Rocky Marciano beats an ageing Joe Louis in the Brown Bomber's last fight, two years after his 'retirement'.

The Argentinian Juan Fangio wins his first World Motor Racing Championship.

Randolph Turpin defeats the legendary Sugar Ray Robinson to take boxing's World Middleweight Championship in front of his home crowd at Earl's Court.

Max Faulkner becomes the first and only golfer to win an Open Championship off the British mainland when he lifts the trophy at Royal Portrush.

1952

Debuts for two of Britain's all-time greats as Cliff Morgan inspires Wales to a Grand Slam, and Fred Trueman rips into India at Headingley.

At the Helsinki Olympics, Emil Zatopek improves on his London Olympics performance, winning three long distance Gold medals in the 5,000 metres, 10,000 metres and the marathon.

1953

Sir Gordon Richards wins his first (and only) Derby, on Pinza, in his last year as Champion Jockey.

In what will always be remembered as the 'Matthews Cup Final', Stanley Matthews inspires Blackpool to come from 3-1 down to beat Bolton 4-3 in a classic encounter.

The American golfer Ben Hogan is unbeatable as he wins The Open, the US Open and The Masters.

Little Mo Connolly becomes the first woman to win the tennis Grand Slam.

Wales defeat the mighty All Blacks 13-8 at Cardiff.

England win back The Ashes in front of a huge emotional crowd at The Oval.

The Mighty Magyars of Hungary, inspired by Ferenc Puskas, hammer a stunned England 6-3 at Wembley.

Mike Hawthorn becomes the first Briton to win a World Championship Grand Prix. Italians and Argentinians had won the 23 races since the championship began in 1950.

1954

Roger Bannister breaks the mystical four-minute mile barrier at Oxford.

Jim Peters' heroic effort to win the Empire Games marathon ends agonisingly short when he collapses 11 times in the final lap.

The balance of football supremacy moves to central Europe as West Germany beat Hungary 3-2 in the World Cup Final.

On 8 April, Peter Dimmock introduces the first Sportsview – BBC TV's midweek sports programme.

Arnold Palmer, after winning the US Amateur Championship, turns professional.

1955

A brave Don Cockell fights his best against the fearsome Rocky Marciano but still loses.

American student Charles Dumas clears seven feet in the high jump. A year later he would take the Olympic title.

Left: Mike Hawthorn made motor racing history when he became the first Briton to win a world championship Grand Prix

1956

Devon Loch, the Queen Mother's horse, ridden by Dick Francis, dramatically collapses in the Grand National less than 100 yards from the finish.

Talks instigated by the Postmaster General establish the list of sporting events in which neither the BBC nor ITV can seek exclusive television rights: The Derby, the Grand National, the English and Scottish FA Cup Finals, cricket Test matches, and Empire and Olympic Games held in Britain.

Off-spinner Jim Laker takes a world record 19 wickets against Australia at Old Trafford. Tony Lock, his fellow spinner, took the one wicket that prevented Laker's clean sweep.

Peter Thomson, often considered the best putter the world has ever seen, wins his third successive Open Championship.

1957

A seemingly ageless Sugar Ray Robinson KOs Gene Fullmer to win the World Middleweight Championship for the fourth time.

The West Indies are on the receiving end of a world record partnership by England's Peter May and Colin Cowdrey of 411.

The Welsh giant John Charles joins Juventus for £70,000 and £60 per week.

Althea Gibson becomes the first black champion of a major tennis title when she wins Wimbledon.

Winger Peter Jackson scores three tries as England win the Grand Slam for the first time in 29 years.

1958

Tragedy strikes in Munich as Manchester United's Busby Babes are decimated in a plane crash.

October 11: Grandstand, BBC TV's Saturday afternoon sports programme, takes to the air. It is now the longest running weekly TV programme in the world. It is Britain's longest live programme, with five or more hours of sport as it happens. Grandstand pioneered many techniques now in everyday use – the video action replay was first seen during the programme's 1966 World Cup coverage.

Two immensely talented sportsmen burst on to the world scene. Arnold Palmer at 28 wins the Masters – the first of his seven Major wins in seven years. Meanwhile Pele, only 17, scores two goals in Brazil's 5-2 win over Sweden in the World Cup Final.

The Formula One World Championship is dominated by British drivers. Mike Hawthorn beats Stirling Moss by one point when he wins the final race in Casablanca.

In a tense match, Christine Truman beats the United States player Althea Gibson to record Britain's first Wightman Cup victory since 1930.

In Gothenburg, Sweden, Herb Elliott lowers his world 1500 metres record by an extraordinary two seconds to 3.36 minutes. Earler in the year he had become the first teenager to run a sub-four-minute mile.

1959

Sweden's Ingemar Johansson wins the World Heavyweight Championship after he batters Floyd Patterson to a third-round defeat in New York's Yankee Stadium. He becomes the first non-American champion since Primo Carnera took the title 25 years earlier.

Career milestones for Billy Wright, who wins a world record 100 international football caps, and the 19-year-old Jack Nicklaus, who takes the US Amateur Championship.

India are at the receiving end of a 5-0 drubbing by England, with the bowling strike force of Statham and Trueman taking the honours.

Second Division Liverpool appoint Bill Shankly as manager.

After nearly 11 hours at the crease, Hanif Mohammad is run out for 499, the highest first-class score.

Wimbledon is graced by Maria Bueno's victory, while the men's final pits American Alex Olmedo against a talented young Australian left-hander called Rod Laver. Olmedo took the title.

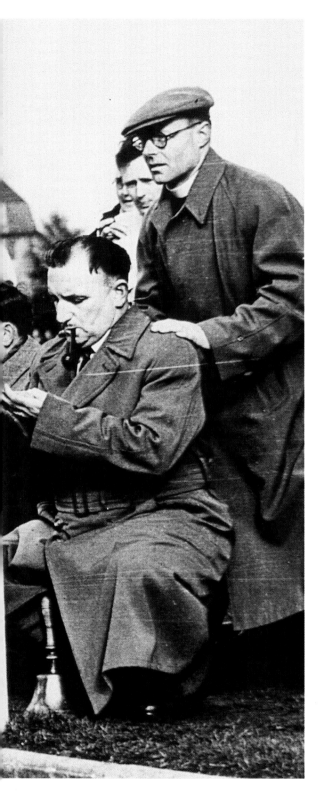

Roger Bannister
Four-minute miracle
AND ALL ON A WINDY DAY IN OXFORD

1954 • ATHLETICS

'With about 230 yards to go, Bannister made his final effort and went past Chataway with that long, ground-eating stride. He literally fell through the tape...'

By Stan Greenberg

In the 1920s the great Finnish runner Paavo Nurmi had tried to run a sub-four-minute mile, but he missed the magical mark by 10 seconds. During the Second World War the Swedes Arne Andersson and Gunder Hägg came closer, battling against each other and breaking the record three times each until Hägg achieved 4:01.4 in 1945.

Young British runner Roger Bannister had broken 4 minutes 10 seconds in 1950, and improved steadily until 1952 when he ran a remarkable three-quarter mile trial in 2:52.9. In the 1952 Olympic 1500 metres he could only finish fourth, but the following year he just missed the mile record with 4:02.0. Within months, the Australian John Landy and the American Wes Santee had run similar times. The race for the 'Holy Grail' was on.

During the winter, Bannister planned an attempt on the mark as soon as weather

When the day dawned, it was overcast and windy, and the project was nearly scrapped.

permitted, aided and abetted by Chris Chataway and Chris Brasher, and his coach Franz Stampfl. The Australian and American seasons began much earlier than Britain's, and they were worried that Landy or Santee might get there first. Indeed, Landy had two good tries, and Santee one, but all fell short.

On the first possible occasion, the Oxford University v AAA match at Oxford on 6 May 1954, the plans were put into operation. When the day dawned overcast and windy, the project was nearly scrapped. Then, just before the race, the wind dropped, and though quite cold, the attempt was back on.

Brasher, later Olympic steeplechase champion, led through the 440-yard mark in 57.4 seconds, and 880 yards in 1:58.0 – at which point Chataway, who later in the year broke the world 5,000 metres record, took over and passed the three-quarter mile in 3:00.4.

With about 230 yards to go, Bannister made his final effort and went past Chataway with that familiar long, ground-eating stride. He literally fell through the tape. Commentator Norris McWhirter built up to the time gradually, finally saying "the time is three...", and the rest of the announcement was drowned out by the 1,500 crowd.

The actual time was 3:59.4, which lasted as the world record for only 46 days, until Landy clocked 3:58.0 in Finland. But by then Bannister was immortal.

Left: Roger Bannister's performance at Oxford on 6 May 1954 made him immortal

THE FOUR-MINUTE MILE

6 May 1954, Oxford ◆ Harold Abrahams commentates

....

"On their marks, they're off again. Bannister second there, and there's Brasher dashing straight into the lead, followed by Bannister with Dole third and Chataway fourth. They've gone about 100 yards, Brasher striding out there beautifully and Bannister running in second position. Chataway now moving up into third position. Just coming up to the first 220-yard mark, we'll get the time here and see how the race is going.

"Brasher still leading with Bannister second and then a gap with Dole of Oxford and then Chataway in third position. And as they pass the first 220 mark I get the time on my watch – 28.7, that's Bannister's time but of course this is early in the race.

"Going round this third bend now, coming into the straight at the moment for the first quarter-mile, still Brasher setting the pace with Bannister in second position running beautifully relaxed and now Chataway's in third position about three yards behind Bannister.

"Coming into the straight for the first time, they'll have completed a quarter of the distance, coming into a headwind and you can see Brasher going back onto his heels a little. Bannister's arms coming up a bit high but he's striding beautifully. They pass the first 440 mark. That makes the time for the first 440 57.7 and looking at my schedule that's 2.3 seconds up on the four-minute mile schedule but it's over a second slower than Gunder Hägg did when he was doing his four-minute mile.

"Round the second lap and still those three far ahead of the other two. Going down the back straight for the second time. And it's Brasher still leading with Bannister second and then a two-yard gap and Chataway in third position. As they go down the back straight for the third time, coming up to the third 220 mark, we'll just try and get the time here, they've just passed it, and my watch says 1.27.5, that's 2.5 seconds up on the four-minute mile.

"Going beautifully now as they come into the straight for the half distance with Brasher still leading, setting the pace beautifully, and these three have been training together in competition, practising so as to get the pace exactly right, and Brasher comes up nearly to the half-mile mark. In another 50 yards they'll pass the half-mile with Brasher still leading, Bannister second and Chataway third, miles ahead of everybody else.

"And they're coming up to the 880 now. And Bannister's just passed the 880

and I make the time one minute 58.3, that's 1.7 inside schedule but it's actually .7 slower than it took Hägg when he ran that famous mile record.

"Now going into the third lap with Brasher still leading, Bannister behind him, and Chataway I think is now going to take a hand because Brasher has done his job and he'll be dropping out. And Chataway goes into the lead followed by Bannister. Third lap, in the middle of the third lap and there is Chataway in front setting a beautiful pace with Bannister going very easily behind. He seems to have a lot in him.

"There's intense excitement all round us and somehow we feel it's going to happen at last as they come round the bend into the straight for the third time with just over a lap to go. Chataway leading Bannister by a couple of yards. Bannister seems to me to be running beautifully easily. All this training he's been doing for the last months is now showing its result. And as they come into the headwind again you can see the wind affecting them slightly but they come up to the three-quarter mile mark. There's Chataway passing the three-quarter mile followed immediately by Bannister.

"Looking at my watch I'm going to try and do the calculation for you. The time is three minutes, nought nought point seven, that means that last lap if my mathematics is accurate and I can't be sure it can be with all the excitement here – 62.4, that's nearly five seconds slower than the first lap but he's got to do 59.3 to get this record inside four minutes.

"I think Bannister will be making his effort in a moment. Going down the back straight. Just over 200 yards to go. And there goes Bannister, he's taken the lead with about 240 yards to go. He's leaving Chataway steadily, he's piling on the pace, he's coming up to the 220 mark, he's just past the 220 mark. Three minutes 30.4 that's 29 and a half seconds to get this four-minute mile.

"Come on, Roger. Coming up to the 1500-metre mark now with 120 yards to go. Just coming up, there he is at the 1500 mark and my watch shows three minutes 43.2. Sixteen seconds for 120 yards. Three 55, twenty-five yards to go. And it's straining every ounce of him, he's absolutely all out and he's all in too and just managed to finish."

Harold Abrahams was one of the timekeepers at Iffley Road during Roger Bannister's four-minute mile. He recorded his commentary after the event while watching a film of the race.

Matthews' magic moment

Stanley stars in the most famous FA Cup Final

Cup Final

'*Preston North End v West Bromwich Albion*
Commentary by Raymond Glendenning and
Alan Clarke, with summaries by Charles Buchan
and Henry Rose.
Before play begins listeners hear community
singing organised by the 'Daily Express' and
conducted by Arthur Caiger, D.C.M.
From the Empire Stadium, Wembley at 2.30'

RADIO TIMES, 23 APRIL 1954

Above: Blackpool after the 1953 FA Cup Final, known as the Matthews Final — even though Stan didn't score. With 20 minutes left, Bolton were 3-1 up. But Matthews laid on the goals for Mortensen and Perry to make it 4-3.

Left: Bolton captain Nat Lofthouse scored twice in the 1958 Final to beat Manchester United 2-0, three months after Munich

Centre: The man who made most impact on British football in the Fifties was not English, Scots, Welsh or Irish. Ferenc Puskas inspired Hungary's devastating 6-3 win over England at Wembley in 1953. Alf Ramsey (left) was in that England team and learned his lesson well enough to win the World Cup in 1966

Sweet Sugar Ray
Pound for pound the best boxer of all time

In his epic career as a professional from 1940 to 1965, Sugar Ray Robinson earned a reputation as, pound-for-pound, the greatest boxing champion of all time. He first won the world welterweight title in 1946, but had to relinquish that when he beat Jake LaMotta for the middleweight crown in 1951. He thus took revenge on LaMotta, 'the Bronx Bull', who in 1943 had given Robinson his only previous defeat in 133 fights.

Then Robinson came to London to fight Randolph Turpin, who on 15 July 1951 at Earl's Court gave one of the finest performances by a British boxer to outpoint Robinson. Just 64 days later, however, Robinson regained the title in New York when the referee stopped the fight after 10 rounds. Turpin was never quite the same fighter again.

Robinson held world titles until 1960, regaining the middleweight championship four times.

British boxer Randolph Turpin takes a punch from Sugar Ray Robinson in their 1951 title fight in New York

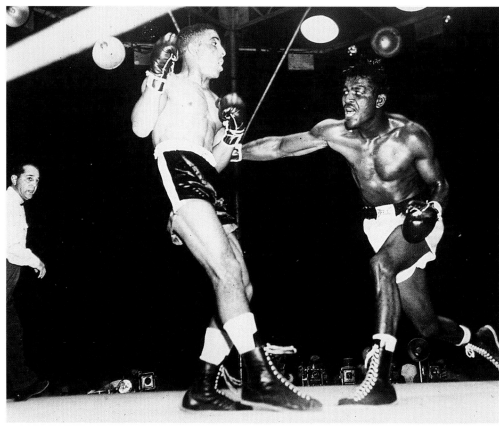

Mighty Marciano

ROCKY MARCIANO was the roughest, toughest heavyweight boxer of them all. He was also one of the greatest, and no boxer can match his perfect record: the only champion to have won every fight of his professional career.

Born Rocco Francis Marchegiano in Brockton, Massachusetts, he turned professional in 1947, but for long found it difficult to get a shot at the world title. He finally did in his 43rd fight, when he knocked out Jersey Joe Walcott in 1952. He defended his title six times before retiring in 1955.

Marciano's final fight was against Archie Moore. Before that he had beaten Britain's Don Cockell, when the referee stopped the fight after nine rounds in San Francisco. Cockell's bravery against such a fierce opponent was remarkable, but many thought that Marciano's barrage of foul blows would have seen him disqualified by a less partial referee.

The invincible Czech

Zatopek's Games is unlikely to be matched

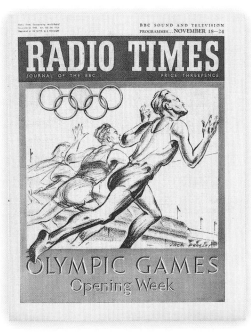

The 1952 Helsinki Olympic Games were dominated by one man – the amazing Emil Zatopek. The 29-year-old Czech not only repeated his 1948 triumph by taking the 10,000 metres Gold medal, he also sprinted past four men on the final bend to win the 5,000 metres. Then, three days later, he ran the first marathon of his life – and won it by a minute and a half. Asked his opinion of marathon running, he announced that he found it boring (this from a man who ran 100 miles a week!). Zatopek set Olympic records in all three events in a performance that is never likely to be matched.

Even his wife Dana Zatopkova got into the act. While Emil was winning the 5,000m, she was busy taking the Gold medal in the javelin. Before Dana and Emil's successes, Czechoslovakia had never won an Olympic event.

Below: The final bend of the 5,000 metres – Zatopek leads as Britain's Chris Chataway goes sprawling

1956 OLYMPIC GAMES

'This will be my seventh Olympic Games stretching over a period of thirty-six years, and during that time I have been lucky enough to see dozens of new Olympic and World records set up. At Helsinki four years ago almost every event gave us a new Olympic record, and while I do not expect quite such a wholesale collection at Melbourne, I have no doubt that there will be quite a number.'

HAROLD ABRAHAMS

RADIO TIMES, 16 NOVEMBER 1956

An era of low scoring but high skill
Morgan makes his mark
THE WELSH WING-HALF CHANGED THE GAME BY SHEER SPEED

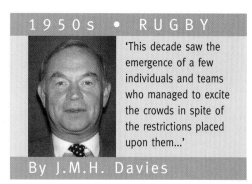

1950s • RUGBY

'This decade saw the emergence of a few individuals and teams who managed to excite the crowds in spite of the restrictions placed upon them...'

By J.M.H. Davies

The next time there is a stoppage of play at Twickenham, for example when numerous substitutions are occurring, reflect on how much the game has changed since the 1950s and how it will change in future.

Rugby in the Fifties was a game about kicking directly to touch without penalty, wing forwards breathing down half-backs' necks from defensive positions now unlawful, needing to play the ball with the foot after a tackle, three-quarters not required to be 19 yards back at lineouts, and other laws which certainly did not encourage open play.

Consequently, the number of points scored in championship games was exceedingly low. For example, Ireland won the title in 1951 with a total of 21 points, and France were winners in 1959 with 28. Even with the changes introduced to the value of the try, the comparison with today's points avalanche is stark.

Does this mean that rugby in the 1950s was dull?

Some of it, yes, as in any era, but this decade saw the emergence of a few individuals

Cliff Morgan's searing breaks in 1952 were moments of magic

and teams who managed to excite the crowds in spite of the restrictions placed upon them.

Who can forget the impact Cliff Morgan made upon Welsh and British rugby? His searing breaks at Twickenham and Lansdowne Road in 1952 were moments of magic, and his arrival began the end of the kicking outside half we had grown to live with. Cliff Morgan continued to sparkle through the decade, winning 27 caps and being on the

losing side just seven times. It was difficult to judge his kicking ability because it was a ploy he rarely used. Interestingly, Morgan never dropped a goal for Wales and probably never tried to.

One of his three tries was against Ireland at Cardiff in 1955. He took the ball at speed, cut through a number of defenders and was moving so quickly as he crossed the line that it appeared the 20 metres of goal would not be enough. This example was his hallmark – acceleration and change of direction at speed.

Along with Morgan, the 1950s championships were blessed with other personalities that stood out, people like Jackie Kyle, Tony O'Reilly, Jeff Butterfield, Peter Jackson and Gordon Waddell, to name but a few. These and many others would have graced any championship decade.

The 1950s saw three successful Lions tours, one the well-documented 1955 visit to South Africa. Here Morgan was at his best on the firm pitches he favoured. He captained the side in the third winning Test, a Welsh record that might last some time yet.

It was no coincidence that the Lions were successful, because club rugby in the British Isles was very strong during this period. Few sides relished visits to Coventry, Northampton, Gloucester, Cardiff, Newport, and many good sides limped away from tours to Ireland, Scotland and Cornwall. Newport and Cardiff played each other four times a season, always before large crowds, with one fixture attracting over 40,000 spectators. What would the professional game give for half that number today?

So some good, some not so good in the Fifties, but what about 40 years on? More substitutes, with attack and defence units on the bench? Goal kickers who do nothing else? Laws further refined to further eliminate defence? Ten players a side? No flair?

I think I will reflect on the Fifties again!

INTERNATIONAL RUGBY UNION FOOTBALL
'2.50 app. The Calcutta Cup
  SCOTLAND v ENGLAND
  The whole of the match from the Murrayfield
Ground, Edinburgh
  by courtesy of the Scottish Rugby Union
  Commentators, Peter West and Leslie Kettley.
  Presented for television by James Buchan.'

RADIO TIMES, 7 MARCH 1958

Black power

Delight shows on the face of Althea Gibson as she is kissed by opponent Darlene Hard, whom she beat in straight sets, 6-3 6-2, to win the 1957 Wimbledon Ladies' Singles title.

The daughter of a South Carolina sharecropper who had moved to New York in 1930, Gibson became a pioneer for black sportswomen. Barred from public courts in the 1940s due to her colour, in 1950 she became the first black competitor at the US National Championships. In 1956 she became the first to win a Grand Slam title, when she captured the French Open.

Gibson was nearly 30 when she won Wimbledon. She won the US Open the same year, successfully defending her title the next year. She later played professional golf and enjoyed some success as a singer and actress.

A SPECIAL TEST MATCH SERVICE
'Ball-by-Ball
  Something completely new happens in British radio on May 30, the date on which the first of this year's five Test Matches opens at Edgbaston. On that day and on all subsequent days of Test play, the British listener will be able to hear a full ball-by-ball account of the proceedings.'

RADIO TIMES, 24 MAY 1957

Right: Colin Cowdrey and Peter May leave the field during an epic second-innings stand of 411 at Edgbaston in 1957. West Indian spinner Sonny Ramadhin had taken seven for 49 in the first innings but May's 285 not out forced a draw

Pirie destroys the opposition

douglas Alastair Gordon Pirie could easily claim to have dragged British distance running, screaming probably, into world class.

One had to go back to the turn of the century and Albert Shrubb to find the previous British distance man of his status – with the exception of the rare excursion beyond the mile of Sydney Wooderson in the 1940s. The young outspoken Yorkshireman infuriated his critics by living up to, or exceeding, his predictions, but they could never accuse him of ducking the opposition.

Gordon Pirie ran against the best runners of his time, beating them more often than not. His inexperience showed in the 1952 Olympics but the next year, under new coach Woldemar Gershler, he came good with world records for six miles and in the 4 x 1500 metres relay.

In 1956 he set world marks at 3,000m twice and took a big slice off the 5,000m record. Later that year, after destroying himself trying to break the Russian Vladimir Kuts in the Olympic 10,000m, he settled for silver behind Kuts in the 5,000m.

In all he broke 22 British records.

Champion
of the Fifties

MAUREEN CONNOLLY

Maureen Connolly is pictured above with the Challenge Trophy after winning the second of her three successive Ladies' Singles Championships at Wimbledon in 1953.

'Little Mo' won her first major tournament, the US Open, at 16 – and lost only four matches throughout the remainder of her career. Her speed around the court and the weight of her ground strokes were allied to remarkable concentration.

She became the first woman to win the Grand Slam of tennis in a single year. In fact, she won six majors in succession, and nine in all. Her career was tragically cut short after her leg was crushed in a riding accident two weeks after her final Wimbledon win in 1954.

In 1955 she married Norman Brinker, a member of the 1952 US Olympic equestrian team that competed in Helsinki. Connolly died of cancer at the age of only 34.

Cliff Morgan joins the BBC

Cliff Morgan made his first radio appearance in 1952 when he was interviewed by Eamonn Andrews for *Sports Report* after Wales had beaten Ireland 14-3 at Lansdowne Road to clinch the Triple Crown.

A leg injury meant he had to be carried up to the BBC commentary box. A week later, the injury was diagnosed as a broken leg.

Cliff joined the BBC in 1960 as sports organiser in Wales. In 1963 he moved to London as editor of *Grandstand* and *Sportsview*. He resigned over a point of principle, but continued as a freelance. He became Editor of the ITV's *This Week* and in 1973 returned to the BBC as editor of Radio Sport. The next year he became head of outside broadcasts. In 1976 he switched to TV.

He retired in 1987, but spent another 11 years presenting Radio 4's *Sport on Four*.

Britain's best follow Fangio

Moss and Hawthorn battle for title after Argentinian ace retires

Above: The dashing British driver Mike Hawthorn succeeded Juan Fangio as world motor racing champion.
Left: In 1955 Stirling Moss, along with British co-driver Dennis Jenkinson, became the first Englishman to win the 1,000-mile Mille Miglia in Italy. His average speed was 97.96mph and it was said to be Moss's greatest drive.
Centre: The Mercedes Silver Arrow Moss drove to victory in the Mille Miglia.
Far left: Fangio wins the French Grand Prix at Reims in 1951

The Argentinian Juan Manuel Fangio was by far the most successful driver in Formula One motor racing in the 1950s. The ace from Buenos Aires was world champion a record five times – in 1951 and every year from 1954 to '57 – and won 24 of his 51 Grand Prix races. In this period he drove for Alfa Romeo, Maserati, Mercedes and Ferrari.

Britain's Stirling Moss had been runner-up to Fangio three years in a row, and when the Argentinian retired at the age of 47 in 1958, Moss looked the likely successor. But he was pipped to the title by just one point by his compatriot Mike Hawthorn.

Both British rivals had been born in 1929, with Hawthorn, the son of a garage proprietor, the quickest to make his name. In 1953 the dashing driver became a national hero with a superb win over Fangio in the French Grand Prix. It was Moss, however, who became the British public's favourite. Universally acknowledged as the best driver never to win the world championship, his name is still taken in vain by policemen who ask speeding drivers: "Who do you think you are – Stirling Moss?"

Hawthorn was tragically killed in a road accident in January 1959. Moss, having won 16 Grand Prix races, retired after a serious crash at Goodwood in 1962.

Champion
of the Fifties

JACKIE MILBURN

Jackie Milburn was a Tyneside legend, his family a football dynasty. Four cousins played League football and the fifth, Cissie, was mother of Bobby and Jack Charlton.

Milburn helped Newcastle United to FA Cup wins in 1951, 1952 and 1955. On the way to the first of these he scored in every round, with two in 'Milburn's Final'. These came in a five-minute spell in a 2-0 win against Blackpool. The second goal was a devastating drive from 25 yards out which came, amazingly, after a mistake by Stanley Matthews, who described it as "the greatest goal I have ever seen, and certainly the finest ever scored at Wembley".

In 11 seasons with Newcastle (1946-56), Milburn scored 177 goals in 353 League matches. He also scored 10 goals in 13 internationals playing centre-forward for England between 1948 and 1955.

The long wait ends
England regain Ashes in a historic match

The 1950s were a great era for English cricket. At The Oval in 1953 the long 15-year wait for a series victory over Australia was ended when England regained the Ashes in a historic match.

After seven wickets for Alec Bedser and Fred Trueman in the first innings, Jim Laker and Tony Lock spun out Australia in the second. Just two wickets fell in chasing the target of 132, leaving England's greatest batting heroes Denis Compton and Bill Edrich together at the close. A huge crowd came on to cheer them all the way to the pavilion.

Above: Edrich and Compton leave the field after scoring the winning runs at The Oval in 1953

The Devon Loch Mystery

Nobody has been able to explain for sure why Devon Loch fell in the 1956 Grand National. Owned by the Queen Mother and ridden by Dick Francis, he had cleared the final fence and seemed to be full of running and on his way to a popular victory.

Suddenly, to the horror of the packed crowd, he fell on the flat some 50 yards from the finish. He picked himself up, but all was lost as ESB swept past to victory.

Dick Francis, who had been champion jumps jockey in 1953/4, but without a National winner in his career, retired the next year to become a successful writer. The Queen Mother remained a great devotee of National Hunt racing – but has never won the Grand National.

Left: Dick Francis hangs his head after Devon Loch had fallen within sight of victory

DEVON LOCH

24 MARCH 1956, AINTREE ◆ PETER O'SULLEVAN AND RAYMOND GLENDENNING COMMENTATE

PETER O'SULLEVAN: "And now Much Obliged is down at fence number 26. And that leaves Devon Loch clear as they race into fence number 27. Devon Loch is clear on the far side of the course with Eagle Lodge in second place. Just behind Eagle Lodge is ESB, who is still going well. Now they're racing into fence number 28 and it's Devon Loch only just about a length in front of Eagle Lodge. Entree in third place, ESB four. Devon Loch the leader by a length and a half. And it's over to you, Raymond."

RAYMOND GLENDENNING: "Well, Devon Loch has been out there well clear of them for quite a while and now, only coming into the last but one fence does Eagle Lodge come up. And ESB moving best of all on the outside. And it's those two, right over together, ESB and Devon Loch, and away goes Entree at the second last.

"They're coming into the last now and Devon Loch, riding straight in, has got a slight advantage in the centre of the fence. In come Devon Loch, ESB and Eagle Lodge – and Devon Loch's over first.

"It's the Queen Mother's horse over first and he's now being chased by ESB. He's coming on to the race course. It's Devon Loch for the Queen Mother with ESB in second place, then Eagle Lodge in third and Gentle Moya coming very hard indeed. But Devon Loch is holding off ESB with 150 yards to go. And Devon Loch is about a length and a half ahead. He's stretching away.

"The hats are coming off. He's three yards clear. It's Devon Loch three yards clear with 100 yards to go.

"Oh, he's gone down! Devon Loch has gone down! He's gone down and been passed by ESB, Gentle Moya in second place and Eagle Lodge coming up into third place, although he's just pipped at the post by Royal Tan. Well, there was a man on the inside of the course and Dick Francis is just holding his hand to his head, he can't believe it. Now across comes Curious Cottage and then Clearing and then Wild Wisdom.

"There must have been a man who raced into the rails there and made Dick Francis just pull when Devon Loch had that race absolutely won for Her Majesty the Queen Mother. He just skidded and couldn't pull himself up in time so he was passed. There was nothing the matter with the horse. It was just one of those unfortunate things.

"And Dick Francis is absolutely the most miserable man. To have got the Grand National of 1956 in his pocket bar an unaccountable slip. And I'm quite sure, from his actions and gestures, that he really must be in tears."

Spin doctor

England's cricket team had much success in the 1950s. The Ashes were regained in 1953 and held in the series against Australia in 1954/5 and 1956 before a surprise loss in 1958/9.

Success came from the fact that England had their best ever array of fast bowling. As Alec Bedser's great career came to an end, Frank Tyson and Brian Statham swept aside the Aussies in 1954/5, and Fred Trueman took more wickets than anyone that decade. Peter Loader and Trevor Bailey gave solid support, and fine bowlers like Les Jackson and Derek Shackleton could not make the team. For spin, too, England had plenty of depth, with Johnny Wardle and the Surrey spin twins Tony Lock and Jim Laker prominent.

Laker, the world's finest off-spinner, reached his peak against the Australians in 1956, when he took 46 wickets in the series at an average of 9.60, including his unique feat of 19 wickets in the fourth Test at Old Trafford – 9 for 37 and 10 for 53. These figures were all the more amazing as Tony Lock was trying for all his worth and took just one wicket in 69 overs.

Below: Off-spinner Jim Laker reached his peak in 1956

Trautmann's heroics
German wins public over after breaking neck

We are now accustomed to substitutes in football matches, but before these were permitted, two successive FA Cup Finals were marred by injuries to goalkeepers.

In 1956 Manchester City beat Birmingham City 3-1 despite City's Bert Trautmann unwittingly playing with a broken neck for most of the game. Then, in 1957, Manchester United lost their goalkeeper Ray Wood due to a broken jaw after only six minutes. With 10 men and Jackie Blanchflower in goal, Manchester United just failed to hold off Aston Villa, who won 2-1.

Trautmann broke his neck diving at the feet of Birmingham inside-right Peter Murphy after just 17 minutes. Initial X-rays after the match showed nothing wrong, but in the next three days the pain became so bad that Trautmann checked into Manchester Royal Infirmary, where he was told the bad news. The second vertebra in his neck had cracked in two. Doctors said he was lucky to be alive.

Trautmann had originally come to Britain as a German prisoner of war, and stayed on. He became one of the game's most popular keepers despite having to overcome considerable anti-German prejudice early in his career.

After his FA Cup Final bravery Trautmann was elected 1956 Footballer of the Year.

Above: Bert Trautmann suffered a broken neck while diving at the feet of Peter Murphy in the FA Cup Final

Right: Anxious moments for England against Hungary in 1953. This photo shows the English keeper Gil Merrick tipping a shot past the post as Billy Wright (left) and Alf Ramsey (far right) look on. Hungary won the match 6-3

1954 • COMMONWEALTH GAMES

Peters' Commonwealth collapse
Marathon runner falls 11 times within sight of the finish line

On the final day of the 1954 British Empire and Commonwealth Games in Vancouver, Roger Bannister had just won his mile clash with John Landy of Australia when news came that the marathon was coming to a close.

A few minutes later Jim Peters stumbled into the arena, and proceeded to give the 35,000 spectators the most harrowing experience they had ever had at a sports meeting.

For the next few minutes, attempting to cover the last lap of the track, Peters fell 11 times.

Peters was over 15 minutes ahead of the next runner when he entered the stadium, but he had paid a high price. The intense heat, well over 32 degrees Centigrade, had induced severe heat exhaustion and dehydration, and he had lost nearly all control of his legs.

Less than 200 metres from the finish line, officials, heeding their own feelings and pleas from the crowd, lifted him off the track. He was taken to hospital and eventually recovered, but he never ran again.

The winner, Joe McGhee of Scotland, had also fallen three times, and was very distressed at the end. Only six of the original 16 runners managed to finish the race.

Below: Jim Peters collapses in the final stage of the 1954 Empire and Commonwealth Games marathon

Evening paper placards broke the news

The day a team died

'BUSBY BABES' WIPED OUT IN MUNICH AIR CRASH

MUNICH DISASTER

'The disaster created a special bond between United and the people, weaving everlasting strands of emotion and sorrow into the fabric of the club...'

By Bryon Butler

tangle of metal surrounded by rescue workers and glaring lights. And it was still snowing.

The crash happened at 3.04pm on 6 February. The Elizabethan aircraft crashed during take-off after a stop to refuel on the way home from a European Cup tie in Belgrade. It claimed 23 lives, including eight players – Geoff Bent, Roger Byrne, Eddie Colman, Mark Jones, David Pegg, Tommy Taylor, Billy Whelan and, two weeks later, Duncan Edwards. The

the disaster created a special bond between United and the people. The tragedy didn't 'make' United any more than it 'broke' it, but, beyond doubt, it wove everlasting strands of emotion and sorrow into the fabric of the club.

It is still the small details that best define the disaster, even 40 years on. Harry Gregg, speaking on *Sport on Four*, provided listeners with a memorably graphic account of the crash. It was so compelling that Cliff Morgan's

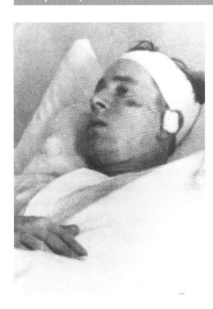

Evening paper placards broke the news as the nation left work on that Thursday evening in February 1958. "United in Air Crash" they read. The worst was confirmed by BBC TV's six o'clock news: the list of dead and injured seemed endless.

The following day the horror of it all was clear, and among the grainy black-and-white images was one of the plane, a smouldering

essence of a champion side known as the 'Busby Babes' was destroyed. Football knew a grief that was beyond the alchemy of words.

Frank Taylor, the only survivor among nine journalists, has told the story in *The Day a Team Died,* a book described as "a tribute to courage and humanity". Taylor still believes English football has never recovered from Munich although, as a companion thought,

interview with Gregg was allowed to fill the programme's entire 25 minutes. Gregg, United's Northern Ireland goalkeeper, was one of the heroes of the tragedy, returning again and again to the wreck to bring out survivors, but that fact was unspoken.

The one regular broadcaster on the plane was Don Davies – 'Old International' of *The Manchester Guardian* – who was among those who died. He was a bouncy little Lancastrian, a romantic, an eccentric, a droll humorist, ideal companion, musician and sportsman who wrote like an angel. He was a charmer on radio, a regular on *Sports Report*, the celebrated five o'clock show on Saturday evenings. Eamonn Andrews and Angus Mackay, the twin barrels of the programme, loved him – along with millions of listeners – though they never quite knew what to make of him.

Once when describing a performance by Scunthorpe in the FA Cup, he recommended a thanksgiving service and chose an appropriate anthem – "How are thy servants blessed, O Lord, how sure is their defence". He once described Nat Lofthouse as "a mud-stained Othello, all hell and damnation".

Davies hated commercialisation, especially all kinds of 'bonuses' or 'inducements', which means we can't be sure he would have enjoyed the modern United or modern football.

Below: Matt Busby and Bobby Charlton after Munich. Opposite page, from far left: Charlton in hospital, the wreckage, and the gifted Duncan Edwards in 1957

Lester Piggott – pictured above at his father's training stable at Lambourn, Berkshire – was born to ride. He won his first race at the age of 12, and his first Derby at 18, in 1954, on Never Say Die (above left). But two weeks later the young prodigy was censured for dangerous riding and advised to ride for another trainer. It did not stop the flood of fan mail (below)

THE DERBY

'As the time draws near to 3.20pm people will gather round their radio sets and in front of their television screens to see and hear the broadcast. The Light Programme commentary is relayed (in the BBC's General Overseas Service) all over the world.'

RADIO TIMES, 25 MAY 1959

The Sixties

THE SWINGING SIXTIES USHERED IN A NEW AGE
FOR SPORT. IT WAS AN ERA WHEN SPORTS PEOPLE
SUDDENLY BECAME PERSONALITIES, MAKING FRONT PAGE
HEADLINES AS OFTEN AS THEY DID THE BACK
– GEORGE BEST, CASSIUS CLAY, LESTER PIGGOTT
AND MANY OTHERS ALL BECAME BIG NEWS FOR
REASONS OTHER THAN SPORTING ACCOMPLISHMENTS

Main photo: The controversial goal that decided the 1966 World Cup.
Above top: Cassius Clay talked as good as he fought in the 60s.
Above left: Graham Hill was world champion racing driver in 1962.
Above right: Jean-Claude Killy won three skiing Gold medals in 1968

Sixties Diary

Above: Tommy Simpson rides in the 1967 Tour de France. This photo was taken just a few days before he died during the race. Right from top: Francis Chichester sailed to glory across the Atlantic. Jimmy Greaves transfers to Milan. Howard Winstone celebrates winning the World Featherweight title. Far right from top: Stirling Moss wins the 1960 Monaco Grand Prix. Abebe Bikila becomes the first athlete to win two consecutive Olympic marathons, four years after winning barefoot. Graham Hill drinks to Grand Prix success

1960

The World Heavyweight Boxing Championship returns to the USA when Floyd Patterson defeats Ingemar Johansson in a rematch, becoming the first boxer to regain the heavyweight title.

In sailing, Francis Chichester sails Gypsy Moth III to capture his first single-handed transatlantic race.

Arnold Palmer wins the US Open Golf Championship.

Abebe Bikila, Ethiopia's barefoot runner, wins the marathon in the Rome Olympics, while Wilma Rudolph wins double gold in the 100 metres and the 200 metres relay.

Spurs win their first 11 games on the way to taking the League title.

1961

In an all-British women's Wimbledon Final, Christine Truman loses to Angela Mortimer.

Mike Hailwood becomes World 250cc Motorcycle Champion, and wins the first of 14 Isle of Man TT races.

Bill Nicholson signs Jimmy Greaves from Milan, but the Spurs manager refuses to make him Britain's first £100,000 footballer, paying £99,999. Greaves scores a hat-trick on his debut.

Despite a shoulder injury, Australian captain Richie Benaud takes six wickets and holds England to just 70 runs to defeat England at Old Trafford.

Jimmy Hill leads a successful campaign to abolish football's £20 maximum wage. Fulham's Johnny Haynes makes history by becoming Britain's first £100-a-week footballer.

1962

Graham Hill wins the World Motor Racing Championship with Scotland's Jim Clark coming second. But Stirling Moss has to retire after an early-season crash at Goodwood.

Sonny Liston hammers Floyd Patterson to a first-round defeat, becoming the new World Heavyweight Champion.

Australia dominates world tennis as Rod Laver takes the Grand Slam, beating Roy Emerson in three of the four finals, while Margaret Smith wins every major title except Wimbledon.

1963

Boxer Davey Moore dies after losing his featherweight title to Sugar Ramos. The same fate befalls Benny 'The Kid' Paret after he collapses against Emile Griffith.

Alf Ramsey becomes England football manager and Spurs defeat Real Madrid to capture the European Cup Winners Cup.

Sussex beat Worcestershire to win the first Gillette Cup limited overs match.

1964

Cassius Clay takes Sonny Liston's World Heavyweight boxing title, and also adopts the name Muhammad Ali.

Colin Cowdrey catches Neil Hawke of Australia as Freddie Trueman becomes the first man to reach 300 Test wickets. When Ken Barrington scores a century against South Africa, he becomes the first man to record 100s against all seven Test-playing countries.

Tony Nash and Robin Dixon win Winter Olympic Gold medals in the two-man bobsleigh. In the Tokyo games, the long jump Gold medals go to Britons Mary Rand and Lynn Davies.

Roy Emerson takes three of the tennis Grand Slam titles when he wins Wimbledon, the Australian Open and the US Open, defeating Fred Stolle in each final.

Ann Packer takes silver in the 400 metres and gold in the 800 metres in the Tokyo Olympics.

Dick Fosbury's unique style set an Olympic record and changed the high jump forever

1965

Leeds lose the FA Cup Final to Liverpool, and the league title to Manchester United on goal difference.

Jack Nicklaus wins the Masters by nine shots over Arnold Palmer and Gary Player.

Jock Stein becomes manager of Celtic.

Muhammad Ali knocks out Sonny Liston in the first round of their championship bout.

1966

Muhammad Ali refuses to serve in the Vietnam War.

Despite being five love down in the final set against Maria Bueno, Billie Jean King wins Wimbledon.

Jack Nicklaus wins his first Open Championship.

Jonah Barrington becomes world number one in squash.

At 21 years old, Derek Underwood makes his Test debut as an England cricketer.

The England football team win the World Cup.

1967

Gareth Edwards debuts for Wales at 19.

In American Football's first Superbowl, the Green Bay Packers beat the Kansas City Chiefs 35-10.

British cyclist Tommy Simpson dies of heat exhaustion in the Tour de France.

Pat Koechlin-Smythe makes history in the equestrian world by becoming the first woman team leader, steering Great Britain to Nations Cup victory at Aachen.

Celtic become the first British football team to win the European Cup when they defeat Inter Milan 2-1 in Lisbon.

1968

At the end of his career, Howard Winstone wins boxing's World Featherweight Championship. He then loses his title and retires.

The MCC cancel a tour of South Africa when the South Africans say England player Basil d'Oliveira is not welcome in their country.

Colin Cowdrey becomes the first player to play 100 Test matches.

Joe Frazier wins Muhammad Ali's vacant World Heavyweight title.

France's Jean-Claude Killy wins all three alpine skiing events in the Winter Olympics.

America's Jim Hines records the first 10 second time in the 100 metres.

Americans Bob Beamon and Dick Fosbury make history in the Olympic long jump and high jump respectively, Beamon by leaping 8.90 metres and Fosbury by inventing the 'Fosbury flop'

Arthur Ashe becomes the first black player to win a major tennis title, winning the US Open.

Manchester United beat Benfica 4-1 in the European Cup Final.

1969

Tony Jacklin becomes the first British player since 1951 to win golf's Open Championship.

Don Revie takes Leeds to their first League Championship with a record 67 points.

In cycling, Eddie Mercx wins the Tour de France, his first of four in a row.

Great Britain & Ireland share the Ryder Cup with the United States after Jack Nicklaus generously concedes a 30-inch putt to Open Champion Tony Jacklin on the final green at Royal Birkdale.

Spurs do the double in 1961

THE TOTTENHAM HOTSPUR football team show their twin trophies to jubilant fans after their FA Cup Final win in 1961 at Wembley.

Spurs were superb as they became the first team since Aston Villa in 1897 to complete the Cup and League double. They began the season with 11 straight wins and won 31 of their 42 matches, with just four losses and 115 goals to top the table by eight points. The Cup Final win was by 2-0 over Leicester City.

Danny Blanchflower was inspirational as team captain, and was later voted the Football Writers' Player of the Year, Dave Mackay was a dynamo in midfield and John White a genius up front, but the entire team combined magically. This was Tottenham's FA Cup Final line-up: Brown; Baker, Henry; Blanchflower, Norman, Mackay; Jones, White, Smith, Allen, Dyson.

Champion
of the sixties

Rod Laver

Rocket Rod Laver is the only man to have won the Grand Slam of tennis twice, first as an amateur in 1962 and again as a professional in 1969. This achievement came from winning Wimbledon and the Australian, French, and US Opens.

The greatest ever left-hander, he was undefeated at singles in four successive Wimbledons. After taking the title in 1961 and 1962, he was then unable to contest the event after turning pro, but with the advent of the Open era, he returned to win in 1968 and 1969.

Born in Rockhampton in Queensland, the redheaded left-hander had first come to the fore as Australian junior champion in 1957, and was a hard-hitting, agile player, with a delicate touch at the net, employing heavy top-spin on his attacking shots. Many well-respected authorities say he was the finest player to ever play the game.

Bill Shankly's Liverpool

Bill Shankly was the driving force behind Liverpool's emergence as a great team. Having won an FA Cup winner's medal with Preston North End and five caps for Scotland prior to the War, he began his managerial career with Carlisle in 1949. After four more clubs he joined Liverpool in December 1959.

Shankly developed a strong youth team that rose to the top as Liverpool won Division II in 1962 and Division I in 1964. Before his retirement in 1974, he won two more League titles, 1966 and 1973, the FA Cup in 1965 and 1974 and the UEFA Cup in 1974.

Shankly created a set-up at Liverpool where even greater triumphs followed, most particularly for his successor Bob Paisley, who had been on the Anfield staff for 20 years.

In the Paisley era, 1974-83, Liverpool won the European Cup three times, the UEFA Cup once, the League six times and the League Cup three times.

✻ LIVERPOOL IN THE SHANKLY ERA

Year	League	FA Cup
1959/60	3 (D2)	R4
1960/1	3 (D2)	R4
1961/2	1 (D2)	R5
1962/3	8	SF
1963/4	1	R6
1964/5	7	WON
1965/6	1	R3
1966/7	5	R5
1967/8	3	R6
1968/9	2	R5
1969/70	5	R6
1970/1	5	F
1971/2	3	R4
1972/3	1	R4
1973/4	2	WON

1964 • OLYMPIC GAMES

Britain's unique jump double

Rand and Davies leap to Olympic Gold medal glory

Great Britain achieved a unique double in the 1964 Tokyo Games when Mary Rand and Lynn Davies won the women's and men's long jumps. It was a year in which British athletes gained much success, winning four Gold medals, seven Silver and one Bronze.

The 1960 Games had been a disaster for British athletes, especially Mary Rand. She failed miserably in the long jump final. Not in Tokyo. She became the first British woman to win an Olympic athletics title, breaking the world record, and also won Silver in the pentathlon.

Davies was a bigger surprise. Having been nearly eliminated in qualifying, he and coach Ron Pickering thought he could take bronze.

For the final it was cold, windy and wet, and Lynn was less unsettled by the conditions than the others. In the fifth round he pulled out a lifetime best, and British record jump of 8.07 metres, to win the Gold medal and record a famous British double.

Rand (left) and Davies with the jumps that won them gold in the 1964 Olympics

ANGELA MORTIMER v CHRISTINE TRUMAN

8 July 1961, Wimbledon ◆ Raymond Glendenning commentates

RAYMOND GLENDENNING:

"It's Mortimer's turn to serve. Christine Truman leading 4-3 and having won the first set 6-4. She serves, Truman into the net."

UMPIRE: "15 love."

GLENDENNING: "Now Mortimer. Chopped back short by Truman. Now Mortimer puts one right down the very back hand corner, and Truman lobs it back out."

UMPIRE: "30 love."

GLENDENNING: "Mortimer into the net. Fault. She serves again. Truman drives fast the forehand. Mortimer tries to pass her. Truman deep to the backhand. Mortimer lobs but out of court."

UMPIRE: "30-15."

GLENDENNING: "Now Mortimer to the left-hand court. She serves, it's a let. First service. She serves to the left-hand court. Mortimer gets it back. Deep off Truman's return. Now Truman goes across court for the forehand. Mortimer deep to the backhand. Truman rather shorter to the backhand. Mortimer deep to the backhand. Truman backhanded drop shot. Mortimer tries to pass Truman. Truman tries another drop shot, but this time it's her side of the net."

UMPIRE: "40-15."

GLENDENNING: "Mortimer now to the right-hand court into the net. She serves again – oh, a double. You can tell the sort of tension she's under."

UMPIRE: "40-30."

GLENDENNING: "She serves to the left-hand court, into the net again. She serves again. Chopped back short by Truman. Mortimer only just dug that one out. Truman deep to the forehand. Mortimer very high up. And out of court."

UMPIRE: "Deuce."

GLENDENNING: "She serves and it's a fault. She serves again, it's good. Truman deep to the backhand. Mortimer a lob. Truman smashes. Mortimer gets it

up, an easier kill this time and down the backhand court it goes."

UMPIRE: "Advantage Miss Truman."

GLENDENNING: "Now Mortimer to the left-hand court. She serves. Chopped back short by Truman. Mortimer deep down to the forehand. Truman rather deep to the centre. Mortimer getting it. Now Truman coming into the net as Mortimer puts it there. I think it's passed Truman. Yes I'm sure it has."

UMPIRE: "Deuce."

GLENDENNING: "A double fault."

UMPIRE: "Advantage Miss Truman."

GLENDENNING: "Mortimer first service right. Truman flat to the backhand. A net caught her there, but Truman is able to get it up. She's on the ground. Mortimer gets it back. A half-volley by Truman but she's holding her leg. I think she's hurt her leg there as she fell."

UMPIRE: "Deuce."

GLENDENNING: "It certainly looks as though she's pulled a muscle. She's certainly holding the back of her thigh. Now Mortimer down the centre line. Truman deep to the backhand. Mortimer, oh, very feebly out of court."

UMPIRE: "Advantage Miss Truman."

GLENDENNING: "Mortimer good service. Returned short by Truman. Deep by Mortimer. Backhanded and shorter still by Truman, putting plenty of slice on it. Deep by Mortimer. Shorter still by Truman. Mortimer just over the net. Truman coming to the net now but she overhits her drive."

UMPIRE: "Deuce."

GLENDENNING: "Now Mortimer to the right-hand court. She serves down the centre line, chopped back by Truman, coming into the net. Mortimer a lob. Truman lets it go, and it's out."

UMPIRE: "Advantage Miss Truman."

GLENDENNING: "Mortimer first service a fault, out over the service line. She serves again and that one was a shooter. Truman got it up, it bounced twice on the net, before bouncing out of court."

UMPIRE: "Deuce."

GLENDENNING: "Now Mortimer, first service to the right-hand court, a fault. Second one's good. Truman deep down the backhand. Mortimer lobs. Truman can't run for it, but she has got it up. She lobs very high now. Back by Mortimer, a rather poor shot. Deep by Truman. Mortimer deep to the centre of the court. Truman deep to the forehand. Mortimer deep to the backhand. Truman rather shorter to the backhand and out."

UMPIRE: "Advantage Miss Mortimer."

GLENDENNING: "Now Mortimer to the left-hand court. She serves. Fault. Serves again to the left-hand court. Driven deep by Truman. Out of court."

UMPIRE: "Game to Miss Mortimer. Four games all, second set."

After Christine Truman strained a muscle in her left thigh, Angela Mortimer took the second set 6-4 to level the scores. Truman put up a strong fight but eventually lost 4-6 6-4 7-5.

THE RUGBY LEAGUE
CHALLENGE CUP FINAL
*Huddersfield v
Wakefield Trinity*
EDDIE WARING *writes:
It will be a White Rose,
all-Yorkshire battle at
the Empire Stadium,
Wembley, this
afternoon when
Huddersfield meet
Wakefield Trinity in
the final of the Rugby
League Challenge Cup.
Grandstand will televise
the whole of the match
and listeners to the
North Home Service
will hear commentaries
from Alan Dixon and
Keity Macklin.*

Both clubs in today's Final have been to Wembley before and both have won the Challenge Cup, too.

Huddersfield were winners on their last visit in 1953 when they defeated St. Helens. Before that they reached Wembley in 1933 when they beat Warrington, and in 1935 when they lost to Castleford. Today they have the chance to equal the record for the highest number of Cup wins, held by Leeds with seven successes. So far Huddersfield have won the Challenge Cup six times.

Wakefield's Wembley victory is of a more recent date. In 1960 they beat Hull, scoring 38 points – the highest number in a Wembley final. Their previous Wembley win was in 1946, in the first final after the war.

At present Wakefield are having one of their best seasons. They have won the Yorkshire County Challenge Cup and are in the League Championship play-offs known in the North as the 'Top Four'.

There will be a rare battle this afternoon between the two packs of forwards, for Huddersfield have shown mighty forward play in their games leading to Wembley, while Wakefield have a strong pack which includes a number of Internationals. Derek Turner, the Wakefield skipper, is the vice-captain of the Great Britain touring side which will be playing in Australia and New Zealand this summer. The Huddersfield captain, Tommy Smales, is a crafty scrum-half with a lot of experience.

With South African players like Alan Skene, the Wakefield centre, and Don Deveraux, former Welsh Rugby Union International forward, on the Huddersfield register, this afternoon's final should be packed with interest.

RADIO TIMES, 10 MAY 1962

The wayward genius

He walked out on United at the age of 27

GEORGE BEST

'Nothing struck more fear into a defender than the sight of George Best running at him with the ball at his feet...'

By Trevor Brooking

George Best was an exceptional talent who probably emerged as the first true superstar of the British game. He was a brilliant individualist who thrilled supporters with his breathtaking skill. However, he also became a wayward genius, who attracted many headlines off the pitch.

He was born on 22 May 1946, and it was obvious Manchester United had acquired someone special when, at 15, he arrived at Old Trafford. He signed professional forms on his 17th birthday, and made his debut four months later at West Bromwich Albion. By the time the season ended he was a first team regular – the George Best phenomenon was underway.

What were his strengths? It is probably easier to point out that he had no weaknesses. Although he was not renowned for his heading or tackling, they were more than adequate.

Nothing struck more fear into a defender than the sight of Best running at him with the ball at his feet. He could mesmerise the very best of opponents, and those many surging runs could unlock the most miserly of defences. His superb balance and control enabled him to produce a wonderful array of feints, twists and turns which consistently bewildered defenders.

The media became fascinated with his antics on and off the pitch, and he found himself propelled into the glamorous, liberated new era of the Sixties. The foot-

> •The media became fascinated and obsessed with his antics both on and off the pitch, and he found himself propelled into the glamorous new era of the Sixties•

balling highs were considerable. United won the League in 1965 and 1967, and revelled in the European Cup.

Best conjured up one of his best individual displays in a quarter-final away tie against Portuguese giants Benfica in 1966. The Northern Ireland wizard scored two early goals as United crushed the home team 5-1, Benfica's first European defeat in the famous Stadium of Light. Partizan Belgrade knocked United out in the semi-finals, but two years later they lifted the European Cup at Wembley in May 1968.

The final was a showpiece and Best scored in a 4-1 demolition of Benfica once again.

My own personal memory of George Best was September 1971 when I visited Old Trafford as a youngster with West Ham. The impish winger simply wore us into submission. I scored from outside the penalty area that day but no-one remembers because George helped himself to a hat-trick. One memorable goal of the three came from a short corner. Receiving a return pass, he dribbled past three defenders, before selling Bobby Moore a peach of a dummy, and blasting the ball into the net.

The only cloud on his greatness was the sudden departure from the game in 1974, when he walked out on United at the age of 27. His endless indiscretions away from football finally took their toll and, sadly, he decided to waste the talent that had made him famous.

My own career peaked between the ages of 27 and 33, and I'm sure Best could have become a greater star if his ambition and fitness had been preserved. However, his talent has comfortably withstood the test of time. He will always remain one of the most gifted, natural footballers the world has ever seen.

The Speed Demons
Campbell clan had it in their blood

Billie Jean King

S peed was in the Campbell family's blood. Sir Malcolm Campbell had been a hero of the great age of challenges to the world land speed record.

Sir Malcolm took the record in nine improvements from 146.16 mph in 1924 to 301.13 mph in 1935. He had also improved the world water speed record three times.

His son Donald broke both these records. On land he raced to 403.14 mph in Australia in 1964 and broke the water speed record seven times from 1955.

The last of these records came on Lake Dumbleyung in Western Australia on 31 December 1964, when he piloted his turbo-jet engined Bluebird to 276.279mph.

Two years later Campbell was killed in another record attempt, just after his boat had reached an unofficial speed of 328 mph on Coniston Water in England.

Above: Sir Malcolm Campbell set nine speed records.

Below: Son Donald broke the water record seven times

B illie Jean King first came to the attention of Wimbledon fans in 1962 when, as an unknown 18-year-old by the name of Billie Jean Moffitt (King's maiden name), she shocked Wimbledon by knocking out top seed Margaret Smith.

Smith got her revenge the following year when she defeated the precocious teenager in the final, winning 6-3, 6-4. It would take King another three years before the she began her domination of the All-England Club.

King took her first singles title in 1966 by defeating Maria Bueno. In 1967 she beat Ann Jones, then in 1968 she made history when she defeated Judy Tegart to become the first woman since Maureen Connolly to win the title three years in succession. King lost the final in 1969, but went on to win three more times in the Seventies, for a total of six Wimbledon singles titles.

FRED TRUEMAN'S 300TH

ENGLAND V AUSTRALIA, 15 AUGUST 1964, THE OVAL ◆ JOHN ARLOTT COMMENTATES

John Arlott: "Trueman back again. Almost with a fidget on as he comes back, head down, furiously scrubbing the ball on his flannels. Moves in again to the edge of the crease, bowls. Veivers tries to get a touch on it to the leg side. He doesn't touch it, Parkes takes it, no run.

"Three hundred and sixty seven for eight. Trueman back, a little sweat off the brow on to the hand and on to the ball, then a little polish on the flannels and then straight away into the right-hander, earlier than usual, and he comes in, bowls again from the edge of the crease. Veivers pulls the bottom hand away, dabs on the leg side, gets a single. This takes him up – did he not get the bat on to it? Three six seven for eight.

"Three six seven for eight, 55 Veivers, 14 Hawke. And Trueman now to bowl to Hawke. Still these four men up close, two slips, two short legs. Trueman comes in, bowls from the edge of the crease, and that goes down the leg side. Hawke doesn't get a touch. Through to Parkes. Three six seven for eight. Trueman with a bit of a scowl at the batsman. Doesn't even look friendly towards his fieldsmen at the moment. In his 31st over. Has two wickets. Wants a third.

"Trueman in again. Bowls to Hawke – and Hawke goes forward and he's caught!

There's the 300th! There was no nicer touch than Trueman congratulating Hawke. Caught by Cowdrey. Neil Hawke can never have come in to the pavilion to a greater ovation in his life – but they weren't looking at him. Fred Trueman's 300th Test wicket. The first man in the history of cricket to achieve the figure when Hawke palyed a half-hearted stroke outside the off stump to a ball that perhaps left him a little, took the outside edge and Cowdrey swooped on it, two hands. It was high in the air, up went Trueman, up went the crowd, stood to him, and as Hawke walked away Trueman congratulated him. And the score – Australia three six seven for nine."

Jack Fingleton: "A nice neat catch by Colin Cowdrey and my heartiest congratulations, as an Australian, to one of the greatest fighters we've ever had against us. This chap is never beaten. He's always tried as long as I've known him. He's put everything he's got into the game and it couldn't have happened to a greater fighter. Three hundred wickets. A lot of them tried to get on the field but that pretty solid force of policemen out there stopped them. I think someone had ideas of putting a garland around Freddie's neck of Yorkshire white roses. Well done, Freddie Trueman."

Fiery Fred takes a record 300 wickets

Fred Trueman has taken his 300th Test wicket, the first ever to reach this milestone. Neil Hawke caught Cowdrey bowled Trueman 14, at The Oval in the Fifth Test of the 1964 Ashes series. The England team gather round, with skipper Ted Dexter on Trueman's left and the fast bowler's arm around Colin Cowdrey.

Trueman ended his Test career a year later with a record of 307 wickets at an average of 21.57 and commented that if anyone were to beat this record he would be "...bloody tired".

Trueman burst into Test cricket with 29 wickets in four Tests against the hapless Indians, who were devastated by his pace in 1952. As 'Fiery Fred' he bristled with forthright views throughout a playing career in which he gave stalwart service to England and Yorkshire, and ever since as a speaker and member of BBC Radio's *Test Match Special* team.

Imperious Piggott

He got the most out of any horse he rode

CASSIUS CLAY v. SONNY LISTON
The World Heavyweight Championship in the Light Programme and on BBC-1 (See page 35)

THE HEAVYWEIGHT CHAMPIONSHIP
OF THE WORLD

'*Cassius Clay, USA, Champion of the World v
Sonny Liston, USA, former Champion of the World
In tonight's special edition of Sportsview, Harry
Carpenter reports on this morning's World Title
fight in Lewiston, Maine, when Cassius Clay
defended the richest prize in sport against Sonny
Liston, the former champion who lost the title to
Clay 15 months ago.*'

RADIO TIMES MAY 20, 1965

A s a horseman Lester Piggott was a genius, the greatest jockey of his age from his first winner at the age of 12 in 1948 to his final retirement from the saddle in 1995. A solitary and withdrawn character due to partial deafness and a speech impediment, he had a series of suspensions for dangerous riding in his younger days, and sadly achieved notoriety with a jail sentence for tax fraud in 1987.

However, nothing can take away his unmatched ability to get the most out of any horse he rode. The public loved him for his ability to ride Derby winners. He had a record nine from Never Say Die in 1954 when he was just 18 years old, through Crepello 1957, St Paddy 1960, Sir Ivor 1968, Nijinsky 1970, Roberto 1972, Empery 1976, The Minstrel 1977 to Teenoso in 1983. Of these he considered Nijinsky the best, followed by Sir Ivor.

Above: Piggott rides Sir Ivor to the winner's circle after the 1968 Derby

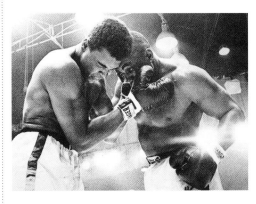

**Former champion Jersey Joe Walcott stopped the 1964
fight between Cassius Clay and Sonny Liston**

Muhammad Ali leaves his mark on history

The Greatest

FIRST TRUE WORLD STAR OF THE TELEVISION AGE

MUHAMMAD ALI

'His was the brilliant fighting talent of his generation, and it swept him first to the Olympic Gold medal, then to the heavyweight title...'

By John Rawling

When the 20th century ends and sages pause to review the impact sport has had on 100 years of human existence, no one will command greater analysis than Muhammad Ali.

Ali was the first true world star of the TV age, and his colourful verbosity proved an inspiration to millions. As one of his greatest rivals, George Foreman, was once moved to say: "He may not have been the greatest heavyweight of all time; that may have been Joe Louis. But he was the greatest man to have ever been a heavyweight boxer, no question."

His was the brilliant fighting talent of his generation, and it swept him first to the Olympic Gold medal in 1960, then to the world heavyweight title when he defeated the feared Sonny Liston on 25 February 1964.

Liston was seen as almost invincible after twice beating Floyd Patterson in one round. Surly, monosyllabic and moody, Liston had also served time for beating up a policeman.

Enter the outrageous young challenger Cassius Clay. Liston was the massive favourite. But the 22-year-old, with the speed of a lightweight and a self-belief which may never have been equalled before or since, upset the champion with psychological stunts which verged on hysteria before the fight.

In the ring, Clay comprehensively outboxed him. The 'Big Ugly Bear', as Clay dubbed him, was humiliated.

Clay immediately changed his name to Cassius X. Later he adopted the title Muhammad Ali as he embraced the teachings of Elijah Muhammad, leader of the Nation of Islam group which was to be at the centre of the black power movement in the USA. It was an affiliation which did little, initially, to improve Ali's marketability, but a succession of dazzling performances between 1964 and 1967 meant he was already being assessed as one of the great heavyweights of all time.

The singlemindedness of principle which separated Ali from the rest became evident when he refused to serve in Vietnam on the grounds of religion, saying famously: "I ain't got no quarrel with them Viet-Cong."

In June 1967, the New York State Athletic Commission suspended his licence to box. Other commissions followed and though he was still the champion, Ali was unable to fight.

He told the media: "There is an alternative and that alternative is justice. If justice prevails, if my constitutional rights are upheld, I will be forced to go neither to the army nor jail. I am confident that justice must come my way, for the truth must eventually prevail."

He was already a brilliant fighter, but he had become an articulate spokesman for a generation capturing an anti-Vietnam mood. Here was a man prepared to surrender his livelihood in the name of his religion. He neither went to jail nor served in the army.

Outrageously handsome and blessed with charisma and charm to match, he was a huge hit as he lectured on the college circuit. Ali's popularity rocketed during 1970, and he came back as a king ready to reclaim his throne.

But the three and a half years away had taken their toll. Ali, despite the great wins and huge paydays ahead of him, was unable to regain the speed which had made him almost untouchable. Years of inactivity had created another fighter. When once he had merely slipped and feinted before dancing away from danger, now he came to rely on the more debilitating virtues which have thrilled boxing spectators for centuries. Ring savvy, guile if you like, conning and coasting, holding and fiddling, all were integral parts of the new Ali. And the ability to take a punch... had any man taken so many? Was a fighter ever so brave? When he stepped back into the ring, it was as though the naivety of youth had been replaced by the reality and pain of adulthood.

Not that the public cared. Ali's public was seduced into believing he was unbeatable. Until 8 March 1971. It was billed 'The Fight of the Century'. Joe Frazier and Muhammad Ali shared a purse estimated at two million dollars, a scarcely believable figure at the time, and the Madison Square Garden crowd was stunned as Ali tasted defeat for the first time.

Ali was to fight Frazier twice more, each time emerging victorious. Their third meeting, in Manila, Ali was to call "the closest thing to death" that he had ever experienced in the ring. Perhaps it was then, in October 1975, with his fortune and fame secured that he should have ended his fighting career.

He had regained the world heavyweight title after an eighth-round knockout over George Foreman a year earlier in 'The Rumble in the Jungle'. That was one of the most extraordinary fights of all. Foreman had destroyed Frazier to win the title and there was real fear for Ali's life as he approached the contest.

"They were right," said Foreman later, "I

Left: Muhammad Ali celebrates after defeating Sonny Liston in 1964.
Below: Against Floyd Patterson in 1965

was a bad man. I was going in the ring thinking sooner of later one of those suckers isn't going to get out of here."

But Foreman proved to be the sucker. In the stifling heat and humidity of Zaire, he punched himself to a standstill as Ali chose to 'Rope-a-Dope' – lean on the ropes and absorb the shots of arguably the hardest puncher who ever lived, before applying the coup de grace.

Post-Manila, Ali was a shadow of his

former self. The once beautiful athlete kept winning, but he kept taking too many punches. After he beat Earnie Shavers in 1977, his respected ring physician Ferdie Pacheco quit saying Ali's neurological state was deteriorating to the point where he wanted no more association with his fighting.

Still, Ali was addicted to the adulation. In 1978, he lost his title then regained it against Leon Spinks, a novice who would once have been treated with contempt. Then came the pathetic spectacle of his loss in 1980, aged 38, to former sparring partner Larry Holmes. Ali, his hair dyed black with his weight reduced by drugs, was already showing signs of a Parkinson's disease related illness. It was self-evident that he should not have fought then, yet he did once more, in 1981, taking a hammering at the hands of Trevor Berbick.

Ali's physical deterioration thereafter was disturbing. When I first met him in 1984, he already slurred like a drunkard and his eyes focused somewhere through you. The overwhelming urge was to say: "You were my hero, why did you do this to yourself?" But, as his trainer Angelo Dundee told me: "Nobody ever told Muhammad what to do. He was the boss." And one of his oldest friends, the photographer Howard Bingham, when asked if Ali had regrets, answered: "No way, he would do it all again."

Ali has walked where nobody else has ever done – who are we to question the motives?

CLAY v COOPER

18 JUNE 1963, EMPIRE STADIUM, WEMBLEY ◆ SIMON SMITH COMMENTATES

....

ROUND ONE

SIMON SMITH: "The referee is now calling them to the middle."

REFEREE: "May the best man win."

SIMON SMITH: "These two come out, salute each other, come together and it's Cooper who leads with his left.

"Clay going backwards, moving out that left hand, stabbing it out as he goes away, suddenly comes in, stabs out the left hand, goes back again. Cooper goes in with the left hand, catches his man high up on the side of the head, a good

explosive left hand from Cooper and that's the sort of stuff we want...

"Cooper comes in again, one left hand to the body, one left hand to the head. What a lovely start for Henry Cooper.

"There's a clash of heads. Now Clay is bleeding from the nose! He's a slow starter, Henry Cooper, but not tonight by golly. What a sensational start.

"Clay goes in with a left hand. Cooper boxes him away. Cooper comes off the ropes with a left hand and Clay is bleeding from the nose. Cooper comes in, Clay gives a hard left hand into Cooper's head.

"Clay appears to be in trouble. He's bleeding from the nose. Cooper lets him have a left hand and right to the body. Back comes Clay, tries to get into the body, and now goes Cooper again, a beautiful straight left into Clay's face.

"Clay's already badly bruised. Cooper is coming after him and comes in with a left hand to the head. Clay pulls his man in to him, in trouble. Clay tries to take him into the ropes. Cooper first with the punch, now Clay swinging out that left hand himself. Now Cooper is after him, gets him in the corner with a good right to the body. Cooper is belting Clay as the bell ends round one. Come in Barrington Dalby..."

W. BARRINGTON DALBY: "This is unbelievable. Cooper, once he gets a man on

the hook, very rarely lets him off. He certainly dished out a lot of punishment, made his nose bleed. Clay was complaining to the referee, what for I don't know."

ROUND TWO

SIMON SMITH: "Cooper moves down. Three good left hands from Cooper in Clay's face, three ramrod lefts and Clay is not a bit happy...

"Clay looking bemused, looking very worried. He's neatly tied up by Cooper. Clay comes in close with a short sharp right. I see one of those cuts has appeared just underneath Cooper's left eye.

"Clay comes after his man and he's trying to open that cut. It's just beginning to trickle blood as the bell ends round two."

W. BARRINGTON DALBY: "Well, Clay managed to wriggle off the hook. He was certainly boxing better in that round but it was Cooper's round. Clay has been much more careful. He realises he's up against a man who can hurt him."

ROUND THREE

SIMON SMITH: "Cooper comes in with good left hook and catches him on the side of the head. He's going after him now with a left and right to the body. A good left from Cooper. And a good right from Cooper. But Clay got one in between, a right-hand, and it's started that eye bleeding again...

"Although Clay isn't throwing as many punches as Cooper, these punches are effective. He's lacerating that cut...

"Cooper's eye is beginning to look bad, it's bleeding a lot. Clay dances away, drops his hands down low, then picks up his guard as Cooper comes in...

"It looks as though Cassius Clay has weathered the storm..."

W. BARRINGTON DALBY: "That was Clay's best round but he still didn't win it. Cooper got home very very well with some straight lefts. Now I think his judgement of distance is faulty because of a certain amount of blood running into his eye and he's probably worried about that."

ROUND FOUR

SIMON SMITH: "Cooper lets him have one, explodes one into his midriff. Cooper still working this left hand exceedingly well but still having trouble with that left eye. It's cut again and it's bleeding again. Cooper is obviously going to have trouble going the distance. He's going after Clay, a little bit desperate. Clay stops him with consummate ease, draws him in, dances away, leaves him stranded on the rope, and then as Cooper turns round Clay pokes out the left hand into his face. It certainly is taking its toll...

"Just seconds left of this fourth round and it's Clay poking out one, two left hands and then getting a good left-hander from Cooper in return into Clay's face. Now Clay tries to get back with the left hook and Clay is down! Cooper has felled him! A beautiful punch. And as the bell goes, Clay has just been dropped by a beautiful punch from Cooper. Barry."

W. BARRINGTON DALBY: "Well, of all the hard luck. Clay just won that round, he was on top in that round. And then Cooper just got the range and hit him with a beautiful left hook. Clay nearly came out on top of us but he managed to get up at four. Clay's left glove has burst. That is an extraordinary thing because it means that if they've got to change the glove, they're going to give Clay a rest. No, he's going to change it at the end of the next round."

ROUND FIVE

SIMON SMITH: "And that was down for four, Cassius Clay at the end of the

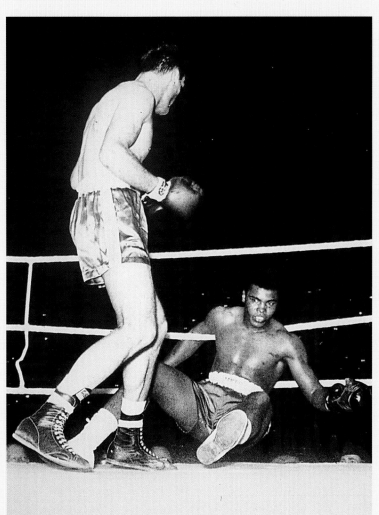

last round, and he's really swinging into Cooper now. No more of the contemptuous stuff. He's after him. Cooper got Clay with a left hand but Clay comes back with a left and right to the head. He's split that eye again.

"And another left hand from Clay, that was really a good one, lashing Cooper's face, and Cooper is bleeding badly. And Clay is picking his punches now, he's making his man pay for dropping him in that last round.

"Cooper is in trouble. He's covered with his own blood and I don't think it can be allowed to go on. Clay comes after Cooper, pokes out that left hand, and Cooper is a terrible sight. Clay comes after him and belts that left hand once, twice, three times into his face.

"And even hardened ringsiders are saying: 'Stop it.' They're chucking newspapers in the ring. The referee has gone across to Cooper. He has stopped it! Clay is the winner."

ANNOUNCER: "After one minute 15 seconds of the fifth round, the referee stops the contest. Clay is the winner."

SIMON SMITH: "Clay has silenced the crowd. He said all along he would win in round five and, well, he's done it."

W. BARRINGTON DALBY: "Yes, that was inevitable. Cooper's scourge, of course, scar tissue round his left eye. I am not taking anything away from Clay, who certainly boxed beautifully. But he must certainly think that he's a lucky man. That last left hook with which Mr Clay had the indignity of being sat on his pants by a British heavyweight — that was a beautiful punch. And had Cooper been able to continue without the dreadful handicap of a cut eye, who knows what might have happened? He put on a fine show."

Nicklaus, Palmer and Player

Golf's big three dominate the fairways of the world

Arnold Palmer (far left) did much to make the game popular, although his time at the top was limited. Jack Nicklaus (left) and Gary Player (below left) each won the Open Championship three times

Arnold Palmer made golf exciting for millions and did much to ensure continued prosperity for a game that has brought huge rewards to some.

Palmer's major victories were confined to a surprisingly short period. He won the US Open in 1960, the Open Championships of 1960 and 1961, and four Masters between 1958 and 1964 – but he has continued to delight golf enthusiasts ever since.

South Africa's Gary Player, a small man at 5ft 7ins but supremely fit, did even better, winning all four majors, for nine wins in all, between 1959 and 1978, but both men were eventually left far behind by the great Jack Nicklaus.

A prodigy, Nicklaus was a superb amateur who won the 1959 and 1969 US Amateur. In his first year as a professional, 1962, he won the US Open, defeating Arnold Palmer in a play-off. That was not appreciated at the time by golfing fans, but over the years Nicklaus' skills have gained him universal admiration. His total of 18 wins in the four Majors may never be surpassed.

These three have played a huge part in elevating the status of golf around the world.

The golden age of british motor racing

Hill, Clark, Surtees, Stewart

In the 12 years from 1962 to 1973, British drivers won the Formula One World Drivers' Championship nine times. Graham Hill started this great run in 1962, driving for BRM, and, after being runner-up each year between 1963-65, won again for Lotus in 1968. He was succeeded by a man that many consider the most talented of all the great British drivers, Jim Clark.

Driving for Lotus, Clark set a record with seven Grand Prix wins in 1963, and won again in 1965. Tragically, he was killed in an accident at Hockenheim in 1968.

John Surtees, the only man to beome world champion on four wheels as well as two (500cc motor-cycling 1958-60) won for Ferrari in 1964 by just one point over Hill.

The final British winner of the decade was Jackie Stewart. He emerged as the most successful, with three titles in 1969, 1971 and 1973, as well as being runner-up in 1968 and 1972. He passed Clark's record of 25 Grand Prix wins with 27 in his Formula One career.

Left: Jackie Stewart was the most successful British driver of the 60s.
Above and top: Jim Clark took over from Graham Hill as Britain's number one driver.
Above left: Graham Hill in action in 1966

Some people are on the pitch,
They think it's all over...
It is now!

When Kenneth Wolstenholme uttered those immortal words to millions of BBC TV viewers in the dying moments of the 1966 World Cup Final, he did so on the spur of the moment. They were not scripted. There was no forethought put in beforehand. Wolstenholme was simply reacting to the situation as he saw it at the time. Yet little did he, or anyone else for that matter, know just how prophetic those words would turn out to be.

"They think it's all over... it is now," eight words to describe delirious English fans swarming onto the Wembley turf prematurely to celebrate England's famous victory over West Germany, and Geoff Hurst hammering the final nail in the German coffin.

Wolstenholme has dined out on the quote ever since. The words made him famous, made him immortal in the annals of English football. Nearly every time that famous victory is celebrated – on screen, on radio, even in print – Wolstenholme's words are repeated. They are even conjured up when the England side is preparing for either the European Championships or the World Cup.

The annoying thing for English fans is that the words have come back to haunt successive England sides until the present day.

English football reached its peak in 1966, the year it showed the world that the country which invented the game could also master it as well. But not for long. England may have won the World Cup but their reign at the top of world football was fleeting. Ironically, the final whistle on that memorable afternoon signalled England's coming of age, and its downward slide as a footballing power.

To the chagrin of managers since, no one has been able to assemble a team that even comes close to Sir Alf Ramsey's blend of aggression and skill. Not Revie, not Greenwood, not Robson, not Taylor, not Venables, not Hoddle.

Ramsey's World Cup-winning side had talent and style in the shape of Bobby Moore, Martin Peters, Geoff Hurst and the Charlton brothers Bobby and Jack. It had tenacious and tireless workers in Roger Hunt, Alan Ball, Nobby Stiles, George Cohen and Ray Wilson. Most importantly, it had the best keeper in the world in Gordon Banks. It had the toughest backbone of any England squad before and since – Banks, Moore and Bobby Charlton, three players any manager could build a successful team around. The rest of the side had no problem blending in.

England bosses since Ramsey have been good managers in their own right, but none has been able to bring England the ultimate reward Sir Alf achieved on home soil. No other British team has managed it either.

Ramsey wasn't a rash manager. Fairly measured in his approach to the game, he was

Booby Moore holds the World Cup as a jubilant England side celebrate victory at Wembley in 1966

AND 3 GERMANY W. 2

Geoff Hurst scores his third, and England's fourth goal in the 1966 World Cup Final

was seen by many experts in the game as nothing more than a brutal tackler, a player out of his depth amidst the talent surrounding him. Yet Ramsey was adamant about Stiles' importance to the team. "If Nobby Stiles doesn't play, then England don't play," was Ramsey's terse comment.

His players respected him because he was willing to stick to such principles. They knew the value of Stiles to the team, the way he terrorised opposing players. When he stuck by Stiles and other players, he drew the team closer to him. That point was made by Bobby Moore in Jeff Powell's excellent book on the late England captain, *Bobby Moore: The Life And Times Of A Sporting Hero*.

"The spirit in the camp had been good more intellectual than inspirational. He thought deeply about the game but, as he was to prove, he was not afraid to make tough, controversial decisions.

As with England's involvement in every World Cup since – indeed, throw in every European Championship, every England game, competitive or friendly – the critics were waiting for the manager to slip up, waiting to slam him for picking the wrong player, going with the wrong formation. That was certainly true in 1966.

Ramsey was hammered for his selection of Nobby Stiles during that year's championship. Many thought he wasn't good enough to make the squad, let alone the starting eleven. He from way back," said Moore, "but with every new blast at Alf the spirit grew. We believed we had a great chance. Alf believed in us. We would show 'em."

Show 'em they did, but not before Ramsey made the most controversial decision of the competition, one still much debated today.

Every team needs a genius, someone

ENGLAND V URUGUAY

'The whole of tonight's match in which England meet the first of their opponents in Group One.

Commentator, Kenneth Wolstenholme with summaries and opinion at half-time and after the match by the Grandstand team of experts, including former England captains Billy Wright and Johnny Haynes.'

RADIO TIMES JULY 7, 1966

around whom the play revolves, someone who makes things happen out of nothing. That man in the England team was Jimmy Greaves. He was to England in 1966 what Paul Gascoigne was to England in 1990. Yet so strong was Ramsey's self-belief that he risked the nation's wrath by leaving him out of the final. Ramsey opted for Geoff Hurst over Greaves, and the move was to be the manager's most inspirational choice ever.

Despite falling behind the Germans early on, England had come back through goals by Hurst and Martin Peters, West Ham teammates of Moore. Ramsey's omission of Greaves had been vindicated, England had won the World Cup. Or so it seemed.

Ramsey had warned his players about the German side well before the final. His warning could be summed up thus – they never give up. He was spot on.

The Germans kept coming at the English defence after they had gone behind 2-1, yet it wasn't until the final minute that their efforts paid off. The German player Karl-Heinz Schnellinger appeared to handle the ball in the England box, but the referee never raised the whistle to his lips. Play continued and in a goal-mouth scramble, the Germans equalised through Wolfgang Weber. Game on.

Ramsey proved between full and extra-time that he was not only a great manager, but great motivator too. While others might have castigated their players for throwing away the World Cup in the dying seconds, Ramsey gave his downtrodden side one last inspirational push.

"All right," Ramsey said. "You've won the World Cup once. Now go and win it again. Look at the Germans. They're flat out. Down on the grass. Having massages. Flat on their backs. Just have a look at them. They can't live with you. Not for another half an hour. Not through extra-time."

He was right, but victory wasn't without controversy.

Undeniably the most talked about incident

in any World Cup is Geoff Hurst's second goal in the 1966 final. Hurst's shot hit the underside of the bar, bounced down and then out away from the net. England shouted goal, Germany claimed otherwise. Video footage has been debated ever since.

Russian linesman Tofik Bakhramov raised his flag to signal a goal. The Germans protested vehemently, but the referee pointed to the centre circle. England were in front.

Moore deals with the incident objectively

Celtic win European Cup

IN 1967 CELTIC WON the treble of Scottish League, Scottish Cup and Scottish League Cup. It was marvellous for their fans, especially such a triumph over rivals Rangers.

These two teams had long dominated Scottish football, so even more important was Celtic's 2-1 win over Internazionale of Milan in the European Cup final. This was the first ever win by a British club in this competition.

Celtic were guided by Jock Stein, manager from 1965 to 1978. Goals from Tommy Gemmell and Steve Chalmers took them to a magnificent victory after Inter had gone ahead just seven minutes into the match.

This was Celtic's first-ever appearance in a European competition, and they reached the final by beating Zurich, Nantes, Vojvodina and Dukla Prague. Sadly they lost in the first round to Dynamo Kiev the following year.

Celtic captain Billy McNeill with the European Cup

in Powell's book when he says: "I believe Roger Hunt got us the verdict. I was 50 yards away on the halfway line and in no position to offer an honest opinion at the time. From my viewpoint it had to be a goal because of Roger's reaction. He was right there, a yard from the line, and the ball came out his way. Yet he made no attempt to knock it back in. Just turned around with his arms in the air.

"I don't know how the linesman could decide. At the time I was in no doubt but on reflection I've got to say I wouldn't have liked a goal like that to be given against England."

Had that goal separated the two sides it would have been a hollow victory, but in the dying seconds of extra-time, Moore calmly took the ball out of his own area and hit Hurst with a pass just over the halfway line.

Hurst ran at the Germans and screamed a shot into the top of net to seal the dramatic victory and make Kenneth Wolstenholme a national icon.

GRAND NATIONAL STEEPLECHASE
'*Sixteen cameras capture the thrills of Becher's, Valentine's, The Chair, and the rest of the formidable National course over 4 miles 856 yards as the world's greatest steeplechasers race for a first prize of more than £17,000.*

Commentators: Peter O'Sullevan, Clive Graham, Michael O'Hehir, Michael Seth-Smith, Robert Haynes.'

RADIO TIMES 28 MARCH 1968

1967 • RACING

Freak Grand National
Foinavon threads way through melée to win

The 1967 Grand National became notorious for the pile-up at the 23rd fence, which was negotiated safely by just one horse. It seemed that a loose horse stopped the first two horses, these stopped the next, and then all but one of the remainder of the field ran into the pile-up and were unable to clear the fence.

Foinavon, a rank outsider ridden by John Buckingham, was far behind the leaders, but managed to thread his way through the mêlée, and battled on home to win the race. His starting price, for a fortunate few, was 100-1, making him the longest priced winner since Caughoo had won at similar odds in 1947.

Other horses were eventually re-mounted and Honey End came in second, 15 lengths behind Foinavon, with Red Alligator, who was to win a year later, third, a further three lengths adrift.

Outsider Foinavon (opposite) won the Grand National as other horses failed to get past the 23rd fence

FOINAVON'S GRAND NATIONAL

8 April 1967, Aintree ◆ Bob Haynes and Michael O'Hehir, Michael Seth-Smith and Peter Bromley commentate

BOB HAYNES: "This is fence no. 17 and there's still an awful lot left standing and the loose horse jumped in first. Just in behind that is Kirtle-lad, Rutherfords, then Princeful, Castle Falls, Kapeno, Rondetto, then The Fossa, then comes Greek Scholar, then comes Leedsy, and Norther and Different Class. After that Quintin Bay…"

MICHAEL O'HEHIR: "Cutting now towards Becher's for the second time it is Castle Falls with Princeful, Kapeno, Rondetto, Rutherfords along the inside, The Fossa, Norther, Greek Scholar and Kirtle-Lad together. And at Becher's the loose horse is now in front...he doesn't appear to interfere with anyone though Rutherfords lost a bit of ground there. But he's alright and they're turning now to the fence after Becher's and as they do the leader is Castle Falls with Rutherfords along the inside. And Rutherfords is being hampered and so is Castle Falls. Rondetto has fallen. Princeful has fallen. Norther has fallen. Kirtle-Lad has fallen. The Fossa has fallen. It's a right pile up. Leedsy has climbed over the fence and left his jockey there. And now with all this mayhem, Foinavon has gone off on his own. He's about 50/100 yards in front of everything else. They're all pulling up having a look now, to see what's happening at the fence. Auzzie is jumping over it now. Quintin Bay is climbing over it and as they go now to Canal Turn, well the one that went to the Canal Turn happened to be Foinavon. He's 100 yards in front of Kirtle-Lad. Then come Quintin Bay and Auzzie together, Greek Scholar is next . They're coming now to Valentine's, at least when I say they're cominng, it's Foinavon who's coming. He is roughly 200 yards in front. And over to Michael Seth-Smith..."

MICHAEL SETH-SMITH: "Well this is the most incredible National. Foinavon, I've never seen a horse at this stage of the race so far ahead. He's going quite easily. He's nearly a fence in front. He jumps it and he's jumping very well, this blinkered horse Foinavon. He's literally 200 yards in front..."

PETER BROMLEY: "As they come now to the second last fence, Foinavon about

150 yards in front of Greek Scholar. Honey End coming into third place. Into the second last, Foinavon on his own. He's over safely. The others are just jumping it now. Honey End over in second place. Greek Scholar is third. Then comes Packed Home, then Auzzie. Then towards the wide outside I can see Ronald's Boy and Red Alligator. Into the last fence now and I don't think they're going to catch him, he's still motoring with about 400 yards to go. It's Foinavon who is going to be the biggest turn up in the National ever. Honey End in second place trying to get on terms. Josh Gifford riding a sterling finish, but he's got about 10 lengths to make up. Greek Scholar is third, Red Alligator is fourth, then comes Packed Home and Auzzie. On the run for the line they've got 100 yards to go and it's Foinavon's National. It's Foinavon all the way. Foinavon has got 25 yards to go. Foinavon has won the Grand National. But the question everyone is asking, is whatever happened at fence no. 23. Michael O'Hehir is out there.

MICHAEL O'HEHIR: It all happened so quickly. A loose horse went across in front of Rutherfords and Rutherfords seemed to go into the wing. Then two or three loose horses ran hither and tither in front of the fence and the next thing we saw was that Rondetto, who had gone into the lead when Rutherfords made his mistake, he was on the ground having been interfered with by the loose horse. Then Kirtle-Lad was interfered with. Different Class was brought down. Rondetto went down. Anglo went down. The Fossa went down. They all went down in a heap and until a few minutes ago, they were still picking themselves up wondering what happened. One or two jockeys tried to catch their horses to go on after the others. But Foinavon, who was almost walking at this stage, miles and miles behind the other horses, who were really in the race, Foinavon came and climbed – and I mean climbed – over what was left of that fence and went off 200 yards in front of the race. And from then on John Buckingham really took his chance. Foinavon the winner at 100 to 1.

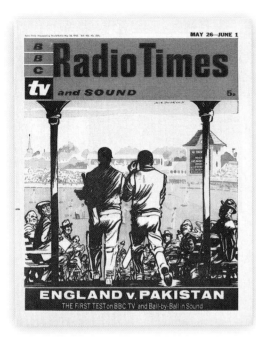

MAY 26—JUNE 1

BBC Radio Times
tv and SOUND 5p

ENGLAND v. PAKISTAN
THE FIRST TEST on BBC TV and Ball-by-Ball in Sound

ENGLAND V PAKISTAN

'The first Test at Edgbaston.

Test Match Special

SOUND

A ball-by-ball commentary on the first, and all the Test Matches in this series, will be broadcast on the Network Three and Third Programme wavelengths. This will begin at 11.15 today (11.25 on subsequent days) and continue during the hours of play until 6.35 pm. On Saturday, however, the last half-hour before the close of play (6.0 - 6.35) will be broadcast in the Light Programme.'

TELEVISION

On all five days of the match BBC TV cameras will make morning, afternoon and early evening visits to Edgbaston. On Saturday afternoon, coverage of the game will be woven into the varied fabric of Summer Grandstand.

RADIO TIMES MAY 24, 1962

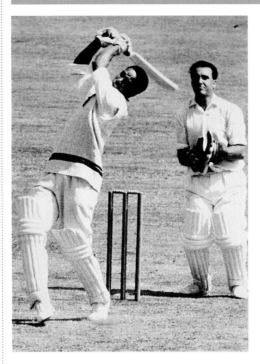

Sobers on fire

Amazing hitting by the complete cricketer

GARY SOBERS' SIX SIXES

31 AUGUST 1968, SWANSEA
WILFRED WOOLLER COMMENTATES

"Fifty-two in 29 minutes. That's another one up in the enclosure! Three sixes in this over. How many balls has be bowled? Three balls, three sixes. Fifty-eight. What an incredible bit of hitting.

"Oh, he's got that! A shorter run, it's up again. There it is, bouncing on the concrete. Four sixes in four balls. We've had some very good hitting, a very good 140 by Bolus. This makes him 64.

"I wonder where Nash is going to bowl this one. And that will just carry — no, it's going to be out. Caught at — oh, he's dropped it over the boundary! Well this is incredible.

"Now if he hits six on the trot it's a world record. Seventy on the board. And he's done it! He's done it! And my goodness it's gone way down to Swansea."

On 31 August 1968 at St Helen's, Swansea, Gary Sobers became the first man to hit all six balls of an over for six in first-class cricket. And this was no 'joke bowling' to expedite a declaration.

Batting for Nottinghamshire against Glamorgan, and coming in with the score at 300 for five wickets, Sobers had scored 40 in 30 minutes when he faced Malcolm Nash, usually an excellent medium-fast bowler, but on this occasion bowling slower.

Sobers was caught off the fifth ball, but the fielder went over the boundary line, and the final ball was dispatched out of the ground,

not be be found until the next day.

At 32, the West Indies captain was at the peak of his form. From 1954 to 1974 he was recognised as the world's greatest all-round cricketer. A superb batsman, who set a world record of 365 not out against Pakistan in 1968, he was also a gifted bowler who first played as an orthodox slow left-armer, but later bowled at fast-medium or in a variety of styles. He was also a brilliant fielder.

In 1975, he was knighted for his services to the game. In a ceremony at Bridgetown race-course, Barbados, 10,000 countrymen cheered as the Queen honoured their hero.

Sunday League cricket brings new fans to the game

I n order to arrest the decline in interest in English cricket, many changes were introduced in the 1960s, in keeping with that decade of freedoms.

One-day cricket excited a new public for the game as the knock-out competition, the Gillette Cup, led the way from its introduction in 1963. That was initially contested by the first-class counties over one innings per side of 65 overs (60 overs from 1964).

In 1969, after the success of Sunday games played by the 'Cavaliers' against county sides, an even more frenetic version of the game was added – the John Player's County League, played on Sundays at 40 overs per side with regular coverage on BBC2. Lancashire, shrewdly captained by Jack Bond, became the first champions; their superb fielding showed just how vital this aspect of the game was in the one-day game.

Above: Jack Bond captained Lancashire to the first John Player's County League title in 1969

Beamon shatters long jump record

A t an altitude of 2,248 metres, Mexico City, site of the 1968 Olympic Games, had differing effects on competitors. In endurance events it often had disastrous consequences. However, in the sprints and jumps startling performances were achieved. The men's long jump was a good example.

Much was expected of the four best jumpers. Lynn Davies (Britain) was defending his title; Ralph Boston (USA), 1960 champion, and Igor Ter-Ovanesyan (USSR) were joint record holders at 8.35 metres; and Bob Beamon (USA) was the year's top jumper.

In the final, the first three competitors had fouled their first attempts. Beamon was next and, fast on the runway, he leapt high in the air and when he landed it was obvious something exceptional had happened. Finally the scoreboard lit up – Beamon had jumped a phenomenal 8.90 metres (29ft 2½ in). His record stood for nearly 24 years.

BEAMON'S LEAP

18 OCTOBER 1968, MEXICO CITY
RON PICKERING COMMENTATES

"On the long jump runway, Bobby Beamon of the United States. The man most feared by every competitor in this competition. Erratic but incredibly talented. Here he goes for his opening leap. Oooh, it's an enormous one! My goodness me, it's an enormous one. That's surely shattered the Olympic record. This is what everybody is here for. It's been said that if he hits the board right he could go out the end of the pit. And that's an enormous one."

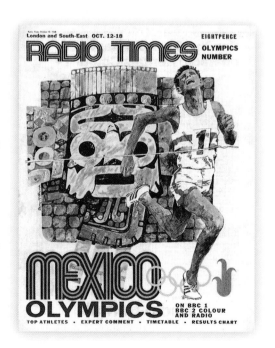

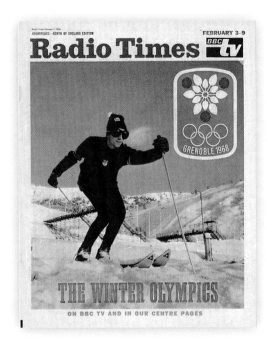

Olympic glory for Britons Tony Nash and Robin Dixon, Gold medal winners in the two-man bobsleigh event in 1964

THE WINTER OLYMPIC GAMES

'Grenoble has literally turned itself inside out, transformed its very character in order to play host to the world's athletes.

Mountains have been moved and sculptured with dynamite, smart highways have replaced rough mountain tracks. Theatres, cultural centres, and hotels have sprung up to make this city of a quarter of a million people a new powerhouse in France.

A town hall, resplendent with black marble, a second more elaborate rink, and new housing centres have been added to the civic amenities.'

RADIO TIMES FEBRUARY 1, 1968

Nijinsky's miracle year

Nijinsky, the name of the great Russian dancer, was carried by a great racehorse who thrilled race fans with his musculature and brilliance in the seasons of 1969-70, just as his namesake had wowed ballet audiences 50-60 years earlier.

Sired by Northern Dancer and bred by Eddie Taylor, Nijinsky was bought for a Canadian record $84,000 by Charles Engelhard, who sent him to be trained by Vincent O'Brien in Ireland. After winning all his six races as a two-year-old, he became the first horse for 35 years to win the Triple Crown (2,000 Guineas, Derby and St Leger) in 1970.

With the priceless ability to accelerate when needed, he was ridden by Lester Piggott to those triumphs and victory over older horses in the King George VI and Queen Elizabeth Stakes. In the same year Liam Ward won the Irish Derby on him, but, after an attack of ringworm, Nijinsky was beaten in his final two races in the autumn.

Lester Piggott on Nijinsky after winning the 1970 Derby

Welsh rugby glory

Gareth Edwards was the inspiration for a wonderful run of success

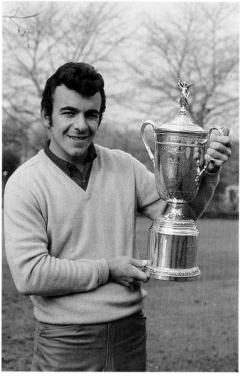

Jacklin the lad

the Welsh rugby union team of the late 1960s and early 1970s thrilled not only their loyal supporters, but enthusiasts all over the world with their brilliant play.

Gareth Edwards, the scrum-half at the heart of the Welsh team, played throughout the glory years of 1967 to 1978, when Wales won the Grand Slam in 1971, 1976 and 1978, and the Triple Crown in 1969 and 1977. He made his debut at 19 and became captain at 20.

Outside Edwards were the great fly-halves, first Barry John and then Phil Bennett, and a superb three-quarter line, with flying wings Gerald Davies and J.J. Williams, and the solid-

ity and panache of J.P.R. Williams at full-back. Centre John Dawes skippered the British Lions team that achieved a first series win in New Zealand in 1971, and on that tour there were 14 Welshmen, as well as coach Carwyn James.

Mervyn Davies was a tower of strength at No. 8 during this period, and from 1975 the formidable Pontypool front-row of Charlie Faulkner, Bobby Windsor and Graham Price packed down together for Wales.

Gareth Edwards goes for the line in Paris in 1969 as Wales rampage to the Five Nations title

TONY JACKLIN poses at home with his 1970 US Open trophy, after returning from Minnesota with wife Vivien and son Bradley.

With a seven-shot win over Dave Hill, he had become the first British golfer to win this major since Ted Ray in 1920 – and no Briton has won since. A year earlier Jacklin had ended a depressing 18-year run of no British successes in The Open with his win at Royal Lytham & St Annes. He followed that by helping Great Britain and Ireland share the 1969 Ryder Cup with the USA, after the match ended in a 16-16 tie.

Jacklin's career at the very highest level proved to be disappointingly short, with no more majors, although he was third in The Open in 1971 and 1972. He later became an inspirational captain of the European Ryder Cup team which won in 1985 and 1987 and fought a tense draw in 1989.

The Seventies

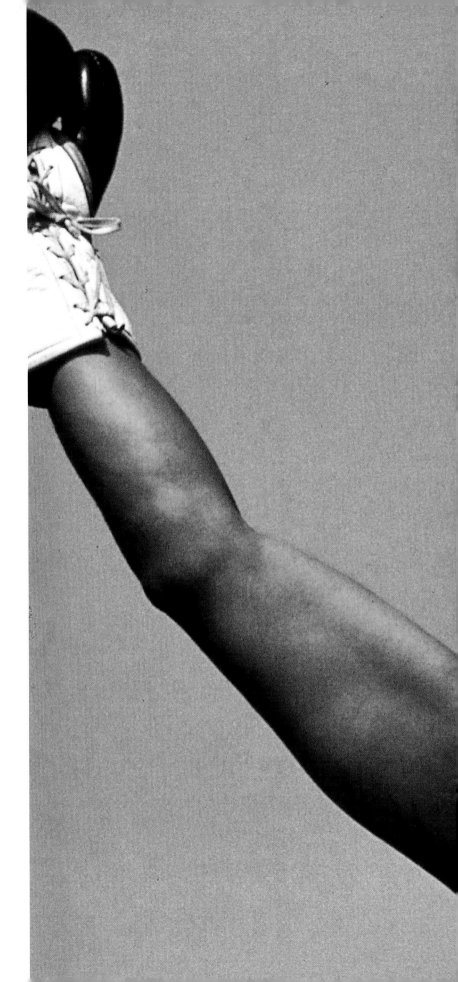

THE DECADE STARTED WITH PELE'S FINEST HOUR.
IT ENDED WITH SEVE BALLESTEROS WINNING THE FIRST
OF HIS THREE OPEN CHAMPIONSHIPS. IN BETWEEN, WE
THRILLED TO AN ERA OF HIGH EXCITEMENT AS BJORN BORG,
MUHAMMAD ALI, ALEX HIGGINS, MARK SPITZ, CHRIS EVERT
AND RED RUM DAZZLED IN THEIR RESPECTIVE SPORTS

Main photo: Muhammad Ali relishes another moment of triumph.
Above top: David Gower making a double century against India.
Above left: Terror comes to the 1972 Munich Olympic Games.
Above right: Conquering British Lions captain Willie John McBride

Seventies Diary

Above: Liverpool's Phil
Thompson after winning the
1978 European Cup.
Right from top: Lee Trevino
and his wife pose with the
Open trophy at Royal
Birkdale in 1971; Joe Frazier;
and David Wilkie.
Far right from top:
Geoff Lewis on Mill Reef
winning the 1971 Derby;
Giacomo Agostini; and
lovebirds Jimmy Connors
and Chris Evert show off
their Wimbledon singles
titles in 1974

1970

Briton Tony Jacklin takes golf's US
Open Championship by seven strokes.

Austria's Jochen Rindt dies in a crash
at Monza but wins the F1 drivers
championship posthumously.

Brazil win the World Cup, defeating
Italy 4-1 in the final.

Boxing laments the death of Sonny
Liston from a drug overdose.

Margaret Court wins Wimbledon,
beating Billie Jean King 14-12, 11-9,
and goes on to win the Grand Slam.

Muhammad Ali returns to boxing
after a three-year absence, easily
beating Jerry Quarry.

1971

India gain their first Test victory in
England on the strength of spinners
Chandrasekhar, Bishen Bedi and
Venkataraghavan.

In a brutal match, Joe Frazier defeats
Muhammad Ali in the 'Fight of
Champions'.

Lee Trevino wins the US and British Open championships.
He went on to retain the British Open title in 1972.

In horse racing, Mill Reef wins The Derby, King George VI
and the Arc de Triomphe.

At the Burghley Horse Trials, Princess Anne rides Doublet
to two Gold medals in the European three-day event.

Edward Heath leads Great Britain to victory in yachting,
by captaining the winning Admirals Cup team.

1972

England beat Australia 2-1 to win the first Prudential
Trophy, with Dennis Amiss scoring cricket's first one-day
international century.

Alex Higgins wins the snooker world championship.

Roberto Duran defeats Scotland's
Ken Buchanan in a world lightweight
championship fight, after Buchanan
is hit with a low blow.

Swimmer Mark Spitz wins seven
Olympic Gold medals.

Palestinian terrorists shoot 11 Israeli
athletes at the Olympic Games.

Giacomo Agostino takes his seventh
consecutive 500cc world
motorcycling championship.

1973

George Foreman knocks Joe Frazier
down six times in two rounds to
take Frazier's world heavyweight
boxing title.

Jack and Bobby Charlton hang up
their football boots.

A bomb scare stops play at Lord's in
England's Test match against the
West Indies.

In the Open Championship at Royal
Troon, 71-year-old Gene Sarazen scores a hole in one.

In athletics, David Bedford takes eight seconds off Lasse
Viren's 10,000 metres record.

1974

South Africa's Gary Player wins the Masters and Open
Championship.

Tanzania's Filbert Bayi breaks the 1500 metres record by
one second.

Chris Evert and Jimmy Connors get engaged and both
win Wimbledon.

Led by Franz Beckenbauer, West Germany defeat Holland
to win the World Cup.

In athletics, Brendan Foster breaks the 3,000 metres
world record.

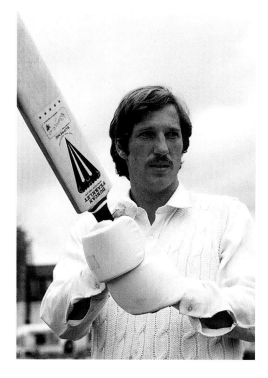  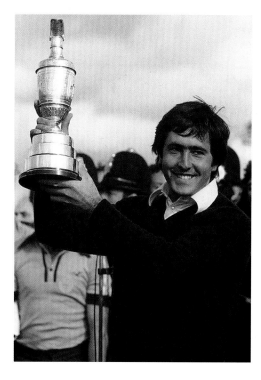

Above from left: Ian Botham, Margaret Court, and Seve Ballesteros with the 1979 Open Championship trophy

1975

Jack Nicklaus wins the Masters by beating Johnny Miller and Tom Weiskopf in an exciting final round.

Non-League Wimbledon defeat First Division side Burnley in the FA Cup, then draw with Leeds.

Czechoslovakian tennis player Martina Navratilova defects to the USA.

Niki Lauda wins the motor racing world championship for Ferrari.

In the 'Thriller in Manilla', Muhammad Ali beats Joe Frazier when Frazier doesn't get up for the 15th round.

1976

Second Division Southampton beat Manchester United in the FA Cup Final after a goal by Bobby Stokes.

Nineteen-year-old golfer Seve Ballesteros finishes second to Johnny Miller in the Open Championship.

David Wilkie takes swimming Gold in the Olympics, winning the 200 metres breaststroke.

The West Indies bowler Michael Holding takes 14 wickets for 149 runs as England crash to a 231-run defeat at The Oval.

Australia win the Centenary Test match against England as Dennis Lillee takes 11 wickets.

1977

In boxing, John Conteh refuses to fight Miguel Cuello and is stripped of his world light heavyweight title.

Red Rum wins a third Grand National and then retires.

Kevin Keegan plays his last game for Liverpool as his side wins the League Cup and European Cup.

Jack Nicklaus and Tom Watson smash Open Championship golf records at Turnberry as Watson wins his second Open.

Virginia Wade captures Wimbledon during the Queen's Jubilee year.

1978

David Gower makes his England cricket debut and hits a four off his first ball.

Leighton Rees makes darts history by becoming Wales' first professional champion.

Martina Navratilova wins her first Wimbledon title, defeating Chris Evert.

In cycling's Tour de France, Bernard Hinault wins the first of a record five titles.

Bowler Sarfraz Nawaz stops Australia beating Pakistan after the Aussies needed only 62 with seven wickets left. Sarfraz takes all seven wickets for five runs.

1979

Trevor Francis moves from Birmingham to Nottingham Forest to become the first £1 million player.

Jim Watt becomes lightweight world boxing champion, while Maurice Hope takes the light middleweight title.

Seve Ballesteros is dubbed the 'car park champion' as he wins the Open Championship. Seve hit a miraculous recovery shot from a parking lot en route to victory.

A golf first as Europeans take part in the Ryder Cup, but lose to the USA.

Ian Botham captures his 100th Test wicket in a record quick time of two years and nine days.

Korbut and Comaneci captivate the world
Olympic darlings
THEY CHANGED GYMNASTICS FOREVER

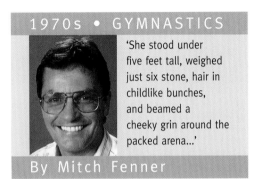

1970s • GYMNASTICS

'She stood under five feet tall, weighed just six stone, hair in childlike bunches, and beamed a cheeky grin around the packed arena...'

By Mitch Fenner

One hundred and ninety years ago, Friedrich Jahn gave the world a system for gymnastics which, by 1952, had evolved into the competition apparatus used at today's World Championships and Olympic Games.

The 1950s and '60s brought developments that established clear distinctions between men's and women's gymnastics. Men performed with strength and daring, while women epitomised grace and elegance. Both displayed great composure under pressure, sharing an impersonal discipline nurtured in the training hall and reaching maturity on the competition podium. There was an inaccessible, almost magical aura surrounding the champions of the day, their self-control, skills and achievements seemingly beyond the reach of mere mortals. It was the champion's duty to stay impassive, whether in victory or defeat.

This was the image of gymnastics by the late Sixties. Its stars never shone brighter than the sport itself. It had been so in Jahn's day, and for every Olympic games since 1896.

But in 1968, a performance at the Mexico

Olga Korbut – tiny phenomenon

Olympic Games from Vera Caslavska gave notice of things to come. A cleverly presented floor routine set to the music of the Mexican Hat Dance flattered the hosts, delighted the spectators, and clearly impressed the judges. It was, in fact, the first flirtation with the then latent 'show business' appeal of gymnastics.

Four years later came a tiny phenomenon that would not only realise this potential, but completely overturn the accepted conventions of serious and intense Olympic competition. Seventeen-year-old Olga Korbut stepped on to the podium at the 1972 Munich games. She stood under five feet tall, weighed just six stone, hair in childlike bunches, and beamed a cheeky grin around the packed arena. By the

time the competition was over she had dominated centre stage, entranced the crowd, and captured the hearts of millions worldwide.

As the competition unfolded, Olga's smile became synonymous with every performance – until the asymmetric bars. In that event she lost style and rhythm several times, and at the end rushed to her seat and dissolved into tears, unable to cope with what she regarded as failure. It was ironic that a sport based on precision and accuracy of performance, and where mistakes had been traditionally met with stoicism, would come to owe so much to the 'failure' of one unfortunate girl.

Olga could not have dreamed that that spontaneous display of emotion was to be the single most important influence on the sport since Jahn. Millions shared the moment through televised pictures, and the devastated Olga won the hearts of every parent watching.

More significantly, little girls the world over identified with her misery.

Here at last was a star with the human touch. In the space of 30 seconds she had removed the barriers erected through decades of tradition. During the days of competition that remained, the world tuned in to follow the fortunes of Olga Korbut, willing her towards eventual victory in the beam and floor events.

On beam she removed another barrier by demonstrating that daring skills were not the sole province of men's gymnastics, her back somersault causing a sensation, even giving rise to speculation that it would be banned as too dangerous. Olga had paved the way towards the increasing difficulty that is a feature of today's medal-winning performances.

It was her floor performance that gave true vent to her personality as she smiled and cavorted through 90 seconds of lively and flexible acrobatics, the crowd roaring their approval of every manoeuvre.

The impact of Olga's performance and personality came as a complete surprise, the aftermath unprecedented. The sport's popularity soared. The demand in Great Britain was such that hundreds of clubs were formed, many of those by parents who had become frustrated at the lack of opportunity for their offspring to take up gymnastics.

The Soviets were quick to recognise the value of Olga's worldwide appeal. Entrepreneurs and sponsors were eager to provide the opportunity to package and present gymnastics through the staging of event spectaculars, with TV coverage a major factor in ensuring commercial success. Touring gymnastic shows had arrived, and Olga Korbut was the star the world wanted to see. She had changed gymnastics, bringing the sport within reach of thousands of young girls.

Korbut's career ended in 1976, her legacy indelible. Olga's distinctive brand of gymnastics brought criticism from purists, though she is unlikely ever to be rivalled in achieving that which eludes even the most technically excellent of gymnasts – star quality.

Today Olga Korbut lives in the American city of Atlanta, Georgia, where she coaches her beloved sport. She also travels the world as a gymnastics ambassador, extolling the virtues of determination and hard work that were so much part of her success.

An entirely different combination, but of no less impact, was to come from a 13-year-old Romanian of Korbut-like physique.

Nadia Comaneci was the product of a late Sixties search for gymnastics talent throughout her country, and by the mid-Seventies she had taken her place alongside Olga as a world star and household name. She was at the vanguard of Romania's attempt to oust the hitherto unbeatable Soviet team from their number one world ranking.

Comaneci's trademark was technical excellence, taking difficulty and risk a stage further than Korbut. Nadia blurred and finally erased the traditional distinctions between men's and women's gymnastics, combining dynamic power, daring, grace and elegance.

Nadia's performance at the 1975 Champions All competition in London mes- merised the audience and whetted appetites for a head-to-head with the world's most famous gymnast.

That confrontation was to come in 1976 at the Montreal Olympic Games. It was a meeting of opposites, for Nadia had none of the sparkling attraction of Korbut. Strangely, her appeal centred around a clinical and

Nadia Comaneci – aura of invincibility

unemotional approach, giving her an aura of invincibility that intrigued both expert and casual spectator alike.

Nadia emerged triumphant and assumed the crown as the sport's new Queen; at just 14 she appeared unassailable. Her victory was emphatic, and she entered the history books as the first gymnast to be judged faultless at an Olympic Games, scoring the maximum 10 points on seven occasions in 12 routines. It was a feat that has never been equalled, and had the immediate effect of provoking a com- plete and drastic review of the judging system.

If Olga had removed the emotional barriers, Nadia had dismantled those surrounding the elusive perfect performance. The phrase 'Perfect 10' was coined and will ever be associated with the name Nadia Comaneci.

As an individual she had demonstrated that the Soviet gymnastics machine was not infallible, and in 1979, amid rumours of poor health and arguments with her coach, she helped the Romanian team to their first World Championships win.

Despite an increasingly volatile relationship in later years, Nadia and her mentor of some 12 years had been a formidable partnership. Never before had a coach stepped into the limelight, and Bela Karoly achieved fame and notoriety for his training methods and competition arena antics – the first 'celebrity' coach on the world stage.

Nadia's meteoric rise and huge success at such a tender age set the seal on the new order. So much was the sport now the exclusive province of tiny acrobatic girls, that by the age of 18 she had retired, thinking herself too old!

Following a controversial defection to the West, Nadia travelled the United States in search of a new life and eventually built a career making celebrity appearances at coaching clinics, gymnastics shows and on TV. Today she is a successful businesswoman, married to 1979 World Championships gold medallist Bart Conner.

Gymnastics owes an incalculable debt to Olga Korbut and Nadia Comaneci. Through their respective styles, and within four short years, these two great stars had taken gymnastics to an admiring public and established it as a major Olympic sport. Olga had inspired thousands of youngsters to accept the challenge of gymnastics, and Nadia showed them that it was possible to make the dream of absolute perfection a reality.

Friedrich Jahn, the 'father' of modern gymnastics, would have been proud of them.

who flung himself to his right and made a seemingly impossible one-handed push over the bar off a header from Pele.

England, with six of the winning team from 1966, were narrowly beaten (3-2) by West Germany in the quarter-finals.

Brazil, however, went to on defeat Italy 4-1 in the final. Fittingly Pele scored the first goal and fed first Jairzinho and then Carlos Alberto for the decisive goals in the closing stages of the match.

Perfect Pele

Banks robs him but Brazil win

The genius of Pele was best seen in the 1970 World Cup in Mexico. He had originally established his international reputation at the World Cup of 1958, but his contributions in 1962 and 1966 were much restricted by injury.

Although both teams qualified, a decisive match was contested by Brazil and England in Group 3. A goal from Jairzinho, laid on by Pele, settled the issue, but the feature of the game was a superb save by Gordon Banks,

Above: Gordon Banks makes one of the finest saves ever seen in the World Cup. Right: Pele after helping Brazil defeat Italy in the 1970 World Cup Final

Gunners on target
League and Cup double for Arsenal

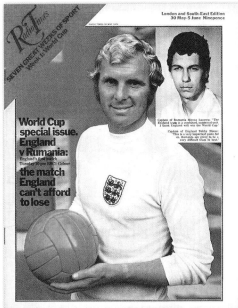

THE WORLD CUP

'The reasons for paying so much attention to the World Cup are simple: football is our national sport; England are the World Champions and BBC1 has a reputation to give not only proper regard to sport, but also to do it better than anyone else.

Over the years, we have fought for and won a good name for our sports coverage. We pioneered new techniques; we drew attention to new sports. We helped to give national prominence to such sports as show-jumping, swimming, athletics, skating and Rugby League. It has been – and still is – a two-way partnership between sport and BBC TV – a partnership that has been of benefit to both. Above all, it has brought pleasure to millions.'

RADIO TIMES, 28 MAY 1970

In 1971 Arsenal, managed by Bertie Mee, emulated the Spurs team of a decade earlier to win the coveted League and Cup double (a feat they were to achieve again in 1998). In the League, Arsenal came from six points down with eight games to play to pip Leeds for the title, 65 points to 64, with Spurs third on 52.

In the Cup, the indomitable spirit of the Gunners was amply demonstrated in the semi-final when they came back from 0-2 down to Stoke City to get an equaliser from a Peter Storey penalty with just a minute to play, before taking the replay 2-0. Liverpool were the opponents in the final, in which no goals were scored until Steve Heighway gave Liverpool the lead in extra time. Still Arsenal did not yield. Substitute Eddie Kelly scrambled an equaliser and then, with nine minutes to go, Charlie George, the darling of the Highbury faithful, struck home a fine winner.

Spitz swims to seven Golds

SEVEN GOLD MEDALS, and in each of them a new world record – that was the astonishing and unparalleled achievement of Mark Spitz at the Olympic Games in Munich in 1972.

Spitz was determined to make up for the disappointment of 1968. Then he had been tipped for six Golds, but came away with two relay Golds, a Silver in the 100 metres butterfly and a Bronze at 100 metres freestyle. He ended by finishing last in the 200 metres butterfly, in which he held the world record.

In Munich his gold trail started, fittingly, with the 200 metres butterfly, to which he added successively the 4 x 100 metres freestyle, 200 metres freestyle, 100 metres butterfly, 4 x 200 metres freestyle, 100 metres freestyle and finally the 4 x 100 metres medley relay, in which he swam the butterfly leg.

In all, from 1967 to 1972, Spitz set 26 world records in individual events.

Tragedy at Munich
They burst in with machine guns blazing

Death came to the 1972 Munich Olympics at dawn on 5 September. At 5.10am a band of 'Black September' Arab guerrillas broke into the Israeli building in the Olympic village.

They burst in with sub-machine guns blazing. Moshe Weinberg, a 33-year-old wrestling coach, died instantly. Yosef Romano, a weightlifter, was mortally wounded as he held a door shut while two of his team-mates escaped through a window. Fifteen others also escaped through windows and side doors. Ten were taken hostage, but one of them, Gad Tsabari, made a dash for freedom, dodging bullets as he ran.

The guerrillas demanded the release of 200 Palestinians held in Israeli jails and safe passage out of Germany. The Olympic village was surrounded by 12,000 police, and the Games were suspended.

The West German Chancellor, Willy Brandt, flew in to take charge of negotiations. The terrorists were told they would be flown with their hostages to an Arab country. They were taken by helicopter to the Furstenfeld military airport 25 miles from Munich.

Just before midnight the guerrillas and their hostages began to walk across the tarmac to a waiting Boeing 727 aircraft. Suddenly the airport was plunged into darkness as all lights were turned off, and German police marksmen opened fire.

The rescue attempt took a tragic turn. All nine hostages were killed, as were four Arabs and one policeman. Three terrorists were captured and one escaped into nearby woods.

NORTH WEST 26 August-1 September 1972 Price 5p
BBC Radio Merseyside

Radio Times

Fastest man alive?

INSIDE: Valeri Borzov, Russia's threat to the black Americans in the 100 metres Plus colour exclusives on this week's favourites The Munich Olympics All week BBCtv and Radio

OLYMPICS EXCLUSIVE Week 1

VALERI BORZOV

'Borzov was stockier than I expected of a sprinter, power concentrated in thick thighs. Hair respectably cut, he might have been a promising bank clerk. He ignored everyone, strutting like a chicken to exercise every available foot muscle, from toe to heel, then throwing off his blue track-suit to practise his start and the hand-over of the relay baton.

He seemed exceptionally self-contained, squatting on the ground away from his mates, talking little, even to the man who has trained him for six years, Valentin Petrovsky.'

RADIO TIMES,
26 AUGUST - 1 SEPTEMBER 1972

(Soviet athlete Valeri Borzov went on to win both the 100 metres and 200 metres at the 1972 Olympics – the only European ever to do so.)

Law unto himself

DENIS LAW was a marvellously exciting inside-forward, one of the finest ever seen in Britain. He began his League career with Huddersfield, but in March 1960 he went to Manchester City and became their top scorer before Torino secured his transfer little more than a year later.

Law did not settle in Italy, however, and was delighted when Manchester United's Matt Busby brought him back to England. In 11 seasons there he achieved huge success, including an FA Cup winner's medal in 1963 and Football League championships in 1965 and 1967. In 1964 he was voted European Footballer of the Year.

He ended his career at Manchester City in the 1973/4 season. It was ironic that United, in temporary decline, needed to win at Old Trafford against City at the end of the season to stay in the First Division. Law, playing his last League game, sent his old club down with the only goal in the match.

Champion
of the Seventies

ALEX HIGGINS

The moment when Alex Higgins tearfully beckoned into the crowd to persuade his wife Lynn and baby son to join him after he won the World Professional Snooker title in 1972 will live long in the memories of all who watched on television.

'Hurricane' Higgins, a one-time apprentice jockey from Belfast, had won the Northern Ireland amateur championship in 1968. He turned professional in 1971 and burst on to the scene in 1972, winning the world title at his first attempt. Aged just 23, he was then the youngest ever world champion. His fast, brilliant play made him a crowd favourite in the 1970s.

It was, however, 10 years before he won the world title for a second time, in an emotional final against Ray Reardon. Thereafter major wins became scarcer as his churlish behaviour brought him increasingly into conflict with officials and fellow players.

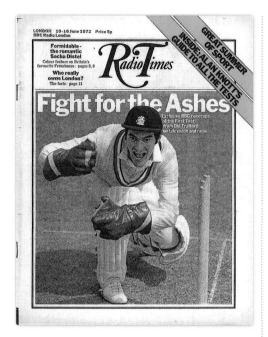

THE ASHES

'First Test Match

England v Australia

Third day

The whole of this morning's play direct from Old Trafford

Introduced by Peter West

Commentary team RICHIE BENAUD, JIM LAKER, TED DEXTER'

RADIO TIMES,
10-16 JUNE 1972

1974 • RUGBY UNION

Willie John's wonders

McBride's pride of Lions are 'best ever'

The most successful British Lions team of all time was that which toured South Africa in 1974. The picture shows skipper Willie John McBride leading his team off the plane on their triumphant return to Heathrow Airport. Their overall record in their 22 matches read: won 21, drawn one, lost none; points for 729, points against 207.

In the Tests the Lions stunned the Springboks with three successive wins – 12-3, 28-9 and 26-9 – before the last match resulted in a 13-13 draw, and that only when a last-minute try by Fergus Slattery was disallowed. Andy Irvine was the leading points-scorer on the tour with 156, but fly-half Phil Bennett (103 points) was the kicker in the first two Tests before Irvine came in to play on the wing, rather than his usual position as fullback, for the last two Tests to help Bennett.

When Willie John retired in 1975, his 63 Irish caps and a record 17 appearances in Tests for the Lions made him the world's most capped forward.

Red Rum, National hero
Record three wins for Britain's favourite

Red Rum, the only horse to win the Grand National three times, became a legend in his lifetime and had an enormous public following.

His first win, as an eight-year-old in 1973, was against public sympathy. In that race he gave 21 lbs to Crisp, whose valiant effort he overcame in the finish. The following year he carried 12 stone to victory and, after seconds in 1975 and 1976, won again with 11.8 in 1977. A National horse par excellence, in his career between 1967-78 Red Rum won 24 of his 100 races under National Hunt rules (three hurdles and 21 steeplechases).

After initially racing on the flat and winning three novice chases, he was bought by Noel le Mare for 6,000 guineas in 1972 and trained by 'Ginger' McCain on the sands at Southport. A life-size statue of Red Rum was unveiled at Aintree in 1988, and he died at the age of 30 in 1995.

Right: Red Rum in 1977, after becoming the first horse to win the Grand National three times

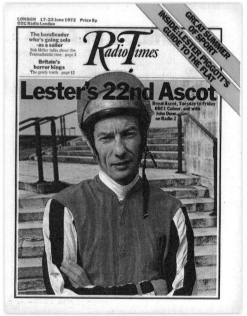

ROYAL ASCOT

'*It is Lester who cracks the whip ... Lester who says where, when and for whom he will ride ... and Lester who, as often as not, is richer and more important than the owner he's riding for.*'

RADIO TIMES,
17-23 JUNE 1972

World Cups of the Seventies

Calypso cricket shines bright

WEST INDIES TAKE CHARGE OF THE ONE-DAY GAME

1970s • CRICKET

'The first World Cup Final was an occasion such as those who were there would surely always treasure in their memory-chests...'

By Peter Baxter

Left and right: Clive Lloyd batting, and with the 1975 World Cup. Centre: Garry Gilmour

ust as had happened with the advent of overarm bowling, it was the women who got there first. They staged the first cricket World Cup in England in 1973. And, indeed, it was England who won it. The men had tried a one-day international – Australia against England – in the early days of 1971, after the Melbourne Test.

There was still something of an air of experimentation in 1975, when the ICC at last sanctioned a full World Cup. Even the BBC seemed not too sure. The Controller of Radio 3 – then the home of *Test Match Special*, of which he was a fan – declared himself not too keen on the one-day game and ball-by-ball commentary was limited to the final.

What was obviously going to be crucial to the success of the enterprise in England in early summer was the weather. Five days before the first game an inch of snow prevented any play between Derbyshire and Lancashire. Things did not look promising. But in the event, that was just the start of a glorious

> **'The stroke of a man knocking a thistle top off with a walking stick – no trouble at all'**
>
> JOHN ARLOTT ON CLIVE LLOYD

summer and sun blessed the entire fortnight.

There were only six Test-playing countries at that time. Their numbers were swelled for the tournament by the inclusion of East Africa and Sri Lanka, still six years away from Test status.

England opened at Lord's against India with a huge score – 334 for four – in their 60 overs, thanks to an Amiss century. India's reply was mystifying, as Gavaskar batted through the innings for 36 not out in a total of 132 for three. It was as if one-day cricket still needed explaining to some folk.

With wins also against New Zealand and East Africa, England's progress to the semi-final was smooth. At Headingley, though, they ran into Australia and, more specifically, Garry Gilmour. In conditions ideal for his swing bowling, he took six for 14 and bowled England out for 94. England's bowlers, though, also liked these conditions and, when they had reduced Australia to 39 for six, Radio 2 (then our main vehicle for sport) decided to join for commentary. That maybe was what prompted an Australian revival and they won by four wickets.

The first World Cup Final was an occasion such as those who were there would surely always treasure in their memory-chests. For us in the radio commenrary box in the pavilion and for millions of listeners round the world there were some purple patches of

forward as that. Lillee and Thomson – with the bat – took Australia to only 17 runs behind, before Brian Johnston described a twilight victory for the West Indies.

Although India had expressed an interest, the ICC decided that 1975 had been such a success they would do it again in England in four years. Perhaps enticed by a first-round

bowler finally came unstuck. Boycott, who had taken five wickets in the four matches so far, Gooch and Larkins had to share 12 overs and they took between them no wicket for 86. Viv Richards made 138 not out, hitting the last ball of the innings from Mike Hendrick for a mighty six.

Though Brearley and Boycott opened with

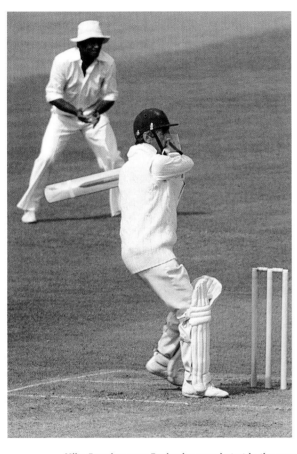

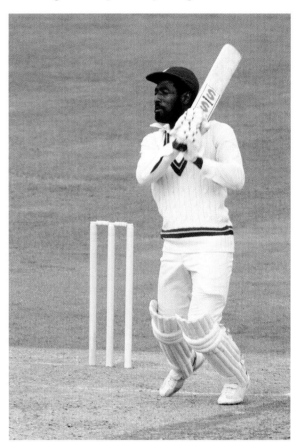

Mike Brearley gave England a sound start in the 1979 Final but Joel Garner took five wickets to seal a West Indies victory based on Viv Richards' sensational 138 not out

John Arlott. On Clive Lloyd, as he cruised to his hundred: "The stroke of a man knocking a thistle top off with a walking stick – no trouble at all." Or on Dickie Bird: "Having a wonderful time, signalling everything including stop to traffic coming on from behind."

"This match," said Arlott, "is just sailing out in front of Australia, like an express train leaving a station." It wasn't quite as straight-

England v Australia match at Lord's, the BBC mounted commentary, too – though, in these Packer years, England won that match easily. England reached the final, too, coming through a fairly tight encounter with New Zealand in the semi-final. It seemed inevitable that their opponents at Lord's would be the West Indies.

There the strategy of 'fiddling' the fifth

a stand of 129, it was never remotely up with the rate required to overhaul the West Indies' 286 and Joel Garner cashed in on the need to accelerate to finish with five for 38. A West Indies victory by 92 runs.

And so the Seventies closed with the West Indies the kings of World Cricket. Their hold on the one-day crown, at least, was to be shaken in the Eighties.

1970s • GOLF

Seve the brave

Impossible shots were his speciality

Spain's Seve Ballesteros first burst upon the golfing stage when he finished second to American Johnny Miller in the 1976 Open Championship at Royal Birkdale.

Seve signalled to the world that he had the audacity to play brave shots others couldn't even conceive when, at the 18th hole, he played a daring chip and run shot between two bunkers to save par.

Seve had to wait until 1979 to win golf's most prestigious trophy, when he triumphed over the links of Royal Lytham & St Annes. Seve would win there again in 1988, but it is his win four years earlier that holds a special place in the Spaniard's heart.

In a thrilling final round over the Old Course at St Andrews, the home of golf, Ballesteros battled against five-times Open champion Tom Watson. Watson blew his chances when he overhit his approach shot at the Old Course's dreaded 17th, the Road Hole. However Seve, playing just ahead of Watson, sealed the victory with a birdie on the home hole, saluting the crowds by repeatedly punching the air after the ball fell into the cup.

Following his 1979 Open title, Ballesteros went on to win the Masters three times. In fact, his victory at Augusta in 1980 made him the tournament's youngest winner ever, a record that stood until Tiger Woods' victory in 1997.

Moment of victory for Seve in the 1979 Open at Royal Lytham & St Annes

King Klammer

FRANZ KLAMMER was perhaps the greatest downhill skier. Certainly nobody can match his record 25 World Cup downhill wins from 1974-84. He was Olympic champion in 1976 and World Cup downhill winner five times.

A farmer's son from Carinthia in Austria, he was famed for his raw courage and determination. Klammer recorded his first downhill win in 1973. He won eight of nine World Cup downhill races in 1975 so, at the age of 22, was the favourite to win the Olympic title on home soil in Innsbruck a year later.

Last of the top seeds to race, he was down on 1972 champion Bernhard Russi en route. However, he overcame the intense pressure and expectation by throwing caution to the wind to take the Gold Medal.

Bionic Barry defies 'death' crash

Sheene machine returns in world-beating form

Barry Sheene had a serious crash at 180mph at Daytona in 1975 which nearly cost him his life. However, he bounced back with remarkable verve to win the World Motorcycling Championship at 500cc for Suzuki in 1976 by a clear margin. He also won the following year.

Sheene was the sixth British rider to win motorcycling's most prestigious title. He followed Leslie Graham, winner of the first world title in 1949, Geoff Duke, John Surtees, and Mike Hailwood who each won four times between 1951 and 1965, and Phil Read, champion of 1973 and 1974. Since Sheene, however, there have been no British champions.

Sheene achieved his first Grand Prix wins for Suzuki in 1971 – one at 50cc and three at 125cc. Moving up to the 500cc class, he had 19 wins in all from 1975 to 1981.

CHRIS EVERT

Chris Evert won the Wimbledon women's singles title three times in the 1970s. Although Evert played with very little emotion – her nickname was the "Ice Maiden" – she became one of the darlings of Wimbledon. Much of that had to do with her romantic relationship with Jimmy Connors.

Evert took over from Billie Jean King as Wimbledon's top women player. Indeed, an 18-year-old Evert lost her first final, in 1973, to King. A year later Evert defeated Russia's Olga Morozova to lift her first championship.

Evert won again in 1976 when she defeated Evonne Cawley. Evert twice lost finals to her great rival Martina Navratilova in the 1970s, before winning the title for the last time in 1981, when she beat Hana Mandlikova.

When Wimbledon belonged to Borg

jorn Borg won Wimbledon for five successive years between 1976-80, and on clay courts he won the French Open a record six times: 1974, 1975 and 1978-81. He was a superlative match player who completely dominated the game during his peak.

Borg had a powerful serve and his counter-attacking topspin shots both on the forehand and on his double-handed backhand were as good as any in the history of the game. He won his first Wimbledon title without losing a set in the tournament, but at the end of his era of supremacy he was challenged by another great player – John McEnroe.

McEnroe and Borg contested two superb Wimbledon finals. In 1980 Borg won his fifth title, coming from two sets to one down to win 8-6 in the fifth. But 1981 was McEnroe's first Wimbledon title, won in four sets after Borg had taken the first set.

Bjorn Borg won Wimbledon a record five times

WIMBLEDON

'*Money alone is not the target for the ambitious young lions of the professional tennis circuit, although over a quarter of a million pounds in prize money is on offer. No, rather it's the distinction of winning tennis' most sought after title under the toughest conditions. Bjorn Borg will be bidding to become the first man since Fred Perry to win three times in a row when he opens the defence of his singles title on the Centre Court at 2.00pm this afternoon, and BBC outside broadcast cameras provide you with 'the best seat in the house'.*'

RADIO TIMES,
24-30 JUNE 1978

Balletic Curry

WITH A BREATHTAKING display of balletic grace, Britain's John Curry ushered in a new era of figure skating when he won the Gold medal at the 1976 Innsbruck Winter Olympics.

Before Curry, men's figure skating was dominated by technical expertise allied to physical strength and spectacular jumping ability. Curry changed that with a style of skating that owed much to his boyhood ambitions to be a ballet dancer. He revealed an athletic agility to match any of his rivals but he used it differently to achieve grace and beauty rather than programmes of power and attack. The outcome was a performance that changed the face of figure skating and left his rivals looking old-fashioned and outclassed.

1976 • CRICKET

Grovelling Greig

England captain's rash prediction rebounds

Before the series began, England captain Tony Greig rashly said the West Indians would be made to "grovel" on their tour to England in 1976. Far from it – the Test series result was a 3-0 victory to the visitors, with two Tests drawn.

Having played brilliantly throughout a wonderfully hot summer, Clive Lloyd's team took the Wisden Trophy with a crushing victory in the fifth Test at The Oval by 231 runs. In this match, two of the sport's all-time greats displayed their skills at their very best. Vivian Richards took his total of Test runs in a calendar year to 1,710, including 829 in this series, with a wondrous 291 from 386 balls, and despite a brave 203 from Dennis Amiss. Michael Holding won the game, displaying exceptional pace and sustained aggression for figures of 8-92 and 6-57, the best ever match figures for a West Indian.

Above: Michael Holding (left) and Clive Lloyd toast success.
Right: The imperious Viv Richards in action at The Oval

WIMBLEDON

'There are many versions of Virginia Wade. To some journalists who follow the lawn tennis circuit and who know the game she is a star – a person who instantly commands attention when she enters the room. And they allow her the privileges of a star. They accept that when she is good she is very, very good and when she is bad she is horrid.'

RADIO TIMES,
24-30 JUNE 1972

Heroic Lauda loses
Hunt seizes title after horrific accident

Left: Niki Lauda had a horrific accident in 1976 but came back to nearly win the Formula One World Championship. Below: James Hunt took the 1976 title from Lauda by one point

Virginia Wade's Centennial fairytale

Niki Lauda had a terrifying accident on the second lap of the German Grand Prix at Nürburgring in 1976, when he hit a kerb and his Ferrari's suspension broke. The car went off the road at high speed and caught fire. Lauda suffered severe burns. The Austrian driver's condition was critical but he fought back so tenaciously that he raced again six weeks later.

At the time of the crash, Lauda, defending the world title he had won in 1975, was leading the championship with 58 points to 35 over the flamboyant Englishman James Hunt. Hunt won the restarted German Grand Prix and later added the Dutch and Canadian races. Lauda's return was sensational, but he could not add quite enough points and withdrew from the final race in Japan due to appalling conditions. Hunt needed and got a third place there to secure the championship by one point.

Lauda, surely the most complete driver of his era, regained the world title in 1977 and won again in 1984, while Hunt had three wins in 1977, but retired after another couple of years in which he struggled to remain competitive.

The Centennial Lawn Tennis Championships at Wimbledon in 1977 were crowned in the finest possible manner, with a British victory in the women's singles. In her 16th championships and approaching her 32nd birthday, Virginia Wade lost the first set of the final to Betty Stove of the Netherlands, but came through to lift the championship by winning 4-6, 6-3, 6-1.

Victory for Wade was a most appropriate highlight to the distinguished career of a woman who won her first major title in 1968 – the US Open – and who played in a record 100 Federation Cup matches for Britain and a record 20 Wightman Cup ties.

A regular BBC commentator, in 1983 she became the first woman to be elected to the Wimbledon Championships Committee.

VIRGINIA WADE v BETTY STOVE

1 JULY 1977, WIMBLEDON ◆ MAX ROBERTSON COMMENTATES

MAX ROBERTSON: "Forty love. Points for 5-1, final set. Wade from the roller end. Everybody hushed and still as she serves now down the centre to the left-hand court. Too long. The group posed on the roller there like an old Victorian photograph. The groundsman's friends, let in for a treat. The second serve right, the forehand down the line into the net!"

UMPIRE: "Game to Miss Wade. Miss Wade leads by five games to one in the final set. Quiet please."

MAX ROBERTSON: "Stove serving, Royal Box end. A good serve to the forehand, just scraped back. And Stove didn't attempt to go for it. Whether she thought it was a fault that wasn't called I don't know. She could have got up and got that. Anyway, love-15 she is. Maybe she's given it away.

"She serves to the backhand, it comes back. Stove a forehand volley across court – and that is just given out. And a wry, rueful grin from Betty Stove as if to say, 'What can I do on this British ground?'

"The Centenary championship. Miss Wade, backhand return, Betty Stove a backhand, a lob from Virginia Wade. Back goes Stove, waits for it to bounce inside the baseline. The Dutch girl plays it deep into the corner – a winner. The brave Dutch girl raises her hands up as if to say: 'Thank you for applauding me now'."

UMPIRE: "15-30."

MAX ROBERTSON: "Everybody willing Virginia Wade at her 16th attempt, when no one thought she could win Wimbledon, to win it now. And she's on her way as Betty Stove comes and nets the forehand."

UMPIRE: "15-40."

MAX ROBERTSON: "The Queen's Silver Jubilee year. Match points to Virginia Wade for that title that everybody else wanted her to win. It's within her grasp now. And Betty Stove is serving from the Royal Box end with the Queen watching as she serves down the centre, backhand return, Betty Stove backhand half-volley. Wade drives and slips as she does so."

UMPIRE: "30-40."

MAX ROBERTSON: "Stove still has a match point to save. An anxious, scrambling point that last one was. Stove serves at match point, it skips off the top of the net, the ball white and floating away like a culprit as it falls a fault. Match point, second serve. Stove serves, it's right, a forehand return by Wade down the line. Stove can't get it.

"Virginia has won! Virginia has grasped the title she thought would never be hers. Virginia Wade has won the Centenary title with the Queen watching her. Virginia will take tea with the Queen. (Massive applause.)

"Well, 16,000 people here at the Centre Court are going to make the umpire wait until he can announce that final score. He has looked up twice, Harry Collins from Surrey, but he can't compete with 16,000 people and frankly with the whole of Britain too. But certainly sympathy for Betty Stove who I thought did everything that she could on a day when really she must have felt that everybody was against her. Betty Stove said this morning: 'If I win I will break 50 million British hearts.' Here's the score..."

UMPIRE: "Ladies and gentlemen, the score was 4-6, 6-3, 6-1." (Laughter.)

MAX ROBERTSON: "So cheers and laughter when Harry Collins finally got out that score. Betty Stove puts on a white cardigan, a little piece of Holland in the midst of British delight. Virginia Wade behind – the new Virginia Wade, the new hairstyle, the new girl, and the new champion.

"Her Majesty the Queen walks out in what I would describe as a pink and white coat and matching hat. The Duke of Edinburgh has a word with one or two of the ballboys. Her Majesty moves to the table and stands there. Alongside her the Union Jack. Virginia Wade – she curtseys, shakes the Queen's hand and has few words with Her Majesty and the Centre Court applaud and applaud and applaud. Virginia has done it. A magnificent representative for Britain as a player, as a captain of our Whiteman Cup team.

"Virginia will turn and she'll hold the silver salver up... NOW. (Huge cheers.) And the moment belongs to Virginia Wade."

Liverpool and Forest did it their way

European Cup: The English years

PAISLEY AND CLOUGH LEAD THEIR TEAMS TO GLORY

THE EUROPEAN CUP

'It was a wonderful spell for English football as our clubs dominated the European sphere... The British influence was so decisive...'

By Trevor Booking

From 1977 to 1981 the names of just two clubs were engraved on the European Cup, and they were Liverpool and Nottingham Forest. It signalled a wonderful spell for English football as our clubs dominated the European sphere. Even Aston Villa kept up the winning tradition by lifting the trophy in 1982, and Liverpool won it again in '84. Foreign players are now an accepted part of any successful Premiership side, but during this exciting era it was the 'British influence' that was so decisive.

Let's look at Liverpool first, who lifted the trophy in 1977, '78 and 1981. When you speak of the Anfield club I think it's fair to suggest that Bill Shankly is the first manager likely to spring into mind. He was an inspirational character and personality who undoubtedly transformed the fortunes of the club between 1959-1974.

Shankly installed the famous 'back-room staff', and it was one of those unsung members, Bob Paisley, who eventually guided them through an unbelievable spell from 1974-83.

Above left: Liverpool's David Johnson with the European Cup.
Above right: John McGovern after Forest won the 1979 European Cup

Their first coveted European Cup Final victory arrived in 1977 when they defeated the Germans Borussia Moenchengladbach 3-1 in Rome. Kevin Keegan signalled the end of his time at Anfield by producing a magnificent display to inspire a superb team performance. The experienced German international Bertie Vogts was detailed to mark Kevin out of the game, but the tireless striker twisted and turned his way to glory before heading off to play for Hamburg the following season.

If the Liverpool faithful were concerned about how they could replace Keegan, the arrival of Kenny Dalglish from Celtic promptly

provided the answer. It was the skills of the Scotsman that were to prove crucial 12 months later as Liverpool kept the trophy by beating FC Bruges 1-0 at Wembley.

Then, in 1981, it was the unlikely figure of left-back Alan Kennedy who turned match winner as he scorched a cracking left-foot drive into the net as Liverpool defeated Real Madrid 1-0 in Paris.

Throughout this tremendous run of success, Liverpool evolved a patient style of play which owed everything to an accurate passing game that enabled them to retain possession for long periods. They encouraged individual flair in the right areas, but the overriding strength was their disciplined teamwork.

Ray Clemence was a reliable last line of defence, while the central defensive pairing of Alan Hanson and Mark Lawrenson became equally vital. Graeme Souness was a major influence beside Ronnie Whelan in midfield, and they were key factors in further European Cup Final appearances in 1984 and 1985.

The two European Cup successes of

Nottingham Forest in 1979 and 1980 were even more remarkable because they achieved their success against the odds. They were a relatively small club compared to some of the major European sides they faced, but somehow their charismatic manager Brian Clough guided them to glory.

Trevor Francis scored the only goal when Forest defeated Malmo in 1979, and in 1980 John Robertson netted the winner against Keegan's Hamburg.

Trevor Francis was of course the first £1,000,000 player to be involved in a transfer deal, but his far post header in the Final quickly paid dividends.

That Forest team was similar in style to Liverpool. Well organised at the back, the team pattern was again based on an accurate, but patient, passing game, and although individuals did capture the headlines, the foundation was very definitely their teamwork.

Goalkeeper Peter

Shilton was an outstanding obstacle in goal, while the unlikely central defensive pair of Larry Lloyd and Kenny Burns proved highly effective.

If I was asked to name their key outfield player I would plump for left winger John Robertson. He always offered them width, and curled a succession of dangerous crosses into the penalty area from seemingly impossible positions.

Brian Clough was one of the best managers of my generation. Although he courted controversy, his record at Derby and Forest was quite incredible. He had the knack of getting the maximum performance out of players. His European Cup successes were his crowning glory, and a great example of how occasionally huge transfer budgets can be overcome.

Top: Kenny Dalglish (centre) scores against Bruges in the 1978 European Cup Final. Left: Liverpool celebrate in familiar style

BBC commentator Bill McLaren selects his favourite scores

My top tries of all time

CHOSEN BY THE MAN THEY CALL THE VOICE OF RUGBY UNION

RUGBY UNION

Phil Bennett's audacious sidestep, Serge Blanco boldly running from his own line, Dean Richards powering through a scrum – these are a few of Bill's favourite things

By Bill McLaren

nothing brings a rugby audience to its feet – and, come to think of it, TV commentators – quite like glorious, long-range tries born out of adventurism, and individual and collective flair.

Australia's 1984 Grand Slam coach, Alan Jones, had total belief in the maxim that "to win without risk is to triumph without glory". Undoubtedly one of the most fertile areas for risk-taking in rugby has to be when the opposition have been attacking but have lost possession. That is when to hit them hard with counter-attack because momentarily they are aligned for attack and not defence. Of course, skill levels and judgement have to be spot on if counter-attack is to be ignited but, when everything gels, there is delight for all – except, of course, the team that concedes the score!

Perhaps the most famous try was scored in what was hailed the greatest game ever – Barbarians v

•Willie John, like a water buffalo on the charge, scored his only international try for Ireland to the unfettered delight of thousand of his fans who invaded the pitch to acclaim the great man•

New Zealand at Cardiff Arms Park in 1973. Remember how Phil Bennett pattered back to within 10 metres of the Barbarians goal line, then sparked the counter with three sizzling sidesteps to launch JPR Williams, John Pullin, John Dawes, Willie John McBride and Tom David with exceptional handling at pace for Gareth Edwards to climax his 25-metres scoring sprint with a soaring dive that brought the house down?

Philippe Saint-André scores a glorious try against England in 1991

Naturally the French, in seeking at times to achieve the outrageous, have thrilled rugby crowds all over the world with their daring and exquisite skills. That was never more evident than at Twickenham in 1991. Although England won 21-19 to clinch the Grand Slam, much of the chat afterwards was about the try scored by French wing Philippe Saint-André. It all was so typically French.

Just short of their own dead-ball line, Pierre Berbizier lit the touchpaper to an amazing move by launching Serge Blanco on a loop. Linkage by Jean-Baptiste Lafond sparked off three magical contributions by Didier

Camberabero. First he exploded Philippe Sella then was reserviced by him before gathering his own chip ahead in tight touchline confines, and placing a cross kick on a sixpence for Saint-André to gather on the run and score between the posts. Magnifique!

It isn't so often that you see a cross kick nowadays from wing to centre field, but it worked like a charm for that amazing French move. It did the same at Murrayfield in 1981 when Australia were awarded an offence kick near the Scottish 25. Everyone expected the Wallabies to kick for goal or set up a tap-kick attack. Instead, Paul McLean took the Scots by surprise by punting across field into the in-goal area and Brendan Moon, bright as a button, anticipated perfectly to score the try.

One score memorable for a personal reason was recorded by the New Zealand hooker Hika Reid against Wales at Cardiff Arms Park in 1980. From a scrummage inside the New Zealand 25, David Loveridge interpassed at pace with the ever-present Graham Mourie before releasing Bill Osborne, Brian Robertson and Stu Wilson, the All Blacks wing then presenting the ball out of the tackle for, of all people, Reid, to swoop, gather and score. "Of all people" because Reid had been among the last out of the original scrummage and yet had covered some 80 metres at speed to be on hand for the final touch. All of which enabled me to tell the BBC TV audience that the try had been scored by "Hika the hooker from Nongataha". I enjoyed that!

Hika was just one of several tight forwards to experience the delight of scoring an international try. There was that remarkable hack and chase try over 70 metres by the Welsh prop Graham Price, a favourite son of Pontypool, against France in Paris in 1975. The French also suffered that season at Lansdowne Road when Willie John, like a water buffalo on the charge, scored his only international try for Ireland to the unfettered delight of thousands of his fans who invaded the pitch to acclaim the great man.

There are all kinds of tries, some of the

RUGBY'S GREATEST TRY

BARBARIANS v NEW ZEALAND, CARDIFF ARMS PARK, 27 JANUARY 1973
BOB IRVINE AND CHRIS REA COMMENTATE

BOB IRVINE: "From 12 yards outside the New Zealand 25, we're going to watch as John Pullin, the England captain and Barbarian hooker today, prepares to throw the ball in. The mark of the game has already been set right at the start. This one's going to be a runner and we're going to have the thrill of our lives this afternoon.

"Towards the end of the lineout Quinnell gets it, goes to the ground. They rip him off it. Picking it up there, Lambert gets it back to Whiting, then back to Going. Going kicks downfield. Underneath it John Williams 15 yards inside his half. He's going to run it. He runs up to the 10-yard mark. Runs into Urlich, Urlich takes him to the ground, kicks it downfield into the arms of Going. Midway between the 25 and halfway, Going is caught with it and the ruck is won by New Zealand. Back it comes from Kirkpatrick, out on the right to Brian Williams. Up to halfway he goes, kicks it down to the 25.

"It's bouncing on the 25 – a bad one for Bennett, going backwards and picking it up. Up there for him is Gowan, he's got past Gowan, he's coming up the middle again. He's feeding it out on the left to John Williams, taken by Brian Williams. It's on the left again to Pullin and then further out to John Dawes, up to halfway he comes. Oh this is excellent. It's Tom David over on the left to Quinnell. Quinnell gives it out to Gareth Edwards. Edwards goes for the corner and Edwards has scored! Edwards the try. What a try. The crowd are going mad and that was after three minutes."

CHRIS REA: "I don't think I'll ever live to see anything quite so magnificent. Phil Bennett had the ball in an impossible position with his back to the opposition. Turned, he beat three men on a sixpence. The ball went to John Williams, Pullin, John Dawes, Tom David and Quinnell before Gareth Edwards, with a magnificent turn of pace, went over in the corner. Four-nil to the Barbarians."

RadioTimes

World snooker
Will Canada's Cliff Thorburn or Britain's John Spencer win this year's world snooker championships? See 'Snooker', from Monday BBC2. Back feature: Cliff, John and the other world-class players

WORLD SNOOKER

'*The Embassy World Professional Snooker Championship*

The first of 14 nightly programmes

The leading 16 professional players in the world compete over the next two weeks for the premier title in snooker and the biggest prize ever in the history of the game, £24,000.

Tonight ex-champion RAY REARDON, seeded No 2, and last year's beaten finalist CLIFF THORBURN, the No 6 seed, are playing their opening matches.

David Vine introduces highlights from the Crucible Theatre, Sheffield.'

Commentator TED LOWE.

RADIO TIMES,
15-21 APRIL 1978

England celebrate a try by Dean Richards (with ball) against Ireland at Twickenham

long-range variety, others of the close-quarter type as when Dean Richards, in England's mighty pack, scored two pushover tries – and should have had a third – against Ireland at Twickenham in 1986.

Then there are the simple ones, as when New Zealand called a two-man lineout against Scotland at Murrayfield in 1979 and Murray Mexted, their elongated number eight, gathered the throw brilliantly and accelerated with such intuitive angle of run as to make it over the 25 metres to the line with barely a hand laid on him.

Contrast that with a Mike Slemen score for the British Isles against the South African Invitation XV in 1980. From a move started by John O'Driscoll's lineout delivery, the ball was transferred 33 times in over two minutes of continuous action. It was an incredible sequence which ended with Bruce Hay giving a scissors pass for Slemen to romp away from an exhausted defence. The com-

mentator must have been breathless afterwards!

Two other scores made for particularly enjoyable commentary. In the Scotland against Wales match at Cardiff in 1980, Scotland scrum-half Alan Lawson covered back into his own 25. With Wales anticipating a clearance to touch, he opened out to create counter handling involving John Beattie, Gordon Dickson, John Rutherford, Andy Irvine and Keith Robertson for Jim Renwick to race over to underline his feat of scoring a try in three consecutive internationals against Wales at Cardiff Arms Park.

Against England at Murrayfield in 1986, David Shedden ignited a sweeping move in which Mike Biggar, Sandy Carmichael and Alan Tomos all handled before Alan Lawson sprinted the last 30 yards for a spectacular try.

What made those two scores special to me personally is that Jim Renwick is a fellow townsman and a former pupil of mine, and Alan Lawson is our much loved son-in-law.

Scots' near miss

Gemmill inspires pyrrhic victory over Dutch

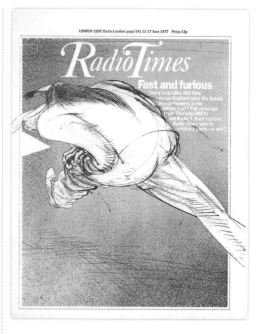

DENNIS LILLEE

'*Melbourne, March 1977. The Centenary Test, and Dennis Lillee is in action. Eyes glaring furiously, moustache bristling blackly, huge hand clamped round the ball as if round a hand-grenade, he turns and begins his long, terrifying run-up. Hair flopping, huge shoulders bent as though against a mighty wind, elbows pumping furiously, he gathers speed.*'

RADIO TIMES,
11-17 JUNE 1977

S cotland's best ever World Cup performance may well be counted as their excellent 3-2 win over Holland in Argentina in 1978.

Archie Gemmill scored twice, once from a penalty, and the other a brilliant goal after he weaved around three Dutch defenders. Graeme Souness added the other Scottish goal to give the travelling 'Ally's Army' hope.

But the win was not enough to overcome the disappointment of the Scots' two previous matches – a 3-1 loss to Peru and a 1-1 draw with Iran. Scotland and Holland finished the group level with three points behind Peru's five, group winners. The Dutch went through on goal average and progressed to the Final, which they lost 3-1 to Argentina in extra time, with Mario Kempes scoring twice.

Above: Archie Gemmill scores against Holland in 1978

The Eighties

Newcomers became heroes and the rewards just kept getting bigger. Seve Ballesteros and Nick Faldo, Jayne Torvill and Christopher Dean, Ian Botham and Carl Lewis all found success. But for some there was a price to pay. Muhammad Ali boxed on too long and was badly beaten by Larry Holmes, and sprinter Ben Johnson was disgraced for taking drugs

Main photo: Carl Lewis – supreme Olympic athlete.
Above top: Graeme Hick scores a brilliant 405 not out.
Above left: Kenny Dalglish and Ian Rush of Liverpool.
Above right: Torvill and Dean glide to victory

Eighties Diary

Above: Ian Botham in full
flow against Australia.
Right from top: Adrian
Moorhouse breaks the
100 metres breaststroke
record. Muhammad Ali
loses to Larry Holmes.
Jack Nicklaus at 46 becomes
the oldest Masters winner.
Far right from top:
Terry Butcher sees red
in World Cup qualifying.
Bill Beaumont leads from
the front. Florence Griffith
Joyner with the medals she
won at the Seoul Olympics.
Scottish golfer Sandy Lyle
wins The Masters

1980

Alan Minter wins boxing's World Middleweight Championship by beating Vito Antuofermo, before losing the title to Marvin Hagler.

Bill Beaumont leads England to victory in rugby union's Grand Slam.

A year after his official retirement, 38-year-old Muhammad Ali loses to Larry Holmes.

Seve Ballesteros becomes the youngest winner of the Masters.

New Zealand are prevented from scoring the six runs they need to defeat Australia in cricket, after Aussie captain Greg Chappell orders his brother Trevor to bowl underarm along the ground. Chappell is accused of poor sportsmanship.

1981

England, following on, beat Australia by 18 runs when Ian Botham scores 149 not out and Bob Willis takes eight for 43.

Rowing history is made when Sue Brown becomes the first woman cox in the Boat Race.

Jocky Wilson wins the first Professional World Darts Championship.

John McEnroe wins Wimbledon for the first time when he defeats Bjorn Borg in the final.

Norway beat England at football – a then unheard-of event.

1982

Steve Davis makes snooker's first televised maximum break.

Bobby Robson becomes the England football manager.

Tom Watson chips in for a birdie two at the 17th to win the US Open Golf Championship. Watson then wins the Open Championship.

1983

India win cricket's World Cup Final at Lord's as favourites West Indies throw the title away.

Torvill and Dean win skating's world title with nine perfect sixes.

Aberdeen win the European Cup-Winners' Cup by beating Real Madrid 2-1.

Carl Lewis wins three Golds in the first Athletics World Championships.

The USA lose yachting's America's Cup for the first time in 132 years when John Bertrand skippers Australia II to the title.

1984

In athletics, South Africa's Zola Budd becomes a British citizen in record time just before her 18th birthday, saving her from a five-year qualification period.

Seve Ballesteros wins the Open Golf Championship for the second time.

After riding 1,138 winners, champion jockey John Francome retires following a bad fall.

1985

Thirty-nine people die and 400 are injured in a riot at Heysel Stadium, Brussels, as Liverpool play Juventus in the European Cup Final.

French cyclist Bernard Hinault equals the record set by Jacques Anquetil and Eddy Mercx with his fifth victory in the Tour de France.

Dennis Taylor takes the World Snooker Championship after being 0-8 down to Steve Davis in the final.

Boxer Barry McGuigan wins the World Featherweight Championship by defeating Panama's Eusebio Pedroza.

Tony Jacklin captains Europe's Ryder Cup side to victory over the USA after 28 years of American dominance. Sandy Lyle is the first Briton to win The Open since Jacklin in 1969.

From left: John McEnroe enjoyed winning at Wimbledon, Bernard Hinault won the Tour de France for the fifth time, and Eddie 'The Eagle' Edwards leaped to the wooden spoon

1986

Jack Nicklaus becomes the oldest Masters winner at the age of 46.

Greg Norman leads all four of golf's Major championships but only wins The Open.

Maradona punches Argentina to victory over England in a World Cup quarter-final match with his famous 'Hand of God' goal. In the same tournament, Gary Lineker scores a hat-trick against Poland. Argentina win the Cup.

Lloyd Honeyghan records a major boxing upset when he hammers Don Curry in Atlantic City.

Iron Mike Tyson beats Trevor Berbick to become boxing's youngest World Heavyweight Champion.

1987

Coventry defeat Tottenham 3-2 in an FA Cup Final that is decided in extra-time by a Gary Mabbutt own goal.

After two years spent rebuilding his swing, Nick Faldo wins the Open Championship with 18 straight pars in the final round at Muirfield.

In athletics, American Ed Moses is beaten at the 400 metres hurdles for the first time in 122 races.

Mike Gatting has cricket's most famous argument when he berates Pakistani umpire Shakoor Rana.

Mike Tyson becomes champion of all three heavyweight boxing titles.

Europe win the Ryder Cup for the first time on American soil when Tony Jacklin's side lift the trophy at Muirfield Village, Ohio.

1988

Somerset are on the receiving end of Graeme Hick's bat as he scores 405 not out.

England cricket captain Mike Gatting gets ousted after it's discovered he had invited a barmaid to his hotel room on his 31st birthday.

Sandy Lyle becomes the first British player to win the US Masters.

Eddie 'The Eagle' Edwards makes history in the Winter Olympics by becoming Britain's first Olympic ski jumper. He finishes last easily.

Ice skater Katarina Witt dazzles audiences with her skating and her daring costumes.

Nineteen-year-old Steffi Graf wins tennis' Grand Slam and the Olympic tennis title.

Rugby union star Jonathan Davies jumps over to rugby league to join Widnes.

1989

Scotland's Stephen Hendry wins the Benson & Hedges Masters snooker title at 19.

Seventeen-year-old American Michael Chang wins the French Open to become the youngest winner of a tennis Grand Slam title.

Nick Faldo wins his first of three Masters tournaments when he defeats American Scott Hoch in a playoff.

Ninety-five Liverpool fans were crushed to death at the FA cup semi-final at Hillsborough, Sheffield.

In a World Cup qualifying match in Sweden, Terry Butcher plays with 10 stitches in his head to lead England to a 0-0 draw.

The 100 metres breaststroke record is broken by 25-year-old Briton Adrian Moorhouse as he wins his seventh Gold medal in European or Commonwealth Games.

No más!

A bizarre twist in the Leonard-Duran saga

"NO MÁS, NO MÁS" (no more, no more) cried Roberto Duran as he abruptly retired in the eighth round of his world welterweight fight against Sugar Ray Leonard in November 1980. This was a rematch after Duran had relinquished the world lightweight crown he had held for seven years to challenge Leonard at the higher weight five months earlier. The slugger Duran won that fight brilliantly, but in the rematch Leonard changed his tactics. Duran could not cope with the speed and long-range sniping of the younger man (24 to 29), and simply gave up, bewildered and humiliated.

Leonard went on to win titles at junior middleweight, middleweight, super middle and light-heavyweight, and Duran also won world titles at junior middleweight and middleweight in the 1980s. In 1989 Duran lost his middleweight title again to Leonard – so, long after "no más", he had indeed come back for more.

Leonard (right) and Duran had some epic battles

The voice of cricket retires

John Arlott was the voice of cricket for millions as his radio broadcasts took the game to listeners all over the world from the 1940s to his retirement in 1980.

Arlott's artistry with words and deep love of the game and its players took him into the hearts of the cricket public. So much so that his attempt to leave quietly at the end of his final stint on air – at the Centenary Test, England against Australia at Lord's on 2 September 1980 – was thwarted. Indeed play was stopped as everyone in the ground stood to applaud him.

A keen reporter, historian, raconteur and wine lover, his breadth of knowledge was immense. He could be quite difficult when he chose to be. He was a fierce upholder of values, notably in fighting the evil of apartheid. His proudest achievement, however, was when the professional cricketers themselves elected him to be President of the Cricketers' Association in 1968.

1981 – The first London Marathon

JOYCE SMITH (below) is the first woman home in the first London Marathon in 1981. On a cold and damp March morning, at the age of 43, she set her fifth British record for the marathon, her time of 2:29:57 being the first sub 2:30 time. In those days the women's race was combined with the men's and she finished 139th overall of the 7,055 starters.

"The late start is due to the time." DAVID COLEMAN

"That's cricket, Harry, you get these sort of things in boxing." FRANK BRUNO

"That slow motion replay doesn't show how fast the ball was travelling." RICHIE BENAUD

"You were treading where no man fears to go." RON PICKERING

People's race

The long-running London Marathon

I t was planned in a pub and launched over lunch. It made its debut on 29 March 1981 and has grown in size and stature each year. Today, the London Marathon is as much a part of Britain's sporting

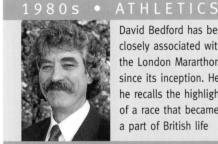

1980s • ATHLETICS

David Bedford has been closely associated with the London Mararthon since its inception. Here he recalls the highlights of a race that became a part of British life

By David Bedford

calendar as the FA Cup Final, the Grand National and the Boat Race. The BBC has broadcast every race live and has helped popularise the event by bringing it into millions of homes worldwide.

The race attracts the best runners in the world. The roll of honour includes men like Dionicio Ceron, Antonio Pinto, Steve Jones and Eamonn Martin, women like Ingrid Kristiansen, Grete Waitz, Rosa Mota and Liz McColgan. At the same time, it is truly a people's race. The weekend jogger and humble club runner and the first-timer compete with the Olympic and World champions.

The Marathon has also become one of the country's largest charity events. Thousands run for good causes and in 1998 raised £15 million. These principles were laid down by founders Chris Brasher and John Disley, who set the wheels in motion over pints with fellow runners in a pub near Richmond Park after their regular Wednesday night run. Brasher developed the idea in an article in *The Observer*. Then a lunch, hosted by *Observer* editor Donald Trelford, and attended by council, police and athletics officials, gave its seal of approval.

There were 7,000 starters for the first race. Norwegian Inge Simonsen and American Dick Beardsley linked hands as they crossed the line together and were declared joint winners. Britain's Joyce Smith took the women's title.

In 1998, nearly 100,000 applied for places, with a record 30,663 lining up at Greenwich and Blackheath to start the 26 miles 385 yards trek to the finish line on The Mall. Some 500,000 spectators lined the

Left: The almost endless tide of runners in the London Marathon comes in all shapes and sizes

course. Millions watched on the BBC as world champion Abel Anton, of Spain, and Ireland's Catherina McKiernan were crowned champions. There have been many memorable performances, none more so among the men than the hat-trick of wins chalked up by the tough little Mexican Ceron in 1994-96. Steve Jones' record of 2:08:16 prevailed from 1985 to 1997 when Pinto ran 2:07:55, while there can have been no more popular win than Eamonn Martin's on his 1993 marathon debut.

Kristiansen, that great Norwegian athlete, will always be associated with the event. She won the women's title four times and her world record of 2:21:06, set in that vintage year of 1985, was not bettered until 1998 when the Kenyan Tegla Loroupe recorded 2:20:47 in Rotterdam.

More recently, McColgan has had a similar affinity with the race. I believe she is unlucky not to have won more than once, particularly in that sprint finish in 1997 when Joyce Chepchumba pipped her by one second. "We were sprinting like Linford Christie," the Kenyan smiled afterwards.

Perhaps the London Marathon was best summed up by action man Chris Moon, who started the 1998 race, ran a personal best time, and captained a team of runners raising money for the Diana Princess of Wales Memorial Fund. Chris, who lost his lower right arm and leg while working for a charity clearing land mines in Mozambique, said: "It is a great coming together of the people and a top sporting event without a hint of trouble. Irrespective of creed or colour, everyone is treated the same. It doesn't matter who they are or what they do. We salute the ability of the elite runners at the head of the field. But everyone who gets round that distance has an achievement they should be proud of."

> "It is a great coming together of the people. Everyone who gets round that distance has an achievement they should be proud of"

Martina and Steffi
Supreme athletes who dominated the courts

Triumph of courage for Bob Champion and Aldaniti

The 1981 Grand National was a triumph of will for both horse and rider. Aldaniti led from start to finish to overcome years of injury problems, including tendon trouble and a broken backbone.

For 32-year-old Bob Champion the victory was even more dramatic. In 1979 he had been given only months to live when cancer was diagnosed. The healthy recovery by both horse and jockey thrilled the racing world and could hardly have had a more emotional and inspiring outcome.

> "It's a photo between Gold Prospect and Shareblank and third is probably just in behind these two." PETER O'SULLEVAN
>
> "Warrshan, the 3.75 million dollar horse, proved itself to be a million dollars."
> JULIAN WILSON

The 1980s and 1990s have been a great era for women's tennis. The depth in quality has not approached that of the men, but the top women have provided the tennis public around the world with matches that sometimes surpassed those of the men,

MARTINA NAVRATILOVA
When Martina Navratilova was a little girl in Czechoslovakia, she says, she always thought she would be famous. 'When I was seven or eight years old and I would go to practise and these people would ask me, "Oh, little girl, what do you have those two tennis rackets for?" I was thinking, "One day you're not going to have to ask me why I have them. You're going to have to know who I am"!'

RADIO TIMES, 21-27 JUNE 1980

with their all-too-quick serve-and-volley points.

Predominant among the women of this era have been Martina Navratilova and Steffi Graf, who can be set apart from any of their predecessors by their supreme athleticism.

Navratilova ranked as world number one for 331 weeks from first attaining that position in July 1978 until 1987. She had a great battle for supremacy with Chris Evert, herself ranked top for 262 weeks between 1975 and 1985, and was succeeded as the world's best by Graf, who had a record 186 successive weeks at the top between 1985-1991 and a record 374 in all to 1997.

A left-hander, Navratilova won 18 Grand Slam singles titles, including Wimbledon a record nine times, as well as 38 doubles titles in the four Grand Slam tournaments. Graf has just one doubles title, but 21 in the singles, including seven Wimbledons.

These two champions met for three straight years in Wimbledon finals – with Navratilova winning in straight sets in 1987, but Graf taking three-set wins in 1988 and 1989, each time winning 6-1 in the third set.

Steffi Graf wins Wimbledon in 1989

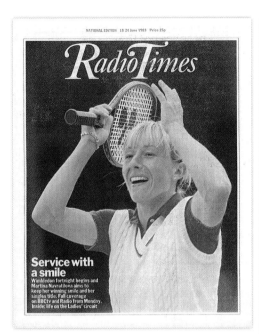

NATIONAL EDITION 18-24 June 1983 Price 25p

Radio Times

Service with a smile
Wimbledon fortnight begins and Martina Navratilova aims to keep her winning smile and her singles title. Full coverage on BBCtv and Radio from Monday. Inside: life on the Ladies' circuit

WIMBLEDON '83

'*The Lawn Tennis Championships*

The second day's play direct from the All England Club featuring The Ladies' Singles. MARTINA NAVRATILOVA, three times champion and the World's No 1, starts the defence of her title on the Centre Court, but the road to the final in 11 days' time will not be easy for the powerful Czech girl.

CHRIS LLOYD, last year's beaten finalist, also has three Wimbledon titles to her credit and this ever popular player heads the 127 challengers to Miss Navratilova's crown.

Play starts earlier on the outside courts than in previous years to accommodate this increased ladies' entry and TRACY AUSTIN, ANDREA JAEGER and perhaps Britain's JO DURIE, who performed so well in the recent French Open, are potential finalists.

Commentators DAN MASKELL, JOHN BARRETT, BARRY DAVIES, MARK COX, ANN JONES, VIRGINIA WADE, BILL THRELFALL and RICHARD EVANS.

With news from the outside courts, results and summaries introduced by HARRY CARPENTER. '

RADIO TIMES 18-24 JUNE 1983

1981 • CRICKET

Botham the conqueror
Ashes-winning displays with bat and ball

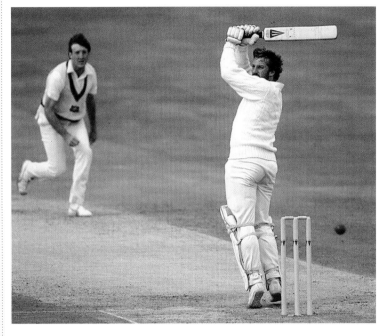

Left: Botham in action during his century in the third Test against Australia in 1981.
Below: Botham is hailed by the fans after being voted man of the match

I an Botham had captained England 12 times in 1980-1, but his side had performed dismally and his own form had deserted him. After two Tests against Australia in 1981 he stepped down and Mike Brearley returned as captain.

The third Test, at Headingley, was all but lost with England 105-5 following-on and still 122 runs behind Australia. But then Botham, after taking 6-95, struck an audacious century off only 87 balls, going on to 149 not out. With Graham Dilley he added 117 in 80 minutes for the eighth wicket. Australia still needed just 130 for victory, but they managed only 111, as Bob Willis destroyed them with 8-43.

Confidence returned to the team and the nation, and the irrepressible Botham took five wickets for one run to take England to another improbable win at Edgbaston and scored an 86-ball century for a third Test victory, to retain The Ashes at Old Trafford.

PITY THE POOR COMMENTATORS

By Stan Greenberg, BBC statistician

Catching out sports commentators is a national pastime. However, I don't think the general public realises the pressures that affect even the best of them. As the statistician to the BBC athletics commentary team for 25 years, I was in a unique position to note the challenges to their expertise.

Perhaps the greatest source of perplexity, especially in athletics, is caused by the names of foreign competitors. There seems to be a law that athletes with the longest, most convoluted names are most prevalent in the shortest races.

Thus, in a heat of the 1972 Olympic 100 metres the line-up included Vassilios Papageorgopoulos (Greece), Jean-Louis Ravelomanantsoa (Madagascar) and Jorge Luis Vizcarrondo (Puerto Rico). To the consternation of the commentators the first two got through as far as the semi-finals.

Similarly, I remember that Sri Lanka (or Ceylon as it then was) had a high jumper in the 1958 Commonwealth Games who rejoiced in the name Nagalingam Ethirveerasingham. Even worse was the Mongolian distance runner at the 1991 World Championships who had the mind-boggling, to Western eyes, name of Tschuuluunbaatar Ariunsaikhan. To the relief of many, he did not get past the heats.

Entries from Madagascar are viewed with a little apprehension as their team included 400 metres runner Randriamahazomanana, and a decathlete named Razafindrakovahoaka – their first names are not known. When faced with such mouthfuls, even the most experienced broadcaster develops doubts.

Another problem occurs when names that are innocuous in their own language have an entirely different, sometimes rude, often funny, aspect in

English. One of the most recent was the Korean runner Shim Duk-Sup. Any Marx Brothers fan will have trouble with that one.

There are everyday phrases that can take on whole new concepts and meanings when used by commentators covering international sport. There has been the giggle-inducing reference to a triple jumper from one Central European country as "the bouncing Czech". Similarly, it is so easy to say that a runner from a Eastern Bloc country took "the pole position".

With China's entry into top-class athletics, the problems have multiplied considerably. While reporting the 1984 Olympic high jump competition, and correctly noting the inconsistency of the Chinese world record holder, reference was made to nerves being "the chink in his armour". On another occasion a competitor from China was described as looking "rather fragile".

There are other names, perhaps simple ones, which can cause trouble. At a Great Britain v Spain indoor match it was pointed out to the late Ron Pickering that one of the Spanish sprinters was Juan Jones. Now the last name is pronounced 'Honesh', but as Ron had once been national coach for Wales it was suggested that he had better not slip up. This obviously played on his mind to the extent that when it came to announcing the line-up, with that runner on the inside, Pickering said over the air: "In lane Juan…"

The tension can build up horrendously during a live transmission when at the mercy of a foreign producer who may not be in tune with visiting broadcasters' requirements. At a meeting in Munich in 1971, there were a whole host of virtually

unknown athletes. Our task was complicated by the fact there was a shortage of competition numbers, and these were often worn on backs only. Identifying athletes became virtually impossible when the German producer insisted on starting with a close-up of the competitor's face each time, so that one couldn't even be sure of which event – of the four taking place – he was showing.

Somehow we coped, luckily recognising, or wildly guessing at, athlete and event. Finally, after a pole vault attempt, Ron Pickering cried out, "Who on earth is that?" The local producer had done one of his switches and went to another event, and poor Ron, usually so cool and laid back, had 'lost it'. I looked at the face on the screen and incredulously said, "It's Lynn". It was indeed Lynn Davies in the long jump, who Ron had coached to a Gold medal and who was a personal friend. Ron had reached the stage at which he wouldn't have recognised a picture of his own mother if it had come up on screen.

At that same meeting there were a lot of African sprinters whose names appeared to be unpronounceable. I rushed around trying to get help from any team managers that were available, and triumphantly returned to the commentary box with my new knowledge. Proudly, I read them out, including, to the best of my ability, the inclusion of the 'clicking' sounds that many Xhosa-type names require. David Coleman, the senior commentator, stared long and hard at me, then picked up the intercom to the producer and quietly informed him we would not be covering the next few sprint races. Though somewhat disgruntled that my efforts had come to nought, I can't say I blamed him.

Determined Daley

Was Thompson the world's finest athlete?

Arguably the world's greatest athlete of the 1980s, Francis Morgan 'Daley' Thompson was born in London of a Scottish mother and a Nigerian father, and developed a competitive edge early on.

Thompson won a county sprint title aged 15 while at boarding school. The following year he joined the Essex Beagles club. In 1975 he won the AAA junior indoor 60 metres, then the outdoor 100 metres – and, significantly, the junior decathlon. He coincidentally celebrated his 18th birthday with 18th place at the Montreal Olympics in 1976, and the next year won the European junior championship.

At the 1978 Commonwealth Games at Edmonton, Alberta, he won the Gold medal, and bettered the Games long jump record during the decathlon. At the European Championships he finished second, but didn't lose again for nine years. In 1980 he set his first world mark, and then won the Olympic title easily.

His vintage year was 1982, when he won both European and Commonwealth titles, and improved the world record twice more. In 1983, though not fully recovered from injury, he won the inaugural World Championship, and successfully defended his Olympic title the next year with another world record. At Los Angeles he also ran first leg for the British sprint relay squad.

In 1986 he again took the European/Commonwealth decathlon double, but that was Daley's last hurrah. He was injured in 1987 and came only ninth at the Rome World Championships. At the Seoul Olympics in 1988 he placed fourth, narrowly missing a medal.

Further injury and an operation caused him to retire in 1992.

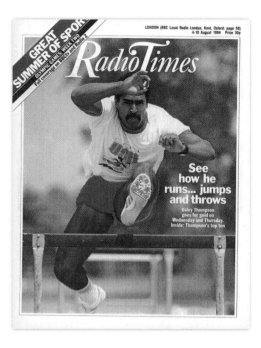

DALEY THOMPSON

'The modern Superman of the athletics arena is unquestionably Francis Daley Thompson, king of two-day Decathlon. His competitive record is unique in our athletics history. Thrice world record holder he is currently Commonwealth, European, World and Olympic Champion. What's more, the stage has once again been set for a titanic clash with the West German giant Jürgen Hingsen. On the eve of the games, as he has done twice in the past, Hingsen has broken the world record for Decathlon. But it should be remembered that he has never yet beaten Daley in a head-to-head competition. The event of the Games starts today and includes 100 metres, long jump, shot, high jump and 400 metres. Day two consists of the 110 metres hurdles, discus, pole vault, javelin and 1500 metres.'

RADIO TIMES, 4-10 AUGUST 1984

Right: The amazingly competitive and consistent Daley Thompson dominated the decathlon during the 1980s

"Watch the time – it gives you a good indication of how fast they're running."

RON PICKERING

Champion
of the Eighties

LUCINDA PALMER-GREEN

Lucinda Prior-Palmer, who married the Australian rider David Green in 1981, won a record six victories at the Badminton Horse Trials. Her first was in 1973 on Be Fair, a present from her parents on her 15th birthday, and her last in 1984 on Beagle Bay. From the age of 17, when she was a member of the winning British team at the 1971 European Junior Championships, to her team Silver medal at the 1984 Olympic Games, she compiled a most distinguished record at three-day eventing. She was European Champion on Be Fair in 1975 and on George in 1977, and World Champion on Regal Realm in 1982, when she also won a team Gold.

1980s • ICE SKATING

When sport became art
The perfect fusion of sport and dance

Some people consider that activities dependent on judging to determine a result should not be classified as sports. Millions who thrilled to Jayne Torvill and Christopher Dean's superb ice dancing would disagree. In the eyes of their fans, Torvill and Dean were the perfect fusion of sport and art.

The British pair started skating together in 1975. Three years later they won the first of six successive British titles. They were fifth at the 1980 Olympic Games before establishing themselves at the top of their sport as world champions each year between 1981-83.

Then came Sarajevo 1984, where they gave a performance that all who saw it will treasure forever. Their interpretation of the pulsating rhythms of Ravel's Bolero transcended sport. After their dramatic close they were awarded 12 sixes, with all nine judges awarding them this perfect score for artistic impression as they took the Olympic Gold. Four weeks later the judges awarded them 13 sixes when they won their fourth consecutive world title.

Torvill and Dean had mesmerised huge television audiences with sublime skill, sporting ability of the highest order and artistic genius.

Perfection personified: Torvill and Dean were world champions three years in a row before their most famous performance at the 1984 Sarajevo Winter Olympics

Sour showdown

Decker and Budd – shootout in LA

The final of the 1984 Olympic 3,000 metres in the Los Angeles Colosseum was the ultimate example of media hype.

Local heroine Mary Decker was the favourite for the title, having won the previous year's world championships at both this distance and the 1500 metres.

A sensation from an early age, she won her first US title (800 metres) at 15, having been the youngest American international runner the year before against the Soviet Union. By the Games in 1984 she was a confident 26-year-old, with national or

Budd (151) and Decker (373) clash in Los Angeles

"Mary Decker Slaney, the world's greatest front runner … I shouldn't be surprised to see her at the front."
RON PICKERING

"Zola Budd: so small, so waif-like, you literally can't see her. But there she is."
ALAN PARRY

"Just look at that. Nine 'six' marks, every one of them a 'six'." ALAN WEEKS

"If our swimmers want to win any more medals, they'll have to put their skates on." DAVE BRENNER

world records from 800 metres to 10 kilometres to her name.

South African-born Zola Budd was also precocious, and early in the Olympic year the 17-year-old had beaten Decker's five kilometres world mark by over six seconds.

South Africa had been banned from the Olympics since 1960, but Budd got to the Games after the controversial granting of British citizenship.

Although the race distance was really too short for Budd, the confrontation was eagerly awaited. For over half the distance all was well. Budd, barefoot, led entering the straight with just over three laps to go, when Decker hit Budd's leg from behind, causing her to stumble. Decker ran on and tripped over the British runner's leg, badly spiking her, and fell on to the infield, unable to rise. She lay frustrated and crying as the race continued, with the partisan crowd booing loudly.

Budd, upset and her leg bleeding, wilted and faded, finishing a dejected seventh, with the race going to the underrated Maricica Puica of Romania. Decker married a Briton, Richard Slaney, the following year and ran, disappointingly, in the 1988 Games. Budd reappeared at Barcelona – for South Africa – but was eliminated in her 3,000 metres heat.

Saved from the scrap heap by TV
Snooker's revival
NEW STARS EMERGE IN EIGHTIES ERA

1980s • SNOOKER

'The public could identify with a player and share his hopes, fears, doubts and triumphs not only when he was at the table, but as he sat in his chair...'

By Clive Everton

The 18.6m BBC viewers who saw Dennis Taylor pot the final black to beat Steve Davis 18-17 in their epic 1985 World Final set three records. It was the largest British television audience for a sporting event (except when BBC and ITV were showing one jointly); it was BBC2's largest ever audience; and it was the largest after-midnight audience for any British channel.

Incredibly, these statistics – or rather snooker's subsequent failure to match them – were later cited as "evidence" that the game was in decline as a television attraction. What has really happened is that snooker's extended honeymoon with television has settled into a solid, enduring marriage.

Familiarity with the sport and the availability of many new channels have made the public more choosy, but exceptional matches still attract exceptional figures. Even unexceptional ones produce eminently respectable numbers. Moreover, it maintains

> • The game was in such a state that the World Championship remained unplayed from 1957-1964. No promoter was prepared to risk staging it •

them over the 300-odd hours of coverage that the BBC's four contract events (the Grand Prix, the Liverpool Victoria UK Championship, the Benson and Hedges Masters and the jewel in the crown, the Embassy World Championship) receive each season.

No one could have predicted such a success story in the Sixties. The game was in such a state that the World Championship remained unplayed from 1957-1964. No promoter was prepared to risk staging it.

In those black and white days, when the whole of *Grandstand* was live, snooker's humble function, invariably in the form of Joe Davis v A N Other, was often to fill in 10 minutes or so between two races from Haydock Park. But then came *Black and White Rag*, the honky tonk piano signature tune of *Pot Black*, whose first series in 1969 arose simply from the infant BBC2's call for low-budget programmes to which colour was intrinsic. It was the first colour channel and sales of sets equipped to receive it had to be stimulated.

The BBC's hopes for *Pot Black* were not immoderately high but it immediately shot to number two in BBC2's ratings. More importantly, it established that the viewing public for snooker was far greater than had been imagined. Even so, while one frame or half an hour a week was fine, championship matches of anything up to 73 frames duration were out of the question.

There was actually a modest snooker

Dennis Taylor after his epic 1985 final with Steve Davis

revival under way. Flush with takings from the newly legalised one-armed bandits, clubs were reviving the exhibition circuit; tobacco sponsorship, even without television, was becoming a factor. Most important of all, there were outstanding recruits from the amateur ranks. John Spencer was one. He had to borrow £100 from his bank manager to enter the 1969 World Championship, the first of three he won. Ray Reardon was another, whose 1970 title was the first of six. In 1972, snooker's first authentic anti-hero, Alex Higgins, became champion at his first attempt with a unique mixture of dash, nerve, charisma and skill.

It took Higgins 13 months from first match until last to win the title but the fledgling West End sports marketing consultancy West Nally obtained sponsorship for and promoted the

1973 championship at City Exhibition Halls, Manchester, on condition it was squeezed into a fortnight. This brought *Grandstand* into play, as it did in 1974 and 1976, when the BBC operation was entrusted to Nick Hunter, who had become convinced that the BBC should develop its coverage from a few glimpses of the final to the entire event.

In 1977 the championship moved to the Crucible Theatre, Sheffield, and, at Hunter's urging, the semi-finals as well as the final were shown. In 1978 a decision was taken to cover every ball from first to last on two tables. The very first late-night highlights programme attracted four million viewers, building to seven million by the end of the championship.

"Backstage at the Crucible," wrote Peter Fiddick in *The Guardian*, "there is a sense the result scarcely matters, that something new is happening. The top players are very conscious of the new audience and its implications. For them the game is at last being shown properly, at length, with all its tactics, and the fact that it could prove even more popular this way opens up a whole new future."

"What the public are getting here," said Fred Davis, "is the feel of what it is like playing under pressure hour after hour for days on end."

It was Davis, immortalised in the song 'When I'm 64', who imprinted his personality on the championship like a monarch from a bygone age, until his attempt to regain the crown was halted in the semi-finals.

The BBC wanted more; ITV followed suit. Within a couple of years, the modern circuit was broadly in place. Snooker's combination of high skill, intense competition and impeccable table manners struck a chord with a public who could identify with a player and share his hopes, fears, doubts and triumphs in full-screen close-up not only when he was at the table, but as he sat helplessly in his chair.

While *Pot Black* had been pleasant entertainment, its single-frame format had not allowed tension, the most interesting ingredient of a match, to accummulate. But

<!--caption-->Left: Supercool Steve Davis ruled in the 1980s, but Alex 'Hurricane' Higgins was the undisputed people's champion

championship snooker revealed players' wills, styles and personalities interacting as they dug deep into their psychological resources.

No match exemplified this better than the 1979 world semi-final in which Terry Griffiths, in his first professional season, finally nailed Eddie Charlton, the dour, relentless Australian who was so often so tantalisingly near the world title without ever winning it. Griffiths was a local hero in Llanelli, where he had been a postman, a bus conductor and an insurance agent, but after 13 days at the Crucible, with millions sharing his battles and becoming emotionally involved in his aspirations, he was a household face. At 20 to two in the morning, Charlton hoisted a white handkerchief on the end of his cue and Griffiths was dazedly saying into David Vine's microphone: "I'm in the final now, you know."

His victory in the final over Dennis Taylor, whose turn would come, was an anticlimax. The 1980 final wasn't, as Cliff Thorburn, a perennial late-night favourite, edged Higgins 18-16 to become Canada's first world champion. When the match coverage was interrupted by the life-and-death drama at the Iranian Embassy siege, the press phones rang as one. When was the snooker coming back on? they all wanted to know.

Higgins played, as ever, as if hungry for the death-or-glory situation, the ultimate test of nerve, in the intense spotlight he craves. In 1982, on the precipice of semi-final defeat by Jimmy White, his 69 to win the penultimate frame on the black, possibly the finest match-saving clearance ever seen, set up his recapture of the title after a 10-year interval. Receiving the trophy amidst scenes of rare emotion, with his tearful insistence that his wife and baby daughter join him in the arena, created an unforgettable image.

As it transpired, this was but a parenthesis in the reign of Steve Davis, champion in 1981

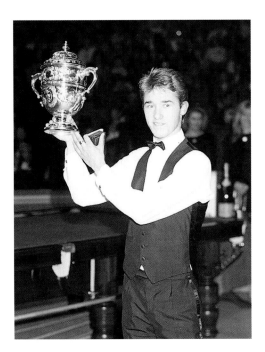

Stephen Hendry took over as No.1 from Steve Davis

and five more times before the decade was out – although the nation may remember his failed final black in the 1985 final against Taylor more than any other ball he potted.

His defeat by Joe Johnson in the 1986 final, while not quite so dramatic, was even more of a shock but, in general, Davis was so clearly No.1 in the Eighties that the whodunnit element of the plot sometimes came as an anticlimax to the unravelling of the sub-plots. Thorburn's 147, the first at the Crucible, in 1983, has been remembered more vividly than Davis drubbing him 18-6 in the final.

Another sub-plot was the emergence of Stephen Hendry, who was to depose Davis as No.1 by becoming the youngest ever World Champion in 1990. Six times in seven years – with John Parrott winning in 1991 – Hendry won the title, consistently producing the highest standard of potting and break-building the game had yet seen.

This ensured the continuance of another sub-plot – White's pursuit of his heart's desire, blocked by Davis in the Eighties, by

Hendry in the Nineties and to some extent by his own flaws.

In the 1992 final, White led Hendry 14-8 but lost 18-14. In 1994, at 17-17, he was heading for victory in the deciding frame when he fluffed a routine black. Six times in the world final, six defeats – but what entertainment, what emotional involvement he gave BBC viewers along the way.

Not all the BBC's archive of memorable snooker originates from the Crucible. There was a 147 from Kirk Stevens, Canada's tragically flawed man in the white suit, at the Benson and Hedges Masters in 1984 ... Hendry's victory over Mike Hallett in the 1991 Masters final from seven down with eight to play ... the Higgins recovery from 7-0 down to beat Davis 16-15 in the 1983 UK final at Preston.

Ronnie O'Sullivan's first UK title in 1993, a week short of his 18th birthday, was an affirmation of prodigious talent and star quality which reached its apogee in his five minutes, 20 seconds 147 at the Crucible in 1997. O'Sullivan's rivalry with John Higgins, the young Scot who made a record 14 centuries to win the 1998 world title, is just about to burst into full flower. It would be simplistic to label this volatile genius v consistent excellence but that is the flavour of it.

Hendry, whose defeat by Ken Doherty in the 1997 world final made it a great day for the Irish, if not such a good one for the Scots, is far from finished and other exceptional talents like the Welsh left-hander, Mark Williams, will come into the reckoning. When Williams potted a tie-break black to beat Hendry 10-9 to win the 1998 Masters, the match had given BBC2 a 56 per cent share of the audience for all terrestrial channels that evening, even against the television premiere of *Jurassic Park*.

Snooker is no dinosaur but a sport endlessly renewed by new generations of great players, who will produce the great matches or great occasions which will maintain the game as a prime television attraction.

After Heysel... the Double

The blackest day for sport in the Eighties was 29 May 1985. Thirty-nine Juventus supporters were crushed to death as they tried to flee from rioting Liverpool fans at the European Cup Final in the Heysel Stadium, Brussels.

Kenny Dalglish became Liverpool's player-manager the day after that horrific event. After a slow start to the 1985/6 season, he played a major role in getting his club to overcome this trauma and fight their way back to the top.

Liverpool ended the season in sensational style, winning 11 of their last 12 League games, to take the title by two points from Everton, whom they then met in the first-ever all-Merseyside Cup Final. A goal from Peter Reid put Everton ahead, but ace goal-scorer Ian Rush scored twice and Craig Johnston added a third to ensure Liverpool's first League and Cup Double.

Above: Liverpool after winning the League.

Below: Rush scores to clinch the FA Cup Final

1985 • GOLF

Europe's Cup at last
Jacklin inspires his team to Ryder victory

1985 – THE BELFRY, Sutton Coldfield. At last! For the first time since 1957 the USA is beaten in the Ryder Cup.

After a series of sweeping American wins, Europeans were introduced in 1979, rather than just British and Irish professionals. But three more US wins came before this triumph.

Tony Jacklin inspired the team as captain. They had come close in his first year in charge in 1983, losing by one point. In 1985 the crucial point came when Craig Stadler missed an 18-inch putt on the final green to allow Bernhard Langer and Sandy Lyle to halve a four-ball match. Then Europe won the singles to seal the victory. Manuel Pinero was the unsung European hero with four wins from five matches.

Jacklin's team won again in 1987 and retained the trophy with a draw in 1989. After narrow US wins in 1991 and 1993, Europe won again (each time by one point) in 1995

Above: Sam Torrance and Tony Jacklin celebrate.
Below left: Pinero, Ballesteros, Canizares and Rivero

and 1997. Passionate affairs all, the European drive has been spearheaded by Nick Faldo, who has played in all 11 Ryder Cups 1977-97 (23 wins, 19 losses and four halves), and Seve Ballesteros, who played in eight Cups (20 wins, 12 losses and five halves), and captained the 1997 team.

Bernhard Langer (9 Cups) and Ian Woosnam (8 Cups) have also been stalwarts in this most successful period for European golf.

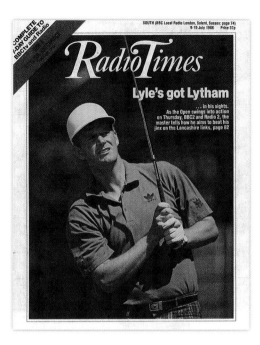

INTERNATIONAL GOLF
'117th Open Championship from Royal Lytham and St Anne's Golf Club.

Royal Lytham and St Anne's has a special place in the history of this great game. Tony Jacklin, amid triumphant scenes, was the last Briton to win here in 1969. Bobby Jones, with the help of a 175-yard bunker shot at the 17th, won the first Open to be held here in 1926. Peter Thomson won the fourth of his five Opens here in 1958, and of course the young SEVE BALLESTEROS enthralled everyone in 1979, winning by three strokes. Double Masters champion SANDY LYLE also provides a strong challenge. Defending champion NICK FALDO knows how difficult it will be to retain the trophy.'

RADIO TIMES, 9-15 JULY 1988

"And there's Ray Clemence looking as cool as ever out in the cold." JIMMY HILL

"That's the sportsmanship you find in snooker – Terry asked Jimmy for a rub of his sandpaper." JOHN VIRGO

"The goals made such a difference to the way this game went." JOHN MOTSON

"Pinero has missed the putt – I wonder what he's thinking in Spanish." RENTON LAIDLAW

"It's a renaissance – or, put more simply, some you win, some you lose." DESMOND LYNAM

A three-ring circus at 200mph

Senna, Mansell and Prost spur one another to record-breaking feats

Nigel Mansell made his Grand Prix debut in 1980, but it was not until 1992, at the age of 39, that the English driver finally achieved his ambition of winning the World Drivers' Championship.

Mansell had been runner-up in 1986 – finishing just two points behind Alain Prost – 1987 and 1991. Having signed for Williams in 1991 after a short-lived retirement, Mansell had a wonderful year in 1992, winning the first five races and achieving a record nine in all to win the title easily.

Such success was well deserved for this fast driver, but few would dispute that the finest drivers of the era were Ayrton Senna, of Brazil, and Frenchman Prost.

Prost was World Champion in 1985-86 and 1989 and runner-up four times. Senna, tragically killed in 1994, won in 1988 and 1990-91 and was runner-up in 1989 and 1993. Before Michael Schumacher matched Mansell in 1998, these three had the most Grand Prix victories, with Prost winning 51, followed by Senna on 41, and Mansell with 31.

Above left: Senna and Mansell collide during the Japanese Grand Prix.
Above right: Mansell gives Senna a lift home.
Left: Senna, Mansell and Prost on the podium

"He's a very competitive competitor, that's the sort of competitor he is."
DORIAN WILLIAMS

"There are four different cars filling the first four places." MURRAY WALKER

"He's obviously gone in for a wheel change. I say 'obviously' because I can't see it." MURRAY WALKER

"...an Achilles' heel for the McLaren team this year, and it literally is the heel because it's the gearbox." MURRAY WALKER

Scudamore's charge
The most successful jump jockey ever

Before becoming a respected media pundit, Peter Scudamore was the most successful jockey in the history of National Hunt racing.

Until 1988 the record number of wins by a jockey in a season was 149, but in 1988/9 'Scu' rode an astonishing 229 winners, with the second best total 92 by Mark Dwyer. No less than 158 of those winners came on horses trained by Martin Pipe, whose 208 winners that season broke his own record by 79. At his stables on the

Devon-Somerset border Pipe had redefined the art of training, and he had the perfect jockey to complement that.

Scudamore shared the jockey's title in 1981-82 and was champion for seven successive seasons from 1985-86 to 1991-92, retiring from the saddle a year later with a career total of 1,678 winners from 7,521 mounts. But his father, Michael, achieved one success which eluded Peter – a Grand National win, on Oxo in 1959.

Peter Scudamore was champion jockey for seven successive years

The kidnapping of Shergar

Shergar became a household word when he was kidnapped. A great racehorse, winner of the 1981 Derby by a record 10 lengths, he was taken from the Aga Khan's Ballymany Stud in County Kildare in February 1983.

The kidnappers, Irish Republican terrorists, demanded a ransom, but this was not met by the syndicate who owned him, and it is presumed that he was killed soon afterwards. For years, however, his name continued to be coupled with that of Lord Lucan, his fate one of the great mysteries of our time.

Trained by Michael Stoute, Shergar had a win as a two-year-old before his great three-year-old campaign. He swept to wins by huge margins in two preparatory races and then won The Derby, the Irish Derby, and the King George VI and Queen Elizabeth Stakes. He lost his sparkle in his last race, placing fourth in the St Leger, before retiring to stud.

Menacing Mike
He chewed up the world of boxing

MIKE TYSON became the youngest ever World Heavyweight Champion, at 20 years 144 days, when he won the WBC version of the title in 1986, beating Trevor Berbick. He added the WBA title with a win over James 'Bonecrusher' Smith and unified the championship when he beat Tony Tucker for the IBF version in 1987.

Tyson established a formidable reputation, particularly for his lethal punching power, so it came as a considerable shock when, after 10 successful title fights, he was knocked out by James 'Buster' Douglas in 1990. The following year he was given a six-year prison sentence for rape.

After release on parole he returned to the ring and in March 1996 was again a World Champion, taking the WBC title from Frank Bruno. After adding the WBA title, he lost to Evander Holyfield and in a re-match in June 1997 there came the disgraceful incident in which he spat out his mouth guard and chewed off a piece of Holyfield's right ear. Warned for that, he then attacked Holyfield's left ear, before being disqualified.

Above: Tyson puts down challenger Bruce Selsdon in 1986.
Left: A formidable fighter

Gatting's highs and lows

From 1986 to 1988, Mike Gatting's career was like a rollercoaster. He had finally become established in the England team with fine batting performances against India and Australia in 1984-85. But misfortune followed as Gatting, now England vice-captain, had his nose broken by a ball from Malcolm Marshall in the first one-day international in the West Indies in February 1986.

That summer he took over the captaincy from David Gower, then led England on a stunningly successful tour of Australia in which The Ashes were retained and they won three one-day tournaments. Gatting was on a high – but then it all went wrong.

In Pakistan, at Faisalabad in December 1987, he was forced to apologise after a furious row with umpire Shakoor Rana that halted play for a day. Then came a dismal tour of New Zealand. Finally he was sacked as England captain after the first Test against the West Indies at Nottingham ... for inviting a barmaid to his hotel room.

Top: The Shakoor Rana incident. Left: Punishing Australia. Right: A broken nose

The era of Coe, Ovett and Cram
Three British middle distance runners ruled the world for a decade

One of the greatest periods of athletics domination came in 1977-1988, when the British runners Sebastian Coe, Steve Ovett and Steve Cram reigned supreme at the mile, 1500 metres and 800 metres.

In 1977 Ovett won the 1500 metres in the European and World Cups, and Coe took his first major title, the European Indoor 800 metres. The next year Ovett won the European 1500 metres title (in third place was David Moorcroft). With Coe and Ovett absent, Moorcroft took the Commonwealth 1500 metres.

In 1979 Coe won the European Cup 800 metres, then set world records for 800 metres (1:42.33), 1500 metres (3:32.1) and mile (3:49.0). Olympic year brought more world records: Ovett twice improved the 1500 metres (to 3:31.36) and mile (3:48.8), while Coe set a 1,000 metres mark of 2:13.40. Yet, to the frustration of athletics followers everywhere, the two rivals never raced each another.

Everything was set up for a tremendous showdown at the Moscow Olympic Games, and it didn't disappoint. Coe was favourite for the 800 metres, but he ran a bad race and Ovett took the tape, with Coe in second place. Ovett looked set to do the double – but a rejuvenated Coe won the 1500 metres with a final burst fired by a furious ambition. Ovett could only come third, while the fast-improving Cram was eighth.

But Coe and Ovett still had points to prove. In the European Cup of 1981, Coe won the 800 metres (Cram was third in the 1500 metres). Coe won again over 800 metres at the World Cup, where Ovett took

Left to right: Steve Ovett, Steve Cram and Sebastian Coe at the 1984 Olympics

the 1500 metres. In June Coe set his long-standing 800 world mark of 1:47.73, and improved his 1,000 metres time to 2:12.18 (which stands today).

In an incredible August they swapped the world mile record three times, Coe running 3:48.53, Ovett 3:48.4, and then Coe 3:47.33.

In 1982 Cram did the European/Commonwealth 1500 metres double, while Coe took Silver in the European 800 metres. Moorcroft won the 5,000 metres

in the Commonwealth Games, then set a world record of 13:00.41. At the end of the year Coe and Cram joined Peter Elliott and Garry Cook to set a 4 x 800 relay mark (7:03.89) which still stands.

After setting two world indoor marks early in 1983, Coe was ill when Steve Cram won the inaugural World 1500 metres title, with Ovett fourth. Three weeks later Ovett broke the world record again with 3:30.77. At the 1984 Olympics he had bronchial problems; Coe and Cram took the first two places over 1500 metres, and Coe won Silver at 800 metres.

Cram went on a record spree in July and August 1985, running 1500 in 3:29.67, the mile in 3:46.32 and 2,000 metres in 4:51.39. The next year he won the European 1500 metres and the Commonwealth 800/1500 metres double. Coe was second in the European 1500 metres, but won the 800 metres, with Tom McKean second and Cram third. Ovett took the Commonwealth 5,000 metres Gold, and in the European 5,000 metres Jack Buckner won Gold and Tim Hutchings was third. But the great things expected at the 1987 World Championships didn't happen, and by the Seoul Olympics this era was coming to an end.

Peter Elliott won the Silver medal at 1500 metres, with Cram taking fourth. Elliott also placed fourth in the 800 metres, and Mark Rowland won a Bronze in the steeplechase. At the end of the year four Britons were in the world's top nine 1500 metres men, but now the great African runners were taking over.

Coe, Ovett, Cram: we may never see their like again...

How many others deserved similar disgrace?

Ben Johnson: Cheat

FLO-JO'S DEATH RAISES URGENT QUESTIONS

1980s • ATHLETICS

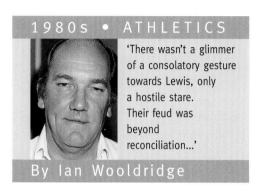

'There wasn't a glimmer of a consolatory gesture towards Lewis, only a hostile stare. Their feud was beyond reconciliation...'

By Ian Wooldridge

It was arguably the most virulent grudge match in Olympic history. That much we knew. It was also, unarguably, to become the most scandalous. But of that we were in blissful ignorance as the eight men crouched on the start-line for the 100 metres final at the Seoul Olympics in 1988.

Bizarrely this highlight of the Games was being staged not long after breakfast – another concession to peak-time television viewers in North America – but not a seat lay empty. More than 70,000 spectators and 3,000 sportswriters had no intention of missing Canada's Jamaican-born Ben Johnson and America's Carl Lewis settle their differences on the track. To say they reviled one another would be to understate their relationship.

Yes, there were six other finalists, including Britain's Linford Christie, but the prediction that this would be a two-man battle of epic dimensions proved utterly correct.

Johnson made a stupendous start. At 20 metres he was marginally up on Lewis. At 50 metres he was five feet ahead and widening the gap. At 70 metres Lewis made the fatal error of glancing sideways. At 90 metres Lewis glanced again, though not long enough to absorb the staggering sight of Johnson's arrogant triumphalism. Fractionally short of the line Johnson threw his right arm skywards, a single finger indicating that he was not only Lewis's conqueror but also the fastest 100-metre runner of all time.

It was an incredible risk to take. Even more incredibly, despite that insolent gesture, he had lowered the world record to 9.79 seconds.

It was the greatest-ever 100-metre run. For the first time in history four men had broken the 10-seconds mark in the same race. Lewis had posted his fastest-ever time of 9.92 seconds to finish second, Christie was third in 9.97, Calvin Smith fourth in 9.99. But, at 26 years of age, the glory was all Johnson's and he wasn't going to share it. There wasn't a glimmer of a consolatory gesture towards Lewis, only a malevolent stare. Their feud was beyond reconciliation.

There had been hints of what caused their mutual antipathy but these were cast aside amid the cacophony and emotion as we began to write our-eyes-have-seen-the-glory eulogies in what passed for purple prose. But what we *still* didn't know was that our eyes had actually seen a charlatan power his way to the most infamous example of cheating to be exposed since the Olympic Games were revived in 1896.

We weren't to know that for precisely another 62 hours. The news flash, South Korean time, came in the middle of the night: "Ben Johnson's been busted. Drugs."

Gold medal snatched back. World time expunged from the record books. Already, surrounded by 50 security men, Johnson was being hustled through a chaotic mass of reporters and cameramen at Seoul Airport on his swift exit to Canada. Back at the Olympic press centre, Michele Verdier of the International Olympic executive was reading this statement to the packed assembly:

"The urine sample of Ben Johnson, Canada, athletics, 100 metres, collected on Saturday 24th September, 1988, was found to contain the metabolites of a banned substance,

Ben Johnson: charlatan

namely stanozolol, an anabolic steroid."

Press retribution – reporters are far more sensitive than politicians when made to look foolish – was venomous. "Thanks a Lot, You Bastard", headlined the *Ottawa Citizen*. But there was a more thought-provoking comment in *Newsday* which said that Johnson and his coaching team were "dirty rotten scoundrels who botched the job and were caught, that's all."

There had been talk of drug abuse in sport as far back as the Rome Olympics in 1960, when Knud Ehemark, a Danish cyclist, had died. But it was the Ben Johnson case, centred as it was on a sensational new world 'record', and the bitter personal feud with Carl Lewis, widely acclaimed at the time as the world's greatest athlete, that meant the word 'drugs' was henceforth to be omnipresent in world headlines.

There would be accusations, counter-accusations, witch hunts, expensive law suits, bans and proven exposure of East German and Chinese chicanery as well as much behind-the-hand whispering that many of the most famous names were similarly flawed.

But at the time it was the *Newsday* comment – "scoundrels who botched the job and got caught" – which was particularly shrewd and perceptive.

The immediate repercussion of Johnson's expulsion from Seoul was that there was a sudden spate of withdrawals from the remainder of the Games. Overnight, athletes highly tipped as medal contenders withdrew with injuries. Others, similarly fancied to do well, flopped and were eliminated in the early qualifying rounds of their disciplines. Had they been scared off by the unmasking of Ben Johnson and feared a similar fate?

One woman showed no such timidity and she was to become the star of the Games. America's Florence Griffith Joyner – the stunningly glamorous Flo-Jo – took Seoul by storm. Cosmetically groomed for the catwalk, let alone the athletics track, with talon-long fingernails varnished in a dazzling array of

different colours, she could also run like the wind. Too close to the wind, some suspected, when she smashed both the 100 metres and 200 metres in world record times so phenomenal – respectively 10.49 seconds and 21.34 seconds – that as I write, more than 10 years later, they remain unchallenged by any woman.

"She's on hormones," it was whispered

Flo-Jo: stunningly glamorous

but, despite the perceptible muscular bulges and the deepening of her voice, no one dare say or write it openly. Flo-Jo, after all, had never failed a drug test.

She quit immediately after the Olympics to cash in on her fame as cover girl, model and clever businesswoman. She was an American icon.

But it was all the prelude to a tragedy. Ten years later, although her records were still intact, Flo-Jo wasn't. In September 1998, aged just 38, she died of a heart attack – her second in two years – and was buried in the graveyard of the Saddleback Community Church, not far from the Los Angeles track

where she had trained on her road to glory.

Or was it glory? Doctors and drug analysts were swift to point out that an excessive intake of hormones blocks arteries and puts extra strain on the heart. Flo-Jo's obituaries were thus tainted with scepticism and some of her contemporary rivals were harsh enough to say that, since she'd stolen their thunder, it served her right. She had cheated, just like Ben Johnson, but in her case the scoundrels in her back-up team hadn't botched the job. They'd beaten science with craftier science.

Flo-Jo's death had skeletons leaping from the woodwork: American footballers, cyclists, field athletes, body-builders who had equally died early or contracted horrendous illnesses from drug abuse.

It also caused many of us who had reported those Olympics to wonder why, if the misuse of drugs had been so widespread, more athletes hadn't been caught.

Could it have been that, following the Johnson scandal, the International Olympic Committee determined there would be no more public exposures to tarnish the image or even undermine its chances of attracting yet more massive sums of corporate sponsorship money for future Games?

The IOC's attitude to drugs tended to be rather more ambivalent than it sometimes claimed. It reduced four-year bans for the guilty to two years. It even, so help me, pardoned Johnson, thus permitting him to run again in 1993.

What happened? Johnson was later tested positive for drugs again and this time the recidivist was banned for life. Down and out at last? Not a bit of it. In 1998 he went back to the courts to claim he was the victim of restraint of trade laws. His lawyer calmly stated that his client would be suing Athletics Canada and the International Amateur Athletic Federation for £65 million each.

How different it might have been had Carl Lewis won that race on that Saturday morning on Seoul.

The great shots of Wimbledon

DAN MASKELL'S FAVOURITE STROKES FROM THE CLASS OF '89

1980s • TENNIS

Dan Maskell died in 1992, aged 84. Shortly before his death, the much-loved doyen of tennis commentators wrote this article, which we are proud to reprint

By Dan Maskell

The golden voice of Dan Maskell conjured up just one image – Wimbledon. He was as much a part of the championships as strawberries and cream and ticket touts.

Dan had been a BBC TV commentator at Wimbledon since 1951, but his association stretched back long before that.

His first sight of Centre Court was in 1924 when, at the tender age of just 16, he watched the Ladies' Singles Final between Britain's Kitty McKane and the legendary eight-time champion Helen Wills-Moody of the United States.

"Every Wimbledon is unique. It is, above all, a great drama," said the 81-year-old Maskell in 1989. "It's fascinating to see the young players from all over the world coming to Wimbledon full of dreams as well as watching the fate of the well-known players. I'm always excited at the prospect of another Wimbledon."

A talented player and a coach to Britain's Davis Cup team in his day, Maskell gave the following critique of the leading players' best strokes prior to the 1989 championships.

(That year's singles titles were in fact won by Boris Becker and Steffi Graf.)

✳ BORIS BECKER'S SERVICE

At 6ft 2ins tall with a powerful physique, the West German is perfectly built for the job. As with all great servers, he has a strong yet sensitive grip.

He transfers his body weight so well from the back to the front foot and, thanks to the present foot-fault rule, he can leave the ground with both feet in a flying leap to give himself even more power.

But the real crux of his action is that he throws the racket head at the ball with speed. He doesn't just guide the racket to the ball, he uses a powerful throwing action at the ball.

Becker's first serve is normally a fast, flattish one – and he can serve equally well to either side of the receiver. He's also quite adventurous with his second serve, sometimes hitting a first serve which brings him quite a few aces. But now he's getting more control by using spin on his second service.

Another shot he has improved is a blocked backhand return of serve from the right-hand court, when his timing is faulty on the uninhibited drive return. He has realised that particularly on fast grass you cannot always drive back your returns from fast first serves.

✳ STEFFI GRAF'S FOREHAND

Graf has the most enviable forehand you could wish to see. It is the complete shot, like a boxer's knockout punch.

The 19-year-old West German is very athletic and runs so beautifully, hitting the ball from a fixed stance, jumping or, perhaps most lethally, on the run.

Hit with a slight top-spin, the main feature

Boris Becker: perfectly built for the job

of the shot is her very late backswing. I've sometimes thought that she's swung the racket back too late, but she has brought off the shot quite successfully. It is a wonderfully powerful forehand and is due to her quick hands and superb racket-head control.

She is getting proficient at running around her backhand and hitting down the line to the opponent's forehand side. She's so fast around the court that when she does run around her backhand, she rarely pays the penalty for sacrificing her court position.

Left to right: Stefan Edberg, Steffi Graf, Ivan Lendl and John McEnroe display their best shots

★ STEFAN EDBERG'S OVERHEAD SMASH

Edberg, the defending champion from Sweden, is a great all-round player. Aged 23, he cuts a fine figure and is quick and athletic.

For the smash, he anticipates the lob very quickly and positions himself early, preparing to throw the racket-head at the ball as he moves. His smashing against really deep and fast lobs is so good because he has the ability to arch his back so strongly, and he can still get his racket well behind the ball before delivering the blow.

His main problem this year has been a nagging back injury, perhaps brought on by the terrific arching of his back that he puts into the smash. He has also lacked a little match maturity at times. Players when they're under pressure need to revert to their 'bread and butter' shots to make sure that they don't lose points needlessly .

He's a fine all-court player, though. If he's fit he has an excellent chance of retaining his Wimbledon title. *(He lost to Becker in the Final.)*

★ IVAN LENDL'S FOREHAND

Lendl used to be a player who did everything by the textbook. On slower courts he had enough time to get into position to play his ground strokes. But on the grass at Wimbledon the ball comes through faster and the bounce is lower.

Lendl's footwork now seems more natural and instinctive, and he plays the shot with less deliberate placing of the feet. It's a much more fluid shot, and indeed his whole game has become more natural.

He hits the forehand with a slight top-spin, but not enough to take the speed off the ball. A shot he has perfected is when he runs round his backhand and hits down the line to his opponent's forehand. It's an easy shot to lose points on but he is beginning to use it well.

He's now an adequate volleyer following behind a confident, deep approach shot, and is good enough overhead – and he's generally becoming a better all-round player.

★ JOHN McENROE'S LOW VOLLEY

McEnroe is undoubtedly one of the best low volleyers I have ever seen. It will be interesting to see him again at Wimbledon after a long period out of the big time.

He may have just lost that little bit of sharpness, but he is one of the most natural volleyers the game of tennis has seen. His special shot is the low volley below the height of the net.

Even if he can't kill the ball for an outright winner, he doesn't just aim to get the ball back in play. He makes sure that he still retains the initiative in a rally by placing the ball deep or at an angle.

McEnroe's supreme volleying skill combines all the virtues of quick reflexes, speedy and balanced footwork, strong and sensitive control of the angle of the racket-face, exquisite timing and anticipation. How often we have admired his glorious talent in doubles matches.

I can't see him going all the way at Wimbledon. He's 30 now and it's a player's nerve, not his legs or his eye, which goes first. Winning Wimbledon can mean seven five-set matches and the tension increases with each succeeding match.

But his return to Wimbledon will create enormous interest. I just hope he keeps his behaviour under control.

★ MARTINA NAVRATILOVA'S SERVE VOLLEY

At her peak, Martina was the best woman player I have ever seen. She's a little older now and perhaps just a little past her best, a little slower. But it's been tough for her being at the top for so long. One wonders whether her nerve will be strong enough to beat Graf if they meet this year.

Her great ambition is to break the Helen Wills-Moody record of eight Wimbledon singles titles. She still has the all-court game to do it – in fact, it was she who single-handedly brought the all-court game back to women's tennis.

Being a left-hander, her serve has a natural advantage as it is immediately unfamiliar to most players. She has a powerful first serve and backs that up with either a kick second serve or slice which takes the receiver's body in the right court.

She is one of the most aggressive volleyers in the women's game and is as happy at the net as she is at the back of the court.

Her 'net sense' is brilliant and her anticipation at times is quite uncanny. She positions herself quickly for the smash, and with it can attack either side of the opponent's court.

But, to me, it's her ability to play exquisite half-volleys following in behind her service that stands out so much.

✴ JIMMY CONNORS' DOUBLE-HANDED BACKHAND

At its best, Connors' double-fisted backhand is an undeniably solid stroke, particularly on a return of serve, and he will pass the in-coming server with controlled trajectory and speed. He can play it with both feet off the ground – and often does.

It's a slightly topped stroke and he puts a lot of effort into the shot – but it's coordinated

effort. Legs, arms, body-turn in harmony.

The great thing about the double-handed shot is that it has a natural disguise. He can wait until almost the last second before deciding where to put it.

If only he had a forehand to match his

Clockwise from top left: Martina Navratilova, Chris Evert, Gabriela Sabatini and Jimmy Connors in full flight

backhand. He's never truly mastered the fore-hand off the low, half-court ball. Connors is a crowd-puller because of his gutsy, all-out per-formances. He's 36, so this could be his final Wimbledon, but they say that every year!

✴ CHRIS EVERT'S DOUBLE-HANDED BACKHAND LOB

This is one of her most beautiful and effective shots. The double-hander immediately bene-fits from its natural disguise. Like Connors, Chris Evert can wait and wait until the very last moment before suddenly hoisting a lob to embarrass her perplexed opponent.

Even under the most extreme pressure from a volleyer at the net, she will move forward to drive the ball right at top of the bounce in order to make a clean winning pass.

The shot often has just a brushing of top-spin. Her consis-tency on the backhand is legendary. I've seen her hit 20 to 30 shots in a rally which have all landed just inches from the base-line time after time.

It's her ability to mix the pass-ing shot drive with the disguised lob that makes her so difficult to volley against.

✴ GABRIELA SABATINI'S FOREHAND/BACKHAND

Sabatini's ground-strokes are not exactly textbook. She out-rageously overswings on the shot and although her strokes are effective, they are energy-sapping and may be the reason why her stamina is sometimes questionable.

Her basic strokes are hit with excessive top spin, but she is not adding a sliced backhand to her repertoire.

I feel that with increasing experience of the very top level of the world-class game, Gabriela may find it necessary to be more economical in the effort she puts into her extravagant style.

1989 • FOOTBALL

The closest finish of them all

Liverpool foiled by last-second goal

In 1989 Liverpool won the FA Cup on May 20. It was a bittersweet victory, coming a month after the Hillsborough tragedy, in which 95 fans had been crushed to death while flocking in to see the semi-final against Nottingham Forest.

However, the season wasn't over. Liverpool went into the final League match just six days after the lifting the FA Cup – and on the back of a run of 24 unbeaten games.

They were at home to Arsenal, who needed to win by two goals to take the title. After a scoreless first half, Arsenal took the lead through Alan Smith after 53 minutes. The tension mounted as full-time loomed. Arsenal threw everything at Liverpool but it seemed their challenge would fall just short.

With two minutes of injury time played, the ball came to Michael Thomas, who coolly flicked the ball over the head of Liverpool keeper Bruce Grobbelaar. Liverpool were stunned, and Arsenal were the champions.

"For those of you who believe in these things, it's taken him 13 points to break the serve, it's the 13th of the month today, this is the 13th Benson & Hedges Championship... and yesterday was his 24th birthday." JOHN BARRETT

"For the first time a record Wimbledon attendance." GERALD WILLIAMS

"He went down like a sack of potatoes, then made a meal of it." TREVOR BROOKING

"I felt a lump in my mouth as the ball went in." TERRY VENABLES

"Being naturally right-footed, he doesn't often chance his arm with his left foot." TREVOR BROOKING

DESERT ORCHID

Surely no horse in history has achieved the fame and love from a devoted public that was accorded to Desert Orchid. Certainly Arkle was the greatest ever steeplechaser, but the striking near-white 'Dessie' may even have gained by his vulnerability – a weakness on left-handed tracks shown by his struggles at Cheltenham. That made his eventual win in the Gold Cup in 1989 all the sweeter.

Desert Orchid overcame overnight rain which made the course heavier than was ideal for him. Even so, his win reputedly cost the bookies £2 million.

His long-striding form and superb jumping were seen to best effect at Kempton, where he won the King George VI Chase a record four times. He first showed his greatness in this race in 1986, when he won by 15 lengths, and he went on to win each year between 1988-90, but retired after a fall there in 1991.

Trained by David Elsworth, he remained a firm favourite, and always looked very sprightly when led out at great races for the rest of the 1990s.

The Nineties

THE DEEDS OF YOUNG SUPERSTARS SUCH AS TIGER WOODS,
BRIAN LARA AND MARTINA HINGIS HAVE ALREADY
WHETTED OUR APPETITES FOR THE MILLENNIUM.
IN BRITAIN, TOO, TALENTED YOUNGSTERS ABOUND:
WITH MICHAEL OWEN, LEE WESTWOOD, IWAN THOMAS
AND TIM HENMAN, THE FUTURE LOOKS BRIGHT INDEED

Main photo: Ballesteros and Olazabal at the 1991 Ryder Cup.
Above top: Brazilian hands grasp the 1994 World Cup.
Above left: Dominic Cork's Test hat-trick against the West Indies.
Above right: Martina Hingis, Wimbledon's youngest champion in 1997

Nineties Diary

Above: Tiger Woods' 1997
Masters win established
him as the world's number
one golfer.
Right from top: Steve
Backley broke the javelin
world record in 1990.
England celebrate their
1995 Grand Slam. And Colin
Jackson's patriotic eyes.
Far right from top: Evander
Holyfield's ear after his fight
with Mike Tyson. Ronnie
O'Sullivan earned £147,000
for his 147 break at the
Crucible. Arsenal's Ian
Wright after setting a new
Arsenal goal-scoring record.
1998 Formula One world
champion Mika Hakkinen.
And Lennox Lewis in
triumphant mood

1990

Stephen Hendry bursts on to the
snooker scene by becoming the
youngest world champion at 21.

Unknown Buster Douglas upsets the
odds-makers with his 10th-round KO
of Mike Tyson in Tokyo.

Golden oldie George Foreman marks
his comeback to heavyweight boxing
by beating Gerry Cooney.

Richard Hadlee retires with a
knighthood after becoming the first
bowler to take 400 Test wickets.

Alex 'Hurricane' Higgins threatens to
have Dennis Taylor shot. Higgins is
banned for 10 months as a result.

The tennis teens take over when
Monica Seles, 16, becomes the
youngest Grand Slam winner after
defeating Steffi Graf in the French
Open, and Jennifer Capriati, 14,
becomes the youngest player ever to
win at match at Wimbledon.

Steve Backley throws a Nemeth javelin all the way to a
world record.

1991

Durham sign Ian Botham and Dean Jones.

Forty-two-year-old George Foreman loses boxing's
Heavyweight Championship title fight to Evander
Holyfield but goes the distance.

Agony and ecstasy for Paul Gascoigne after he scores a
wonder free kick for Spurs in the FA Cup semi-final, then
gets carried off the park in the opening minutes of the
Final after a crazy tackle on Nottingham Forest's Gary
Charles. Spurs win the Final 2-1 in extra time.

Golf's longest hitter, John Daly, caps a rags-to-riches
story by winning the US PGA Championship.

Bob Beamon's 23-year-old long jump record is finally
broken by Mike Powell at the Tokyo World
Championships. Kris Akabusi leads Britain to Gold in the
4 x 400 metres relay race.

1992

Will Carling leads England to a
second straight Grand Slam with a
record 118 points.

Frenchman Eric Cantona guides
Leeds to the First Division title over
Manchester United before being
transferred to Old Trafford.

Andre Agassi sets Wimbledon alight
on his way to a five-set final victory
over Goran Ivanisevich.

The tennis world mourns the death
of Dan Maskell at 84.

Gary Lineker is denied the chance to
break Bobby Charlton's 49-goal
England record when he is
substituted 29 minutes from the end
of England's European Championship
match with Sweden.

Nigel Mansell wins the season's first
five Grand Prix races, nine in total,
and takes the world title with five
races left then quits in a contract dispute with Williams.
Damon Hill replaces Mansell, who goes to Indy Car.

1993

The first World Heavyweight Championship fight between
two British boxers this century sees Lennox Lewis defeat
Frank Bruno in the seventh round at Cardiff.

Nigel Benn and Chris Eubank batter each other in a
brutal 12-round super middleweight title fight that ends
in a draw.

After two false starts when the starting tapes fail to rise
correctly, the Grand National is declared a non-runner.
Trainer Jenny Pitman bursts into tears after watching
Esha Ness ride to a meaningless victory.

Nottingham Forest are relegated from the First Division
and Brian Clough retires.

Colin Jackson and Sally Gunnell break world records in
the Athletics World Championships at Stuttgart, while
Linford Christie takes the 100 metres Gold medal.

Left to right: Devon Malcolm skittles South Africa, Frankie Dettori's victory leap, Andre Agassi wins Wimbledon in 1992, Eric Cantona jumps for joy, and Brian Lara in action

1994

American Nancy Kerrigan takes figure skating's Gold medal in the Winter Olympics, but only after Tonya Harding is accused of plotting to break Kerrigan's legs.

Manchester United lose the League Cup Final but do the League and FA Cup Double, beating Chelsea 4-0 in the FA Cup Final.

Brian Lara breaks the world record for the highest individual Test score with 375 for West Indies v England in the fifth Test in Antigua.

Spain's Jose Maria Olazabal finally lives up to his potential by winning the Masters.

At 51, Willie Carson rides Erhaab to victory in The Derby.

Chris Boardman dons the yellow jersey in the Tour de France, but Miguel Indurain takes the title for the fourth year in succession.

Fanie de Villiers rashly knocks over Devon Malcolm. Malcolm replies by taking 9 for 57 in 99 balls at The Oval to level the series against the South Africans.

Brazil win the World Cup Final by defeating Italy on penalties in America.

Death haunts Grand Prix racing when Ayrton Senna dies in a car crash on the seventh lap at Imola, and Roland Ratzenberger dies in practice.

1995

Eric Cantona plunges football into controversy when he leaps into the crowd to kick a belligerent fan in a match against Crystal Palace at Selhurst Park.

In rugby union, South Africa take the World Cup by defeating New Zealand 15-12 when Joel Stransky kicks a dramatic extra-time drop goal.

Dominic Cork takes a hat-trick as England beat the West Indies at Old Trafford by six wickets.

In the Tour de France, Miguel Indurain triumphs for a record fifth consecutive time.

1996

England lose on penalties to West Germany in the semi-final of the Euro 96 as football "comes home" to England.

Terry Venables steps down as England manager and Glenn Hoddle takes over.

History is made at Ascot when Frankie Dettori rides seven winners in one day.

Aston Villa win the League Cup for a record fifth time by beating Leeds United 3-0 at Wembley.

Greg Norman takes a six-shot lead into the final round of the Masters only to lose to Nick Faldo.

Boxer Frank Bruno retires after losing to Mike Tyson.

Sri Lanka win cricket's World Cup, as Australia and the West Indies forfeit games by not playing in Sri Lanka.

1997

Tiger Woods makes history by becoming the first black man to win the Masters, by a record 12 shots.

Eric Cantona retires from football after leading Manchester United to the Premiership title.

The Snooker World Championship sees the fastest ever maximum break as Ronnie O'Sullivan clears the table in five minutes 20 seconds.

Cricket great Denis Compton dies at the age of 78.

Mike Tyson takes a bite out of Evander Holyfield's ear in their Heavyweight Championship title fight. Tyson is banned.

Martina Hingis becomes Wimbledon's youngest champion when she takes the women's final.

1998

Arsenal are the first team to do the double Double, winning the FA Cup and the Premier League 27 years after they first did it in 1971.

Home team France win the World Cup Final against a below-par Brazil who are accused of throwing the match.

Cricket umpire Dickie Bird announces his retirement.

Mark O'Meara captures two of golf's major titles when he wins the Masters and the Open Championship.

Mika Hakkinen holds off Michael Schumacher to win the Formula One drivers' world championship.

Cricket rediscovers the art of spin
Wonderful Warne
THE WORLD'S BEST SLOW BOWLER

1990s • CRICKET

'The names of Brian
Lara and Shane Warne
already deserve to live
alongside the very best
in cricket's rich and
colourful folklore...'

By Jonathan Agnew

There can have been few decades in the long and complicated history of Test cricket which have been so dramatic as the 1990s. The game has been subjected to just about every conceivable scandal including allegations of match-fixing, ball-tampering, bribery and, most remarkable of all, the claim by a captain of Pakistan that a Test umpire had doctored the ball during a drinks break!

The steady breakdown in both discipline and the spirit of fair play required urgent action. So a code of conduct was introduced, complete with match referees to oversee it, and firm action was encouraged to stamp out intimidating fast bowling and 'sledging'.

South Africa, its house finally put in order, was welcomed fully into the international fold for the first time. Calcutta hosted the opening match of the post-apartheid era, Mother Teresa gave the occasion her blessing and over 100,000 people packed Eden Gardens to watch India win a game which was dwarfed by the significance of it all.

Sadly, even that moment of history was spoiled by further accusations of ball-tampering. So it is with huge relief that cricket-lovers have relished the emergence of two truly great players who should, in time, mature to become cricketing giants.

The names of Brian Lara, who broke the records for the highest Test score and the highest first-class score within seven weeks of one another, and Shane Warne, the prodigious Australian wrist spinner, already deserve to live alongside the very best in cricket's rich and colourful folklore.

However, while Lara set the world alight in 1994, it is Warne who has made the greater overall impact. Remarkably, he has been able to keep his feet firmly on the ground despite his meteoric rise both in fame and income, and it was a joy to discover, as I interviewed him at the start of the 1997 Australian tour, that he was exactly the same amusing, likeable and relaxed man I had met for the first time four years earlier.

And who could ever forget his stunning introduction to Test cricket in England in 1993? Certainly not me, having been the one who had to commentate on his first delivery to Mike Gatting. I remember giving Warne, then aged only 23, quite a build-up as he prepared to bowl – only to have my view of the ball completely obscured both by Gatting's ample frame and Ian Healy, the wicketkeeper, who was standing up to the wicket.

It was only when Gatting, who had stood rooted to the spot while the Australian fielders danced in celebration all around him, finally began to trudge towards the pavilion with an occasional bewildered glance at the off bail which still lay on the ground, that the first slow motion was shown on television.

It was quickly called 'the ball from hell' and for the life of me I cannot imagine anyone playing it securely. It is all too easy to study the replays and criticise Gatting for not being a few more inches further forward. The fact is that it was a loosener for bowler and batsman alike: neither had any right to expect that particular delivery to behave as it did.

Mike Gatting and that unforgettable wicket

The savage spin was only the final ingredient. Homing in towards Gatting's pads, the ball began to drift down the leg side until it was at least 18 inches wide of leg stump. At this stage, Gatting appeared to be content to allow it to spin back into his pads, only for the ball to rip out of the rough and hit the top of the off stump. Gatting was so mortified, he momentarily suspected that Healy might have knocked off the bail with his wicketkeeping gloves.

Shane Warne: cricket's best spinner

Warne's success is founded on three vital assets: his physical strength, his accuracy and his voracious appetite for learning new tricks. His shoulder and spinning fingers, which have been a source of concern through wear and tear, are massively developed and, particularly when accompanied by a Monica Seles-style grunt, he spins the ball further than, possibly, anyone with a legitimate action has ever done on a dry pitch.

He preys on the area outside the right-handed batsman's leg stump which has been roughened up by the bowler's footmarks. Sometimes Warne goes round the wicket to exploit it still further and to make run-scoring almost impossible (which increases still further the pressure on the batsmen). This has given rise to some extraordinary, almost freakish dismissals: Graham Gooch being bowled behind his legs at Edgbaston in 1993, for example. At Sydney in 1997, Shivnarine Chanderpaul was bowled by a massive leg-break which exploded from fully two feet outside the off stump and hit leg.

These dismissals, along with Gatting's delivery, are all on a video tape which Warne carries in his bag at all times just in case, as in early 1997, his confidence takes a dip.

Wrist spinners instinctively get on well with one another – they speak the same confusing language, after all. Theirs is a world of googlies, flippers, boseys and chinamen, and Warne had found an especially close soul-mate in the brilliant Pakistani leg spinner Abdul Qadir. They met during an Australian tour of the sub-continent and Warne returned to talk effusively about a couple of hours they had spent together at either end of a silk carpet, spinning a cricket ball to one another, developing and even inventing new skills. The result was the 'zooter', a Warne prototype which is unveiled periodically to baffle batsmen still further.

One effect is clear to see. There has been a mini-renaissance in the art of wrist-spin bowling, not just in Australia but here, too, on the village greens of England. And for that we should all be thankful.

> "That was a tremendous six: the ball was still in the air as it went over the boundary." FRED TRUEMAN
>
> "The first time you face up to a googly you're going to be in trouble if you've never faced one before." TREVOR BAILEY
>
> "The only possible result is a draw. The alternative is a win for England." RICHIE BENAUD
>
> "Glen McGrath bowled so badly in his first Test, as though he'd never bowled in a Test Match before." GEOFFREY BOYCOTT
>
> "On the first day Logie decided to chance his arm and it came off." TREVOR BAILEY

SALLY GUNNELL

Heading into the 1992 Olympics in Barcelona, Great Britain had a pretty poor record in women's track events. Not since 1964 had a British woman won an Olympic track Gold medal, when Ann Packer broke the world record in the 800 metres in Tokyo. Essex girl Sally Gunnell – the woman's team captain – would change that.

Along with men's captain Linford Christie, who won Gold in the 100 metres, Gunnell inspired the British team at Barcelona. Just 26 years old, Gunnell was at her peak. She was one of the pre-race favourites to take the 400 metres hurdles, and she did not disappoint. Her Gold medal came with a time of 53.23 seconds.

A year later Gunnell capped her career by setting the 400 metres hurdles world record at the 1993 World Championships in Stuttgart, Germany. Gunnell clocked a time of 52.74 to take the top prize. She retired at 31.

John Motson selects his favourite goals
FA Cup Final classics
FROM 35 YEARS OF WATCHING AT WEMBLEY

1990s • FOOTBALL

John Motson has described more FA Cup Final goals than anyone. Here he reveals the best he has seen – and some from an earlier age he wishes he had witnessed

By John Motson

The audience for an FA Cup Final today is around 300 million worldwide: a far cry from 1938, when the Final was first shown on television. Then, the audience was only 10,000 people – and they were all in south-east England, because that was the only area that could get the TV signal.

From those small beginnings, BBC TV covered the FA Cup Final for 60 years, until Sky and ITV took it over in 1998. The Cup Final was the centrepiece of *Grandstand* and I think it's fair to say the BBC's coverage was part of the FA Cup tradition, from 'Abide With Me' right through to the presentations at the end. Other nations admired the FA Cup because they didn't have a Cup Final day with quite the pomp and ceremony that we do.

Nowadays the build-up is so intense that it's very difficult for the game itself to match the hype. With such a lot at stake, people tend to be very apprehensive about making mistakes, and I have commentated on a lot of very tight, tense one-nils. How many really great finals have there been? People with much longer memories than me will look back to the 1953 Matthews Final. Of the finals I covered as a commentator, Tottenham-Coventry in '87 stands out an excellent football match. But the most memorable of all was the Spurs-Manchester City replay in '81, with probably the best Wembley goal of all, that great solo effort by Spurs' Ricky Villa.

What made that game so special was more than just Villa's superlative goal. People forget that Manchester City contributed hugely to the match, and had it not been for Villa's goal, Steve Mackenzie's volley would be remembered as one of the greatest final goals. Moreover, the way the match went was so exciting, with Tottenham taking the lead, then Manchester City going 2-1 up, then Tottenham coming back to win 3-2, all in normal time. There haven't been many Cup Finals that have fluctuated quite like that.

The last of my classic FA Cup Final goals comes from the 1997 final – the last one the BBC covered live. It was my 18th final, and it was very different from the first one I commentated upon. Back in 1977 the FA Cup was very much a British affair. Overseas players were almost unheard-of, because it wasn't until the following year that Spurs signed Ardiles and Villa. But my memories of the Cup go back much further than that, and the first goal I have chosen is from the first FA Cup Final that I ever saw 'in the flesh'.

> *Looking back, I didn't have a very good game. It was only through the goal that I tend to be remembered – particularly as it was a late winner. It was unusual for me to get up that far, as I tended to hold in the middle. But when Peter Brabrook crossed, I ran into the box and connected with it. The funny thing is that it seemed an eternity before you got a reaction from the crowd. It was an unbelievable moment.*
>
> **RONNIE BOYCE**

> *The whole match seemed to be over in a flash. But I'll never forget that goal.*
>
> **NEIL YOUNG**

1964: RONNIE BOYCE (WEST HAM UNITED)
WEST HAM UNITED 3 PRESTON NORTH END 2

In injury time, with Second Division Preston holding West Ham 2-2 after twice being in front, the Hammers broke away down their right. I still remember Alan Kelly limping on his goal line like a wounded bird after an earlier injury, and I wondered how he could possibly cope with Peter Brabrook's cross.

The answer was he couldn't. It was flighted away from him and in came that tireless midfield player Ronnie Boyce to head a dramatic winner.

Alan Sunderland's goal from a kick-off stunned Manchester United

1969: NEIL YOUNG (MANCHESTER CITY)
MANCHESTER CITY 1 LEICESTER CITY 0

By 1969 my career had moved from newspapers to radio, and I was sent by *Sports Report* to get a feel for the post-match interviews.

Mike Summerbee forced his way to the goal line before pulling back an inviting cross which Neil Young thumped past Peter Shilton, who was only 19. That was the only FA Cup Final in which he ever played, and he couldn't stop Young's sensational goal.

1972: ALLAN CLARKE (LEEDS UNITED)
LEEDS UNITED 1 ARSENAL 0

I have special reason to remember Allan Clarke's headed goal for Leeds against Arsenal in 1972. It was the end of my first season with *Match Of The Day*, David Coleman was the Cup Final commentator, and I had to 'grab' the leading players for interviews as they came off the pitch. For that reason, I was sitting behind the goal with the photographers when Mick Jones got behind the Arsenal defence and cut the ball back for Clarke to direct a stinging header past Geoff Barnett, the Arsenal goalkeeper in the absence of the injured Bob Wilson. A great view of a great goal

> **'That was my third FA Cup Final, but what made it special was that it was the first time Leeds won the trophy. I happened to get the winning goal, but we were such a team then that it didn't matter who scored.'**
>
> ALLAN CLARKE

1979: ALAN SUNDERLAND (ARSENAL)
ARSENAL 3 MANCHESTER UNITED 2

By 1979 I had been elevated to the BBC commentary box on Cup Final day and I can still hear myself saying "With four minutes to go and Arsenal leading 2-0, Manchester United must score from this free kick to give themselves any hope of a dramatic recovery." Well, Gordon McQueen did score from the free kick

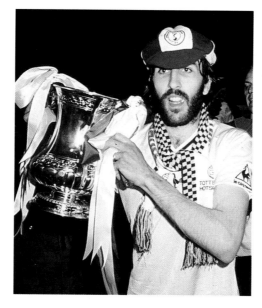

Ricky Villa lifts the Cup after a sensational goal

– and then, less than two minutes from time, Sammy McIlroy equalised.

Straight from the kick-off and with everyone expecting extra time, Liam Brady dribbled into the heart of the United defence and laid the ball left to Graham Rix. His cross deceived goalkeeper Gary Bailey and was swept in at the far post by Alan Sunderland. I'm sure you remember his ecstatic reaction to scoring the winner with literally seconds remaining.

1981: RICARDO VILLA (TOTTENHAM HOTSPUR)
TOTTENHAM HOTSPUR 3 MANCHESTER CITY 2
IN A REPLAY, AFTER DRAWING 1-1

In the 1980s, one goal stands out. The 100th final between Spurs and Manchester City always promised to be memorable – although don't tell that to City's Tommy Hutchison, who scored at both ends in the first match!

Come the Thursday night, and the first FA Cup Final replay ever to be staged at Wembley, and Tottenham manager Keith Burkinshaw decided to give his bearded Argentine midfield player Ricky Villa a second chance after he had been substituted a few days earlier. Ricky's Argentina colleague Ossie Ardiles set

up his first goal early on, and then Steve Mackenzie equalised for City with one of the best volleys Wembley has ever seen.

Spurs had come back from 2-1 down to 2-2 through Garth Crooks, when Villa picked the ball up just inside Tottenham's left touchline and proceeded to pick a path through the City defence. It was a breathtaking piece of individual artistry, and goes down as arguably the best individual goal seen in a Wembley Final.

THE FA CUP FINAL

In perhaps the greatest of Wembley's finals, Matthews inspired Blackpool, trailing 3-1 with just 20 minutes remaining, to a famous 4-3 victory. Despite Mortensen's hat-trick, unique in Wembley Cup Final history, and the midfield brilliance of Taylor, Matthews made the final his own with a magical display of wing play. Novelist H E Bates later wrote: "I do not think Wembley has ever seen anything like the miracle of Blackpool's recovery and the sheer beauty and skill of Matthews' part in it, and I shall be surprised if it ever does again."

RADIO TIMES, 15-21 MAY 1993

Keith Houchen's spectacular diving header against Spurs in the 1987 final

1987: KEITH HOUCHEN (COVENTRY CITY)
COVENTRY CITY 3 TOTTENHAM HOTSPUR 2

Keith Houchen's goal for Coventry against Tottenham remains for me one of the best constructed and best executed goals I've ever seen in an FA Cup Final.

After good work by Houchen himself and Cyrille Regis, the ball went out on the right wing to David Bennett. When his cross came in, Houchen scored with a brilliant diving header. There haven't been many of those in Cup Finals. It was a thrilling finish to a good move: a real sweeping team goal.

Houchen's goal brought Coventry back to

"And Wilkins sends an inch-perfect pass to no one in particular." BRYON BUTLER

"On this 101st Cup Final day, there are just two teams left." DAVID COLEMAN

"Here's Brian Flynn. His official height is five feet five and he doesn't look much taller than that." ALAN GREEN

2-2 and the match eventually went into extra time – which is when Gary Mabbutt's own-goal went in for Coventry. Mabbutt's own-goal was sad for him, but he got a bit of revenge four years later when he lifted the Cup as Tottenham captain after Des Walker put a goal into the Nottingham Forest net.

1990: IAN WRIGHT (CRYSTAL PALACE)
CRYSTAL PALACE 3 MANCHESTER UNITED 3
(MANCHESTER UNITED WON THE REPLAY 1-0)

Ian Wright didn't start the match as he had broken his leg earlier in the season, but Steve Coppell brought him on as a substitute. Three minutes after coming on, he pushed in from the left past two United defenders, spread-eagled the defence and scored a fantastic goal to take the match into extra time.

He then scored again in extra time to give Palace a 3-2 lead. Then back came United to make it 3-3 and we had a replay.

Wright's exuberant confidence altered the course of the Final. His first goal was a classic. It had a hint of Ricky Villa about it, the way he kept possession and finished it off. Outstanding.

1997: ROBERTO DI MATTEO (CHELSEA)
CHELSEA 1 MIDDLESBROUGH 0

The obvious choice from recent years is Roberto Di Matteo's 1997 goal for Chelsea against Middlesbrough, scored within 42 seconds – the fastest ever Wembley Cup Final goal. It was a terrific strike that flew in underneath the crossbar.

Di Matteo's lightning strike made Wembley history and I was privileged to be commentating. In fact it was a bit of a relief to me, because for many years I had always noted down that Jackie Milburn's goal after 45 seconds for Newcastle in 1955 was the fastest ever. I don't take many notes along with me, but I had written the quickest goal down every year just in case it happened and finally, here we were in 1997 – the BBC's last live FA Cup Final. So when the ball hit the net I was glad to look at my stopwatch and realise that he had in fact surpassed Milburn's record.

...AND FIVE GOALS I WISH I HAD SEEN

From the Fifties I've picked another goal by that great Newcastle United hero JACKIE MILBURN, when they beat Blackpool 2-0 in 1951. I've only seen it on the old film coverage, but here's what happens: the little inside right, Ernie Taylor, backheels the ball to Milburn and he strikes it from about 30 yards and it flies in the top corner. I would say it was one of the most powerful long-range goals in Cup Final history. It probably comes somewhere near Di Matteo's.

Then two years later we mustn't forget the Matthews Final, when Blackpool recovered from 3-1 down to beat Bolton 4-3. Stanley Matthews didn't actually score, but he bewildered the defence with his right-wing runs. In the last minute he went down the right wing, jinked his way past three players, then pulled the ball across and BILL PERRY struck the winner.

My thoughts on the Forties will be very brief because the newsreel coverage that has survived is not particularly good. But in 1947 Charlton Athletic beat Burnley 1-0 with a great goal in the last minute of extra time by CHRIS DUFFY.

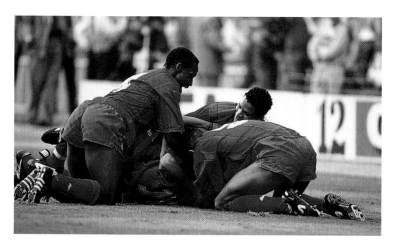

Crystal Palace players pile on Ian Wright after he scored against Manchester United

He whacked it in from outside the penalty area and it flew in the top corner. He was overcome with emotion at that once-in-a-lifetime goal.

In 1948 Manchester United, managed by a young Matt Busby, beat Blackpool 4-2. Blackpool took the lead, United equalised, then Blackpool went 2-1 up. At half-time Busby said: "Just keep playing football" – and they won 4-2. Two goals came from a fellow called JACK ROWLEY, the brother of Arthur Rowley who later became a prolific league goal-scorer. Jack Rowley was an astute striker. His best goal came when he clipped the ball over the goalkeeper's head then ran round and finished it with a sweet movement.

Going back to the 1930s, there's no BBC video tape because it didn't exist. But the BBC did televise the 1938 Final live between Preston North End and Huddersfield. It was settled in the last minute by a penalty from GEORGE MUTCH

of Preston. Mutch got brought down, got up and took the penalty himself and thumped it in off the bar, so Preston beat Huddersfield 1-0. There was a newsreel camera behind the goal and you can see the shot go in off the underside of the bar.

And finally, from the Twenties, the goal I've picked is from the 1928 Final between Blackburn Rovers and Huddersfield Town. Blackburn scored in the first minute when centre-forward JACK ROSCAMP charged the goalkeeper and the ball into the net – and the referee allowed the goal.

Roscamp had lobbed the ball forward and followed up quickly, and as Mercer the goal-keeper went to catch it, he was hit with both feet off the ground by Roscamp, leaving Mercer and the ball in the net. It was a very controversial goal, although players didn't protest like they do now. Blackburn won 3-1.

Roberto Di Matteo (left) celebrates scoring the quickest ever goal in an FA Cup Final

Champion *of the Nineties*

COLIN MONTGOMERIE

Between 1993 and 1998, Colin Montgomerie was undisputedly Europe's number one golfer. In 1997 he took his fifth consecutive European Order of Merit title, breaking the record of four straight set previously by England's Peter Oosterhuis. By winning his sixth title in 1998, the Scotsman equalled the six Seve Ballesteros won between 1976 and 1991, although Seve only ever won three in a row.

Through 1998 Montgomerie had won 17 European Tour events, amassing almost £8 million in earnings. However, Montgomerie has yet to land the major championship he desperately needs to justify his place among the game's elite players. But he has been close in the US Open, where he has finished second twice, and the US PGA Championship where he has lost in a playoff.

Colin Montgomerie was awarded the OBE in November 1998.

Young guns go for it

Tiger Woods and Lee Westwood – two golfers for the new Millennium

Not since Jack Nicklaus has a golfer dominated the game the way Tiger Woods has in the late 1990s. He's been labelled a phenomenon – the tag is justified.

According to his father, Earl, Eldrick 'Tiger' Woods was always destined for greatness. From a young age he showed a grasp for golf that was almost unbelievable. He was making headlines before he was five years old.

As an amateur he won an unprecedented three straight US Amateur Championships (Nicklaus only managed two). It was no surprise then that Woods made such a big impact on the paid game when he turned professional.

When Nicklaus turned pro, he came equipped with the one thing every player desires – length. Nicklaus hit the ball so far that he was sometimes playing pitching wedge second shots when others were hitting five-irons. Tiger Woods had the same advantage.

Woods' 1997 US Masters victory was reminiscent of Jack Nicklaus in his prime. Over four rounds, Woods hit no more than a seven-iron second shot to any par-four hole. He ran away with the tournament, winning by a record 12 shots. His four-round total of 270 broke the previous record of 271 held by Nicklaus and Raymond Floyd. Nicklaus paid him the greatest compliment by stating he thought Woods could win more Masters than he and Arnold Palmer combined – and they won 10!

Woods was the first to earn $2 million in a season (1997), and he ended the Nineties as by far the world's number one player.

As the 1998 season came to a close, England's Lee Westwood stood out as the probable European challenger to Woods' undisputed world supremacy.

At only 25 years old, Westwood has already won over £2 million from just five seasons on the European Tour. He fell just short of dethroning Colin Montgomerie as European number one in 1998, having won four times in Europe (and once on the US Tour).

In their only singles head-to-head challenge, Westwood lost to Woods in the 1998 Cisco World Match Play. But golf fans everywhere are looking forward to these two pitting their skills against each other well into the new Millennium.

Tiger Woods, victorious at the 1997 Masters

Lee Westwood is the probable contender to Woods

1997 • RUGBY UNION

The making of a cult hero
John Bentley inspires the British Lions to South African glory

To many, John Bentley was a controversial choice for the 1997 British and Irish Lions tour to South Africa. How could a player whose last international appearance was nine years ago, and whose career was mainly in rugby league, be taken seriously for a tour party that was setting out to face the world champions on their own home turf? Surely the intensity, speed and style of play had changed completely since Bentley's last England cap in 1988.

However, Fran Cotton and Ian McGeechan thought differently. It was the mental and physical strengths that Bentley had honed in his time away from rugby union the selectors wanted.

John Bentley stamps his authority against South Africa

From their own playing experiences and recent visits to South Africa, they knew exactly what was needed to fight the speed and physical size of the Springboks.

Bentley and his fellow rugby league returnees – Allan Bateman, Scott Gibbs, Scott Quinnell, David Young and Alan Tait – provided the hard-nosed professionalism Cotton knew would be needed to resist the physical challenges awaiting the Lions. Another change introduced by the manager was that all Test places were up for grabs. Those players showing the best form would be in the team, so there was not the disharmony of previous tours that used the first choice and 'dirt trackers' system.

There were many fine individual performances during the victorious tour that complemented the Lions team spirit – the pinpoint accuracy of Neil Jenkins' kicking, Martin Johnson's tough captaincy, Scott Gibbs' rampaging runs and bone-numbing tackles, Matt Dawson's audacious 'dummy' try in the first Test, Keith Wood and his 'never say die' spirit, and Jeremy Guscott's silky and incisive running are just a few examples.

There were two other events which epitomised the players' courage and fierce determination to win and, both times, John Bentley was the man involved in both.

James Small, the brilliant but hot-tempered Western Province winger, liked to psyche out the opposition by using the media and a 'running commentary' during the match. After an initial flourish when Small rounded Bentley and almost scored, the crowd was intimidating in its vocal support. In his own words, Bentley "knew I had to hit him hard and quick. Fortunately for me Small got the ball almost straight away and I put in one of the best tackles I ever made. And while we were on the ground I had a little word in his ear." This incident seemed to lift the Lions while silencing the crowd, and

Bentley finished on the winning side with two tries.

The second event was his 'try of the tour' against Gauteng in Ellis Park Stadium, Johannesburg. Receiving the ball from Neil Jenkins deep in the Lions' own half, Bentley rounded the two opponents and ran into the Gauteng half. He cut inside the full-back and then two more opposition players. Now on the 22 and in front of the goal posts, Bentley went for the line. After evading a tackle, he scored his astonishing solo try, carrying two Gauteng players over the goal line with him.

John Bentley finished the tour as joint top try-scorer with Tony Underwood (seven), having played most games (eight) for the British Lions. The Lions won the Test series 2-1 when an audacious last-minute drop goal by Guscott clinched the crucial Second Test. The world champions were beatable after all.

RADIO TIMES, 20-26 JAN 1996

> "That could have made it 10-3, and there's a subtle difference between that and 7-3." BILL McLAREN
>
> "It's Great Britain in the all-white strip, with the red and blue V, the dark shorts and the dark stockings." RAY FRENCH
>
> "If you didn't know him, you wouldn't know who he was." NIGEL STARMER-SMITH

Ruler of the ring

Don King: boxing's dominant promoter

1990s • BOXING

'Don King – the name alone conjures a picture of a mythical character, part mobster part royalty. Despite all the litigation he is still there, a 20th century P.T. Barnum'

By John Rawling

his booming voice and sheer physical presence command attention. He stands six feet three inches tall and weighs around 300lb, his huge bulk topped off by a shock of candyfloss grey hair. Don King – the name alone conjures a picture of a mythical character, part mobster part royalty.

"My magic lies in my people ties," he boasts, mimicking the rhymes and wordplays used by Muhammad Ali 30 years earlier. For any writer or interviewer, he has time to speak – or rather murder – the English language, searching for ever more outrageous hyperbole to glorify any fight he is promoting.

His cheerful bonhomie is calculated. Seats

"They said it would last two rounds – they were half wrong, it lasted four." HARRY CARPENTER

"No fighter comes into the ring hoping to win – he goes in hoping to win." HENRY COOPER

"He's got a cut on his left eye … it's just below his eyebrow." HARRY CARPENTER

sold in arenas and, more importantly, pay-per-view television sales translate into hard cash. And hard cash is what King has accumulated with greater enthusiasm and panache than any other boxing promoter. He has faced fraud charges and accusations of tax evasion, and seems constantly engaged in some form of litigation against rival promoters or fighters who claim to have been ripped off. But he is still there, a 20th century successor to P.T. Barnum, putting on the biggest and best shows. One hard-bitten cynic of the US press actually told me: "Don King may be evil and corrupt, but he has a brilliant mind and an incredible capacity for hard work. If he had come from a different background he could have been anything he wanted to be. Maybe even President."

King is open about his shady past – he served time for beating a man to death over a debt – and glories in portraying himself as a self-educated man who rose from the ghetto to become one of the most conspicuously wealthy and successful black men in America.

"Only in America, I love America," is his favourite catchphrase. Although some cringe or feel intimidated by him, he generates a genuine sense of admiration. How many people can walk into a crowded restaurant and provoke spontaneous applause? Don King does.

Mike Tyson claimed King had cheated him

out of a staggering $100 million in 10 years. Tim Witherspoon, another ex-world champion, successfully challenged King for lost earnings and ultimately accepted a sizeable out-of-court settlement. The list of the aggrieved goes on.

Yet fighters still sign for him, knowing that his power and influence guarantee the possibility of title fights. And there are those prepared to stand by King, notably Larry Holmes, who has become a wealthy man on the back of a long career mainly overseen by King. He knows that King has probably earned more out of him than he has himself, but "without King, I may not have got the chance".

King's involvement with boxing began in 1972 when he persuaded Muhammad Ali to fight an exhibition to raise funds for a black hospital in Cleveland which was in danger of closure. "It drew $80,000 – the most money ever made at an exhibition," King boasts. "Whatever I do, it has to be the first, the biggest, the best."

He was a key figure in taking Ali and George Foreman to Zaire for the 1974 'Rumble in the Jungle', one of the pivotal fights of the 20th century in terms of projecting boxing to a global audience. He has remained the dominant figure in boxing, especially in the heavyweight division.

Although nearly 70, he shows no sign of slowing down. In Evander Holyfield he has the biggest draw in the sport. And if Holyfield faces Tyson again, in a grudge rematch, King will be the man to drive the deal. For the foreseeable future, the 'Richest Prize in Sport' will stay under the control of the self-styled 'World's Greatest Promoter'.

War of the sluggers

McGwire and Sosa eclipse Babe Ruth's record

The 1998 season was a big turning point for America's national sport. After four years in the doldrums, Major League Baseball was finally returned to the American public.

The game's transformation had nothing to do with the New York Yankees setting a record for the number of wins in a single season on their way to the World Series, which they won by four games straight over the San Diego Padres. But it had everything to do with two men whose exploits at the plate excited the nation and even made headlines around the world.

The legendary Babe Ruth set an astonishing home run record when he hit 60 in 1927. Many predicted it would be a long time and take a special player to beat it. How right they were.

For a few glorious years in the 1950s the New York Yankees' young centre-fielder Mickey Mantle was heir apparent to baseball's most prestigious crown. Throughout the Fifties Mantle attempted to overhaul

Ruth's record, hitting 52 in 1956, but never reaching the magic number of 60.

It was not until 1961 that Mantle figured in a new world record – but perhaps not in the way he would have wanted it. That year Mantle and his fellow Yankee Roger Maris went head-to-head throughout the season, keeping crowds and the media at fever pitch every time they stepped up to bat. In the end a tired and drained Mantle finished on 54, but it was Maris accomplished the impossible by hitting 61.

Perhaps because Maris had 162 games in which to break the record, as opposed to Ruth's 154, Maris's record was never truly appreciated. Ruth was such a huge figure in baseball history that most baseball fans felt Maris had no right to break his record. In a funny way, Babe Ruth's great home run record would remain unless it was broken by a bigger margin. That's exactly what happened in 1998.

The 1998 home run race belonged to two men – the

Sammy Sosa broke Ruth's record but not McGwire's

St Louis Cardinals' Mark McGwire and Sammy Sosa of the Chicago Cubs. Their race to break Maris' 27-year-old record kept the nation enthralled. Newspapers printed daily updates, with photos of McGwire and Sosa and the number of home runs each had.

Having opened up the season with a grand slam home run, McGwire kept ahead of Sosa until the Chicago player went in front on 48 homers. But it was then McGwire all the way until he broke Roger Maris' record. In one of those strange quirks of fate, the Cardinals' opponents that day were the Chicago Cubs and the right-fielder was Sammy Sosa.

The spotlight then shifted to Sosa when he went ahead on 66 (his eventual season total). But McGwire soon regained the lead and finished with an incredible 70 home runs.

Baseball has never witnessed such power hitting in its history, and it is tempting to say it will be a long time before it is ever repeated. But with McGwire and Sosa still in their prime, who knows what these players will ultimately achieve?

Mark McGwire hits a home run out of the ballpark, a feat he accomplished 70 times in the 1998 baseball season

"That was a booming service, it took off like a parachute." GERALD WILLIAMS

"Sadly, the immortal Jackie Milburn died recently." CLIFF MORGAN

Bad day for the bookies
Frankie's magnificent seven
A FEAT UNLIKELY TO BE MATCHED

1996 • RACING

'The atmosphere was extraordinary. Everyone realised this would never be equalled, not on such a competitive day of racing, not at Ascot'

By Clare Balding

Saturday 28 September 1996 was a typically busy day of sport: the Old Firm derby at Ibrox was the commentary match on 5 Live and, with half a dozen Premiership matches, Ascot was halfway down the running order for the afternoon.

It was the first day of the 'Festival of Racing': seven good races with the Queen Elizabeth II stakes the highlight, one of the year's most valuable and prestigious mile contests.

Peter Bromley, our distinguished racing correspondent and commentator, did the usual preview, looking ahead to the big race and discussing the merits of the main contenders.

The talking point that day was the accident a week before at Newbury. Willie Carson had suffered horrific injuries in the paddock when he was kicked by a filly, and had been taken to hospital with a lacerated liver.

Little did we know that next morning racing would be the front-page lead in all the newspapers for the *right* reasons, that people

'Frankie Dettori was the best thing to happen to racing since the days of Piggott and Carson'

would be talking about another jockey, about the extraordinary achievement of a bubbly little Italian. He had a wonderful gift: he could not only make a Ford Capri of a racehorse run like a Ferrari, but he enjoyed it – no, loved it! Grinning from ear to ear after every winner, leaping from their backs like a human jack-in-the-box, exploding with enthusiasm for the sport, Frankie Dettori was the best thing to happen to racing since the days of Piggott and Carson at their best.

Dettori had missed most of the summer with a broken elbow and had spent Royal Ascot on the sidelines, trying his hand as a TV pundit and making it look easy. Now he was back in more familiar clothes. He had a ride in all seven races that day, some fancied, others not.

His low crouching drive took Wall Street to a workmanlike victory in the first race and he won in a photograph on Diffident in the second. The afternoon had started well.

Frankie rode a text-book race in the third, waiting until the furlong marker to make his move and accelerating with a turbo boost to pass Bosra Sham. He came in to a wonderful reception, and despite being asked by an official if he would mind not doing his flying leap, went ahead when he saw Sheikh Mohammed looking perplexed. After all, when the Sheikh says "jump", you jump.

I thought I would wait until after the fourth race to interview Frankie, because he

was busy with TV and I didn't want to rush it. There were 26 runners in the Tote Festival Handicap and, although he had a good chance on Decorated Hero, he was badly drawn. He came from way off the pace to win at 7-1 for his principal trainer and mentor John Gosden. Holding up his hand to signify "four out of four", he was bubbling.

"When a jockey's confidence is high, horses can feel it," he said. "What a day!"

Joanne Watson, *Sport on Five* producer, had more foresight than the rest of us, and told the engineers not to start de-rigging the commentary equipment, just in case. Peter Bromley was scribbling away at his piece, and as we watched the monitor in the little control room Fatefully battled to beat 17 other runners in the fifth, with Dettori in the saddle again.

"You might have to wait to file that piece," our producer Rob Smith suggested to Peter. "If Frankie wins again you'll have to change that five-timer to six."

Three jockeys had ridden all six winners on the card before – Alec Russell, Sir Gordon Richards and, most recently, Willie Carson in 1990 – but never on such a competitive day.

Dettori was on a two-year-old filly called Lochangel in the sixth, trained by Ian Balding, my father. Dad was in a dreadful state, terrified of letting Frankie down if she didn't win and talking down her chances, despite the fact she had shown bags of speed and was a half-sister to the sprinter Lochsong with whom he and Frankie had enjoyed success.

Lochangel looked surprised at the number of people around the paddock. The orders were to come from off the pace and hope she would quicken up. She popped out of the stalls, ears pricked, and made all the running.

"Sometimes you have to improvise," said Frankie. "The instructions went out the window!" That's the difference between a good jockey and a great one. He could assess the situation in a second and had the confidence to change the plan. With this little bit of brilliance he had equalled the record.

Peter Bromley has always said the secret of his longevity is leaving before the last race to beat the traffic. Now he was happy to stay. The 20,000 spectators were, too; only the odd bookmaker ducked for cover. In the seventh race Dettori was riding an unpredictable horse called Fujiyama Crest, quoted at 12-1. Trainer Michael Stoute said the horse couldn't win.

By the time Dettori walked to the paddock to climb on board, the sheer weight of expectation had forced the odds in to 2-1 favourite.

At 5.45, *Sports Report* played the package summing up Dettori's day. Peter picked up off the back of it for the last half-mile. Frankie and Fujiyama Crest had set out to make the running for the full two miles of the long-distance handicap. The bell went as the field turned into the straight, he was still in front and the crowd realised they were about to witness history. A huge roar went up, and I swear the noise literally carried the horse to the line.

Bromley gave his all in a memorable commentary, his rumbling voice reaching a crescendo: "They're into the last furlong, and I don't think you'll hear a word I'm saying because you'll realise that Fujiyama Crest and Frankie Dettori have the lead, but Northern Fleet is going after him ... Fujiyama Crest has won it," he bellowed. "Frankie Dettori's Seven. That is history made, the crowd are running towards the unsaddling enclosure to greet today's hero – Frankie Dettori!"

A mad rush to the winner's enclosure was rewarded by the sight of men hugging each

Frankie Dettori leaps for joy during a great day for horse racing

other, Dettori screaming with delight and holding up his fingers in disbelief to signify SEVEN!! Cynical journalists had tears in their eyes, people were cheering and clapping. Frankie hugged the horse and gave his second leap of the day, jumping on Michael Stoute, hugging him like a giant teddy bear.

He applauded the crowd surrounding the amphitheatre of an enclosure. It was a cauldron of excitement. The atmosphere was extraordinary. Everyone realised this would never be equalled, not on such a competitive day of racing, not at Ascot, not like this.

Another bottle of champagne appeared, this time sprayed over everyone as he ran

round the winner's enclosure. "Don't touch me, I'm red 'ot! I'm gonna do the Lottery tonight, I tell ya!" he laughed in his half-Italian, half-cockney accent. "Whatta day. I've had some great days in my life but this will take some beating – it's incredible. It's been a dream come true."

It made the news bulletins that night, and was the front-page lead in all the morning's papers, as they recognised what was one of the greatest sporting achievements. A Magnificent Seven that paid out at odds of 25,095–1 for the few lucky enough to combine all of his mounts in an accumulated bet. Smaller bookmakers were put out of business, the larger ones lost £25-30 million.

It took a while for the enormity of what he had done to sink in, but later Frankie reflected with typical humility. "It might look as though it was my day, but for me it was horse racing's day. The people's day. An occasion to show that a day at the races can be as fun as any football match, tennis final or golf tournament."

Who could ask for a better advertisement for racing? Who could ask for a better day of sport?

"I imagine that the conditions in those cars today are totally unimaginable." MURRAY WALKER

"An interesting morning, full of interest." JIM LAKER

"This is the sort of pitch which literally castrates a bowler." TREVOR BAILEY

British athletes win nine Gold medals

British athletes win nine Gold medals
Brilliant in Budapest
RENAISSANCE FOR A TROUBLED SPORT

Denise Lewis had a personal best high jump

1998 • ATHLETES

'Colin Jackson added to his long list of honours by becoming the first to win a third European title at 110 metres hurdles...'

By Peter Matthews

before the 1998 European Championships in Budapest, athletics was a troubled sport, weighed down by the financial collapse of the British Athletics Federation and a lack of Gold medals at recent championships. So for British athletes to come home with nine Gold medals was nothing less than a renaissance.

Steve Backley and Colin Jackson each won their third successive European Gold to top the following list of medallists:

DARREN CAMPBELL realised his long-held promise by winning the 100 metres in 10.04, a time which made him Britain's second

"There's going to be a real ding-dong when the bell goes." DAVID COLEMAN

"He's doing well ... he's letting his legs do the running." BRENDAN FOSTER

"You have to talk in metres because nobody under 16 understands feet nowadays. The course is 1.6 miles long." DAVID VINE

fastest ever and exceeded the championship record (with allowable wind) of 10.09 run by Linford Christie in 1990. Campbell stormed to victory, with team-mates Dwain Chambers taking the Silver in 10.10 and Marlon Devonish fifth in 10.24.

DOUG WALKER led a sweep of the medals in the 200 metres, winning in 20.53 from Doug Turner (20.64) and Julian Golding (20.72). Walker, born in Inverness in 1973, played rugby for Scottish schools before becoming a sprinter. He took a Bronze in the sprint relay at the 1994 Commonwealth Games and was a semi-finalist at 200 metres at the World Championships in 1997 before

A victorious Colin Jackson

his great year in 1998, when he won all finals at 200 metres.

IWAN THOMAS completed Britain's domination of the men's sprints by winning the 400 metres in superb style in a new championship record time of 44.52, not far off the British record that he had set at 44.36 in 1996. Solomon Wariso was disqualified after finishing sixth. Controversially the selectors had preferred Wariso to Roger Black, the champion of 1986 and 1990 and second to Du'aine Ladejo in 1994, and Black was undoubtedly in the form to have taken a medal if he had run.

COLIN JACKSON added to his long list of honours by becoming the first to win a third European title at 110 metres hurdles, and for

good measure he lowered his 1994 championship record of 13.04 to 13.02 in both his semi-final and, 75 minutes later, in the final.

JONATHAN EDWARDS had taken triple jumping to a new level in 1995. He produced an extraordinary 18.43 metres in the European Cup, but a following wind marginally over the limit of 2.4 metres per second meant it could not be recognised as a record. Two more wind-assisted 18 metres-plus jumps followed before his day of days at the World Championships in Gothenberg, when he set world records on his first two jumps at 18.16 and 18.29.

He remained the world's top triple jumper overall in the next two years, but could not again reach beyond 18 metres and had to settle for Silver medals at the Olympics and World Championships. In 1998 he won the European Indoor title and the European Cup, and jumped 18.01 in Oslo before dominating the field in Budapest.

STEVE BACKLEY proved once again to be a consummate competitor. He led the qualifiers

Iwan Thomas won the 400 metres in superb style

for the final by 3.74 metres with a magnificent championship record 87.45 (beating his own 87.30 of 1990) and pretty much settled the issue in the final with a further improvement to 89.72 on his first throw. No one could get close, but Mick Hill far exceeded his previous season's best with 86.92 to take the Silver medal, and with sixth place at 84.15 Mark Robertson showed that Britain had now passed Finland to rank as Europe's top javelin nation.

Allison Curbishley in the 4 x 400 metres relay

Amazingly no British team had won the 4 x 100 metres relay in European Championships history; the baton had been dropped in a heat at the previous Championships, but this time there was no mistake. The squad of Allyn Condon, Darren Campbell, Marlon Devonish and Dwain Chambers were much the fastest, at 38.47 in the heats. For the final Doug Walker and Julian Golding replaced Devonish and Chambers, so that the same team that had won at the European Cup

was in place, and they won easily in 38.52.

British teams had won the men's 4 x 400 metres relay six times, including at the three previous Europeans. Gold again went to Britain, and it would have been a major upset had it not done so. However the talented British team were pushed all the way by Poland and the margin, 2:58.68 to 2:58.88, was closer than anticipated. Mark Hylton led off with a fine opening leg timed in 45.42. Jamie Baulch, returning to the form he had showed in 1997, ran the second leg (from a flying start) in 44.61 and the top two, Iwan Thomas (44.21) and Mark Richardson (44.39) ensured that the job was done.

Jonathan Edwards dominated the field

DENISE LEWIS was the one woman to win Gold for Britain. Injury had spoilt her preparation early in the season, so she was not quite at her best, but she still won the heptathlon, her first multi-event competition for a year – the first indeed since her Silver medal in Athens 1997. She had an average start with 13.59 for the 100 metres hurdles (some way down on her best ever of 13.18), but then had a good high jump of 1.83m (best ever 1.84) and a splendid shot, in which she added 50 centimetres to her previous best with 15.27 metres. She then ran a modest 200 metres (24.75, compared to her best

of 24.10) and so ended the first day in second place, 28 points off the lead. On day two a season's best long jump of 6.59 and a javelin throw of 50.16 were better than anyone else and she completed the 800 metres in 2:20.38 to win comfortably with 6,559 points, 99 points ahead of the runner-up.

Finally, Dalton Grant took Silver in the high jump, when he conquered 2.34 for second behind Artur Partyka (Poland) 2.36. Then the women's 4 x 400 metres relay team of Donna Fraser, Vikki Jamison, Katherine Merry and Allison Curbishley took Bronze.

It was a terrific effort and a great boost to British sports fans.

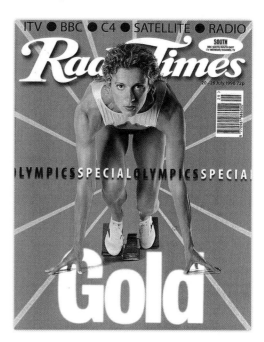

SALLY GUNNELL

'Sally Gunnell has already won a podium place in British athletics history, but new hurdles await her in Atlanta.

"As soon as you cross the line you think, 'That was wonderful', and you realise why you do it, although I hardly ever remember anything of the race because I'm so within myself when I run." '

RADIO TIMES, 20-26 JULY 1996

Left to right: 4 x 100 metres relay champions Condon, Golding, Campbell and Walker

World Cup defeat but a star is born
The Owen factor
A BRITISH TALENT TO MATCH THE BEST

1998 • FOOTBALL

'Owen is one of the youngest of a generation, some now with World Cup experience, which should have their best days still to come...'

By Barry Davies

For 20 minutes or so in France in the summer of 1998, the England football team glimpsed the promised land. Ironically, the undisputed team leader was Michael Owen, the youngest in the side.

Owen earned England a penalty in their World Cup quarter-final against Argentina when he was brought down by Ayala. Then he scored a wonderful individual goal. Having recovered from conceding an early penalty, England were in charge and playing well enough to justify the feeling in the camp from the outset that the Cup would ultimately be theirs.

According to Owen and others, the dressing room at half-time remained upbeat despite Argentina's well-worked free kick just before the interval which had brought them level at 2-2. But the dismissal of David Beckham changed the style of the match and confused the post mortem. The certificate says 'Beaten in a penalty competition', leaving everyone to speculate about 'What if' with some markedly varying conclusions.

In spite of the furore over his book on World Cup 98, Glenn Hoddle will have the chance to put his much-debated theories to a further test in the European Championship; though such is the antipathy between the coach and some sections of the media that to write that is tempting fate.

The World Cup changed Michael Owen's life, but it will be very disappointing if the delight in doing what he enjoys and always wanted to do is ever changed by the increasing demands on a modern superstar.

In contrast with his movement on the field, Owen's style off it is to tread warily with a maturity which belies his years. He admits to irritation at the camera lenses which interrupted his pre-season holiday. But he accepts

that interviews and "standing there letting people snap away at you goes with the job" and does so in a friendly, helpful manner.

Looking back at the World Cup, his simple comment of "I think I have proved that I can play against the best players in the world" is testament to a character unfazed by the mountain of compliments his performances there induced, among them the judgements of many of the great players of the past. "Little Ronaldo", as Mario Zagallo, the coach of Brazil, dubbed him, was the find of the tournament; there was no more dangerous striker around. And at the autumn meeting of the coaches of EUFA teams he was the only Englishman included in the 'All Star XI'.

His performance was helped, I believe, by Hoddle's decision to nurse him into the side. The coach is right in his view that "If he'd gone in in his first game and we'd had a dodgy result and he hadn't scored, people would have said that he was too young and shouldn't have been thrown in at the deep end."

Scoring and hitting a post as a substitute against Romania suggests he should have started the second match when England were guilty of being over-cautious. But if (that little word again) England, having beaten Colombia with Owen playing the 90 minutes, had gone on beat Argentina, wouldn't the careful introduction have been seen as totally justified?

Of "the goal", Owen's most telling memory is: "I saw another white shirt and I thought, he's

Michael Owen celebrates after scoring a brilliant goal in France 1998

not going to have the ball here" (only after-wards did he learn that the shirt was worn by Paul Scholes).

Knowing when to be selfish is a key attribute in a goal-scorer. He will remember the moment all his life.

Wondering just how his older team-mates whose World Cup days had come to an end were feeling, and anticipation for himself and his younger colleagues of the next chance, were the conflicting thoughts running through Owen's mind as he sat in the losers' dressing room in St Etienne.

"When you look at the players we've got and the younger ones coming through I think there's a good reason for hope": a quote of Alan Shearer proportions.

Owen is one of the youngest of a genera-tion, some now with World Cup experience, which should have their best days still to come. With the likes of Beckham, Scholes and Jamie Redknapp around to exploit his pace, touch and ability to tease defenders by running across them, there should be plenty of opportunities for Michael Owen.

✳ MICHAEL OWEN SCORESHEET

Born: Chester 14.12.79

Liverpool debut: 6.5.97 substitute v Wimbledon (Selhurst Park). Lost 2-1, scored penalty

International debut: 11.2.98 v Chile (Wembley). Lost 2-0. Age 18 years 59 days. Youngest player to be capped by England this century

First international goal: 27.5.98 substitute v Morocco (Casablanca). England's youngest goalscorer at 18 years 164 days

World Cup debut: 15.6.98 substitute v Tunisia (Marseille). Won 2-0

First World Cup goal: 22.6.98 substitute v Romania (Toulouse). England's youngest World Cup scorer and the third youngest in World Cup history behind Pele (Brazil) 1958 and Manuel Rosas (Mexico) 1930.

1990s • TENNIS

Henman and Rusedski
At last Britain has two world tennis stars

Not since Fred Perry won three successive titles from 1934 to 1936 has a British tennis player won the Wimbledon men's singles title. Until the mid-1990s such a success seemed an impossible dream, with no British man even ranked in the world's top 10.

Roger Taylor had ranked at 11 when world rankings were first introduced in 1973 but no one made the top 10 until Greg Rusedski broke through in September 1997 following his defeat in the US Open final, when he became the first British man since Bunny Austin in 1938 to contest a Grand Slam singles final. He progressed to

number four a few weeks later.

Rusedski, with an English mother and Canadian father, had switched nationality from Canadian in 1995. His success came with his British passport, but even more popular was Tim Henman (left), who reached the top 10 for the first time in September 1998, ironically when Rusedski dropped out.

'Henmania' at Wimbledon started when he beat No.5 seed Andrey Kafelnikov (Russia) in the first round in 1996, and went on to reach the quarter-finals, as he did again in 1997. In 1998 he did even better, losing to Pete Sampras in the semi-finals.

Rusedski's best performance was in November 1998, when he beat Sampras to win the Paris Open. He and Henman know they can beat anyone in the world; that elusive Wimbledon win just might be coming at last.

"These ball boys are wonderful. You don't even notice them. There's a left-handed one over there. I noticed him earlier." MAX ROBERTSON

"We haven't had any more rain since it stopped raining." HARRY CARPENTER

"You can almost hear the silence as they battle it out." DAN MASKELL

Radio Times, 20-26 Jan 1996

Youth takes the lead in a landmark Sports Review of the Year

BBC viewers vote for the future

MICHAEL OWEN IS 1998'S SPORTS PERSONALITY OF THE YEAR

1998 • BBC SPORT

The BBC Sports Review of the Year was an annual highlight throughout Brian Gearing's career as Editor of Radio Times. But none gave him more pleasure than that of 1998

By Brian Gearing

Looking back over the sporting year 1998 – a year described by Desmond Lynam as "momentous" – encourages, perhaps surprisingly, the millions of us who love sport to look to the future with genuine hope. In these troubled times of gold and greed, that is saying something.

Much of the credit for this uplifting outlook springs from the slight figure of the 18-year old who was chosen by the viewers as the BBC's 45th Sports Personality of the Year. Michael Owen, as Lynam said on the awards programme, "captivated the world of football". He is clean-cut and well-mannered, the son any parents would be proud of.

The goal he scored against Argentina – described on the previous page by Barry Davies – electrified the World Cup finals and he earned high praise from John Motson as "the most promising young talent of France '98". His performance prompted a perfect piece of commentary: "Just think what he will be like when he grows up!"

Owen carries himself with a composure beyond his years – he received the BBC award

Michael Owen receives the BBC Sports Personality of the Year trophy, with Des Lynam, Sue Barker and Steve Rider

the day before his 19th birthday. The presentation to the Liverpool and England footballer was made by David Hemery, the former hurdler, who himself was acclaimed BBC Sports Personality in 1968, more than a decade before Michael Owen was born.

Hemery and Owen are linked by their sporting prowess, but their talents graced very different eras. Hemery won his medals before

television's riches arrived to make sporting stars wealthy (while unhinging a few).

Sport is littered with performers who became victims of their own success, destroyed by the big money that sometimes seems to come too easily, and the fickle adoration of hangers-on. Michael Owen gives every indication of being well-advised by the people who have this prodigious talent in their care.

★ BBC SPORTS PERSONALITY OF THE YEAR

1954	CHRIS CHATAWAY
1955	GORDON PIRIE
1956	JIM LAKER
1957	DAI REES
1958	IAN BLACK
1959	JOHN SURTEES
1960	DAVID BROOME
1961	STIRLING MOSS
1962	ANITA LONSBROUGH
1963	DOROTHY HYMAN
1964	MARY RAND
1965	TOMMY SIMPSON
1966	BOBBY MOORE
1967	HENRY COOPER
1968	DAVID HEMERY
1969	ANN JONES
1970	HENRY COOPER
1971	HRH PRINCESS ANNE
1972	MARY PETERS
1973	JACKIE STEWART
1974	BRENDAN FOSTER
1975	DAVID STEELE
1976	JOHN CURRY
1977	VIRGINIA WADE
1978	STEVE OVETT
1979	SEBASTIAN COE
1980	ROBIN COUSINS
1981	IAN BOTHAM
1982	DALEY THOMPSON
1983	STEVE CRAM
1984	TORVILL AND DEAN
1985	BARRY MCGUIGAN
1986	NIGEL MANSELL
1987	FATIMA WHITBREAD
1988	STEVE DAVIS
1989	NICK FALDO
1990	PAUL GASCOIGNE
1991	LIZ MCCOLGAN
1992	NIGEL MANSELL
1993	LINFORD CHRISTIE
1994	DAMON HILL
1995	JONATHAN EDWARDS
1996	DAMON HILL
1997	GREG RUSEDSKI
1998	MICHAEL OWEN

TOMMY SIMPSON

MARY PETERS

IAN BOTHAM

John Motson acclaimed Michael Owen as the most promising young talent of France '98

Denise Lewis: Fulfilling her destiny as the world's number one heptathlon athlete

Also, he is backed by a loyal and loving family.

Des Lynam said that the sporting year of 1998 was memorable for individuals whose contributions were "absolutely outstanding" and who left an indelible impression with their talent and personality. One such is Michael Owen. Two more are the athletes Denise Lewis and Iwan Thomas, who were placed second and third respectively behind Owen as the viewers' choice.

While the administration of British track and field collapsed in financial crisis – with the bankrupt British Athletics Federation being replaced by UK Athletics as the sport's governing body – the athletes themselves flourished, achieving successes that

> ● Eighteen-year-old Owen's performance at the 1998 World Cup in France prompted a perfect piece of commentary: "Just think what he'll be like when he grows up!" ●

rivalled even the triumphs of the Coe, Ovett and Cram era in the 1970s and '80s when Britain ruled the middle-distance events.

Denise Lewis, with the smile to match her dazzling achievements, became the world number one in her gruelling event, the heptathlon. She won gold medals at both the European Championships and Commonwealth Games.

The heptathlon consists of seven events – 100-metre hurdles, high jump, shot putt, 200 metres, long jump, javelin and 800 metres – and Denise tackles them all with equal confidence. With her ability and looks, and the World Championships and the Sydney Olympics in her sights, she is on course to be the most photographed woman in world athletics.

Iwan Thomas is one of the great 400-metre runners – he put this beyond doubt in 1998 by completing a golden hat-trick of victories in the European Championships, the World Cup and the Commonwealth Games. The gold medal in Kuala Lumpur was very special for him, as the Commonwealth Games is one of the very few opportunities he has to represent Wales. He arrived in Kuala Lumpur at the end of a long, exhausting season, "very tired and with very little left in the tank". But he regards running for Wales as "a great honour. My heart pulled me through."

There were those who said that British athletics was in trouble. Don't you believe it! In sprinting, Dwain Chambers, Darren Campbell and Christian Malcolm are all potential world-beaters. Mark Richardson is a formidable rival for Iwan Thomas in the 400 metres. Hurdler Colin Jackson is European champion for the third time. Jonathan Edwards took the European triple jump title and holds the world record, and Steve Smith has recovered from injury to join Dalton Grant in challenging for the high jump honours.

The BBC *Sports Review of the Year* is about disappointments as well as triumphs. At the 1998 Open Championship at Royal Birkdale, 17-year-old amateur Justin Rose enthralled the nation with his inspirational golf. He

Iwan Thomas:
1998 saw him take his
place as one of the great
400-metre runners

appeared to be Britain's answer to Tiger Woods as, round after round, he grew in confidence and eventually tied for fourth place.

Rose turned professional after The Open, and his last shot as an amateur was unforgettable. He pitched at the pin on the 18th hole. The ball flew towards the flag, clearing a bunker on the way, landed safely on the green and, with the crowd calling "Get in!", it did just that. But after that pinnacle came the letdown. By Christmas Justin had played in 10 tournaments, and missed the cut in every one. Fortunately, he has two crucial factors on his side – one is his talent, which was there for all to see at Royal Birkdale, and the other, as Lee Westwood pointed out, is time.

The pressures on sporting stars are greater than ever before, a stressful combination of the rich rewards available and the expectations of sponsors and public. Few of the previous BBC Sports Personalities of the Year had to deal with demands as daunting as today's. Our heroes seem to get younger all the time – but their very youth, together with support and guidance from parents, agents and managers, is a factor in equipping them to cope, and gives the rest of us cause for hope.

Photographic Credits

**Freddie Mills tries to punch his way out of a paper bag,
watched by Eamonn Andrews**

All photographs, except where specified, are by Allsport, and The Allsport Historical Collection © Hulton Getty.
Immense gratitude to Rob Harborne at Allsport for his invaluable help and enthusiasm.

Radio Times covers supplied by Wallace Grevatt, to whom many thanks.

Photography by Patrick Eagar appears on pages 116, 117 and 160 (left).

Photography by Empics appears on page 174 (bottom) and jacket.

Photography by Michael Steele appears on page 171 and jacket.

Photograph of Clare Balding © BBC.

Photograph of Clive Everton © Eric Whitehead.